# 'Over to Home & from Away'

D1570224

*"In Maine there are four directions — upriver, downstate, over to home and from away."*

— Old Maine Saying

*Books by Jim Brunelle*

Maine Almanac 1978
Maine Almanac 1980
'Over to Home and From Away'

# 'Over to Home & from Away'

### Edited by Jim Brunelle

*Drawings by Michael Ricci*

Guy Gannett Publishing Co.
Portland, Maine

Copyright, James E. Brunelle, 1980.
All rights reserved.
Library of Congress Card # 80-83104
ISBN # 0-930096-11-8
First Printing, January, 1981
Published by Guy Gannett Publishing Co.,
390 Congress Street, Portland, Maine 04101
Printed in the United States of America by
Gannett Graphics, Augusta Maine

# Acknowledgements

Inclusion of works by the following authors was made possible by the generous permission of these authors, publishers and representatives:

Peter Agrafiotis. Selections from TEN YEARS OF CLUEs by Peter Agrafiotis. Copyright 1977 by Peter Agrafiotis. Reprinted by permission of the author.

Cleveland Amory. Specified material from THE LAST RE-SORTS by Cleveland Amory. Copyright 1952 by Cleveland Amory. Reprinted by permission of Harper & Row, Publishers, Inc.

Harold J. Boyle. Selections from HAL BOYLE RECALLS, Portland Evening Express, 1974. Reprinted by permission of Guy Gannett Publishing Co.

Allen D. Brown ("Cap'n Perc Sane"). Selections from SATURDAY COVE by Cap'n Perc Sane. Copyright © 1969 by International Marine Publishing Co., Camden, Maine. Reprinted by permission of International Marine Publishing Co.

Erskine Caldwell. "The Corduroy Pants" by Erskine Caldwell. Copyright © 1931, renewed 1959 by Erskine Caldwell. Reprinted by permission of McIntosh and Otis, Inc.

William M. Clark. Excerpts from TALES OF CEDAR RIVER, copyright 1960 by William M. Clark, and MORE

1965 by Edmund Ware Smith. Copyright 1959, 1960, 1961, 1962, 1963, 1964, 1965 by Holt, Rinehart and Winston. Reprinted by permission of Holt, Rinehart and Winston, Publishers.

Kent Ward. Selections from MAINE WATCH, Bangor Daily News, 1979, 1980. Reprinted by permission of Kent Ward and the Bangor Daily News.

E. B. White. Portion of "Letter to Katherine S. White (North Brooklin, Me.) (Early September 1937) Thursday night" (pp. 159-160) from LETTERS OF E. B. WHITE. Copyright 1976 by E. B. White. Reprinted by permission of Harper & Row Publishers, Inc.

# Foreword

As John Gould suggests in his vinegary introduction to this collection, "Over to Home and From Away" is probably too rich a repast to be digested in a single sitting. Although loosely arranged along chronological lines, it is not intended for cover-to-cover reading. Rather, it is a good bedside or bathroom book, something to be picked up, flipped through, dipped into, put aside and picked up again. It really doesn't matter whether the reader begins with Chapter One or Chapter Ten. Each section, each selection, stands by itself.

This book takes in a century-and-a-half of Maine humorous writing, from the early days of statehood to the present. And despite Gould's cider-tart — and accurate — warning about the dangers of "misguided pedantry" in a collection of this sort, the reader need have no fear that this is another somber autopsy of American humor. As editor-collector, I have been guided by E. B. White's observation: "Humor can be dissected, as a frog can, but the thing dies in the process and the innards are discouraging to any but the pure scientific mind." Apart from a few instinctive, non-scholarly remarks at the outset about the nascent character of Maine humor, I have left it to the reader to judge what is funny and what is not. The nearly three dozen writers represented here speak for themselves.

I owe a debt of gratitude to scores of people in the assem-

xiv

bling of this collection. Some deserve singling out. Jim
McLoughlin of Harpswell Press first suggested the idea to me
more than a decade ago. Two of my oldest friends, Stan
Milton and Lew Colby, supplied many of the Maine stories
in the first chapter. John Gould, complaining all the way of
his antipathy to anthologies, contributed not only the introduction but much wise advice. Portland book antiquarian Francis
O'Brien provided a number of suggestions for sources. My
friend and colleague, Donald C. Hansen, read the manuscript
and supplied encouragement at each stage. Brian Irish of
KJ Printing worked his usual magic in seeing that the difficult
was accomplished immediately and the impossible a day or
two later. Finally, my dear wife Ellen held my hand tightly
throughout the usual agonizing process of book-birthing, re-
viewed the manuscript several times and gave me more practical editing advice than anyone. It's a better book because
of her.

— Jim Brunelle

Cape Elizabeth, 1980

# Contents

# 8 OVER TO HOME

# 9 FROM AWAY

# 10 CHARACTERS

# Introduction

By John Gould

This seems to be the first anthology of humorous Maine writings, and it may be a mistake. Well, there is nothing more tedious than a joke book, and to pile all the Maine funnies in one heap is a similar risk. The dullest thud in the history of letters was the clinical study of wit and humor by Dr. Sigmund Freud. His examples of laugh-makers were merely cadavers in his laboratory, and he proved himself a mirthless man. In that kind of caper, laughter vanishes. Making gentlemen laugh, wrote Molière, is a strange business. Bill Nye, tenuously Maine, said the "youmorist" would be the sad-looking little man keeping to himself and wishing he hadn't come to the party. Alfred Kerr, a German critic, wrote, "Someone who says things amusingly is saying them no less seriously for that." Joseph Clay Neal, a humorist as well as a Philadelphian, put the same thought this way:

> Those gifted with truly humorous genius are more useful as moralists, philosophers, and teachers, than whole legions of the gravest preachers. They speak more effectually to the general ear and heart, even though those who hear are not aware of the fact that they are imbibing wisdom.*

---

*I am told that in Philadelphia, every once in a while, somebody tries to drink through his ear.

It is easy to relate this sobering assessment of hilarity to Maine. James D. Hart, in his biographical sketch of Seba Smith for the *Oxford Companion,* wrote:

> This use of his character (Major Jack Downing) and Smith's freedom from party politics made him the inaugurator of the American tradition of commenting on current events with great shrewdness cloaked under a guise of simplicity, and gave to the country a line of homespun political philosophers that has included Hosea Bigelow, Mr. Dooley, and Will Rogers.

(Mr. Hart's suggestion that Biglow, Dooley, and Rogers are merely writers of Maine humor from away is intriguing, but Smith is the only one of this bunch to get included in this book.)

If there is risk of boredom in this anthology of Maine humor — too much of a good thing all at once — there is also a chance of misguided pedantry. You have here a sort of case history of American literary pleasantries, a demonstration in depth that amounts to a how-to-do-it. Remember how pleased the *Bourgeois gentilhomme* was when he found out he had been speaking prose for forty years and didn't know it? Here we've had these jokers in Maine all these years and didn't know they were philosophers, teachers, inaugurators, moralists — and geniuses. Doc Rockwell, who became a Maine humorous writer when he retired from vaudeville, used to wonder why some words are funny and some are not. He never figured it out, but he knew which was which instinctively. Gelett Burgess said the rhymed double sestine is "hard as the deuce." So it is, and so is grinding guffaws,

xxiii

and there was nothing light-hearted and flippant about the making of the pieces in this book. They came from midnight oil, from careful shaping and jointing, and from a special know-how that sets the humorous writer above the others. So this may be a book to be studied in colleges, a guide to the simplicity of homespun philosophy, etc., and so forth.

— John Gould

In Friendship, 1980

# 1

## Just About Anybody Can Tell a Downeast Story

The lore of downeast humor abounds in stories of the Maine rustic taking terse advantage of the city slicker's smart-alecky vulnerability. There is *always* a farmer leaning against a country fence lying in wait for the lost urban traveler.

"Excuse me," says the motorist coming to a fork in the road marked by signs pointing both ways to Portland. "Does it matter which road I take to Portland?" Our farmer gives the unfortunate wretch a long look, removes the straw from his mouth, spits and says, "Not to me it don't."

Elsewhere, another hopelessly lost tourist pulls to the side of the road and hails the inevitable native predator. "Say, fellah, where does this road go, anyway?" Another long look and a gentle rustle of bones: "Wall, Mister, don't go nowhere. Stays right here mostly."

It can be argued that such stories of mild-mannered meanness are not really typical of the Maine character, but I have a personal recollection which indicates they are not entirely apocryphal.

Shortly after moving to Maine several years ago I managed to get lost on the back roads of Androscoggin County while on a reporting assignment. True to the classic form I overtook a pipe-smoking native standing idly by a fence on the outskirts of a village.

"Excuse me, but is this Monmouth?"

The fellow removed his pipe and, following the compulsory pause, replied, "Ayuh."

"Well, can you tell me where the town hall is?"

"Ayuh."

He replaced the pipe in his mouth and patiently awaited the next question. With a sinking feeling, I realized I had been "downeasted," converted into a summer complaint.

"Just checking," I yelled and drove off.

People really do say "Ayuh" in Maine, although many visitors mistakenly consider the phrase the embodiment of downeast humor. Anybody who can drop his Rs and say "Ayuh" a lot thinks he's an accomplished Maine story-teller. He also believes that the ability to say "Oy vey" is the essence of Jewish humor, or that "Sure an' begorra" makes him an Irish jokester.

Every region of the country has its body of humor, of course, but Maine is one of the few places where the state itself serves as locus to a recognized strain of amusing story. After Vermont, Texas and perhaps Rhode Island, we quickly run out of states which lend their names to a readily identifiable store of jokes. Nobody ever heard of a Michigan joke or a Delaware joke.

And where Texas stories are essentially boastful, the jokes hinging on the size of the state, Maine stories tend to be more self-deprecating.

From time to time New Englanders tell stories which pit the Texan's braggadoccio against the Maine Yankee's understated wit. The Mainer always wins this tussle.

For instance, a Texan once boasted about a steer that measured 24 ax handles between his horns. A man from Maine listened quietly, then mentioned that in his hometown there was a kettle 36 handles wide.

"What can you do with a kettle that big?" the Texan asked.

"We could cook that steer you're talking about."

That's a very old Texas-versus-Maine story and not particularly typical of the genre. Usually the downeaster is considerably more subtle in puncturing the western windbag.

A Texan was bragging to a Mainer about the size of his ranch.

"Why, I could hop in my truck, drive all day and never reach the end of my property line," he said.

"Ayuh," replied the Mainer with an understanding nod. "Had a pickup like that once myself."

The typical Maine story permits the central character to be at once the butt of the joke and its perpetrator. He is the simple rustic — or fisherman or hunting guide or logger — who deflates the patronizing visitor with a rejoinder both naive and calculated, often infused with a tangy dose of native common sense.

Unlike the subjects of most regional and ethnic humor, the downeast character is almost never simply a comic victim of the jest. Confronted by stupidity or rudeness, he remains calm and unflustered. No matter how grinding the human condition, he maintains a flinty sense of the philosophical.

A summer visitor, making conversation with an oldtimer from Rockland who made lobster traps for a living, asked how business was.

"Well," said the oldtimer, "on Monday I didn't sell any. On Tuesday a feller come in and took ten, but on Wednesday he brought 'em back. I didn't sell any on Thursday and on Friday I went fishin'." He paused reflectively, then concluded, "I guess you'd have to say that Tuesday was my best day."

Then there was the time Doc Rockwell's home, "Slipshod Manor," a beautiful, comfortable cottage overlooking Townsend Gut in Southport, caught fire and burned to the ground. His neighbors came over to offer help and cluck their sympathy. "Well, I don't know," said Doc, viewing the ruins, "you can always look at the bright side. The place was getting old. Some of the doors were beginning to stick."

Looking at the bright side is practically a compulsive strain of the Maine character, a defense mechanism against the harsher ridges of life designed to prevent a person from catching up, let alone getting ahead.

Bill Clark catches this ironic optimism in his Cedar River chronicles: "Jonas Hall always said a man was better off to be eight months behind than four months behind. Jonas argued that once the man got eight months behind he could pretend he was four months ahead. He'd lose a year but he'd gain peace of mind and probably what he was going to do in the year he lost wouldn't amount to anything anyway."

At its most effective, downeast humor is a carefully spun yarn, taking full advantage of comic pronunciations, ancillary digressions, descriptions of the foibles of the principals involved and colorful details designed to produce a series of chuckles on the way to the frequently understated punch line. A good downeast story teller might take 15 or 20 minutes to tell a single joke, building the hilarity of the tale gradually to the climax.

Mark Twain identified this relaxed brand of humorous story telling as peculiarly American, in contrast to the more tightly contrived English comic tales or the witty sallies of the French: "The humorous story may be spun out to great length, and may wander around as much as it pleases, and arrive nowhere in particular. Very often, of course, the rambling and disjointed humorous story finishes with a nub, point, snapper, delivered in a carefully casual and indifferent way."

The genealogy of Maine humorous stories doesn't always bear close scrutiny. Consider the oft-told tale of Ed Potter, who lived 50 years in the same house in Oxford County on the Maine-New Hampshire border. He voted in Fryeburg and paid his taxes in Augusta. One year they resurveyed the area and found out Ed's property was actually in New Hampshire. When they told him about the error, Ed heaved a big sigh of relief. "Thank God," he said, "I don't think I coulda stood another one of them Maine winters."

It's a good story. The only trouble is it's not really Maine. It turns up in a dozen Vermont anthologies. But there's been a lot of freebootery in Yankee humor between Maine and Vermont over the years, despite their geographical separation by New Hampshire, and it is not easy to determine just where one state's authentic story leaves off and the other begins. The confusion comes from a kinship of character, of taciturnity and economy of expression.

Incidentally, it has been scientifically established that New Hampshire has no store of folk humor whatever.

Just about anybody can tell a downeast story with reasonable effectiveness. It helps if you can master a few dialectical rudiments — the flat As, the unhurried monotone, an understated metaphor or two — but the only essential quality is a certain solemnity of demeanor and an absence of expectation. Never tell a Maine story with the idea of producing a big laugh; it won't work and you'll be disappointed. The high water mark is an appreciative chuckle.

Two books can help: John Gould's *"Maine Lingo,"* a definitive compendium of words, phrases and locutions peculiar to the region, and Gerald E. Lewis's *"How to Talk Yankee,"* a spirited guide to usage in the Maine language.

What follows is a sampler of downeast stories anybody can tell.

\* \* \*

During the fall foliage season a chartered bus pulled into the Rangeley Lakes region with a load of tourists. The passengers disembarked to buy some cider at a roadside stand located next to an apple orchard. The farmer who operated the stand sat under a nearby tree, making change out of a cigar box.

"My, but this tree seems to be loaded with apples," said a customer by way of making conversation. "Are all your trees as productive as this one?"

"Nope," said the farmer. "Only the apple trees."

\* \* \*

A well-dressed out-of-state matron stopped for provisions at Clif Hutching's grocery store in West Pembroke, and asked to inspect an "oven fowl." Clif went out to the freezer and came back with the only chicken he had in stock.

"How much is that?" the customer inquired.

"$2.49," said Clif.

"Well, it seems a bit scrawny," said the lady. "Could I see one a little larger?"

Clif wasn't about to lose a sale just for the lack of inventory, so

he walked back to the freezer, waited a minute and returned with the same chicken.

"That's better," said the customer. "How much is this one?"

"$3.69, ma'am," said Clif.

"Fine," said the customer, smiling sweetly. "I'll take them both."

\* \* \*

Some of the boys were sitting around the marina swapping summer complaint stories and Blake Hanscom says, "I had one jasper rent one of my boats earlier this season, went out and caught a mess

of togue. He was some excited. Said he put an X on the bottom of
the boat to mark the spot so he could fish there again next year."

"Damn fool," snorts Bill Wintner. "All the boats you got, Blake,
he'll never get the same one."

\* \* \*

A Boston couple bought a summer place in Eustis and started
down the road to find a man named Ben Higby whom they were
told lived in the neighborhood and would be willing to undertake
some repairs to the cottage. About a mile down the road the couple
came upon a man working in a field.

"Excuse me, but do you know where Ben Higby lives?" asked the
husband.

"Ayuh," said the man, looking the two over and volunteering no
further information.

"Well, could you tell us where he lives?" asked the wife. The man
pointed to a small house about a mile up the mountain.

"That's quite a walk," said the wife. "Do you suppose Mr.
Higby is in?"

"Nope, he ain't home," said the man.

As the couple looked at each other, pondering their next move,
the man in the field asked, "What do you want with him?"

Replied the husband: "We just bought the Varney cottage and
we were told Mr. Higby might be willing to do some repairing for
us."

The man regarded them for a moment, then said, "I'm Higby."

\* \* \*

Cap Stover was a Maine guide from Oxbow noted for his taciturnity. Although he didn't say much he was a damned fine guide
and always knew just where the fish were biting best. A pair of
New Yorkers once found his services so satisfactory that they re-

turned the following summer. They found Cap rocking on his front porch.

"Hello, Cap," said one of the sports.

Cap said hello.

"I'm Bob Blackstone, remember me?"

"Ayuh."

"And this is Lenny Poole."

"Ayuh."

There was a pause while the guide kept rocking. Then Blackstone said: "Well, Cap, you don't seem very glad to see us."

"Ain't glad. Ain't sorry. Just don't give a dang."

* * *

The circulation manager of Down East magazine sent a form letter to Abner Mason in Damariscotta notifying him that his subscription had expired. The notice came back a few days later with the scrawled message: "So's Abner."

A retired schoolteacher from Boston who always rented the same cottage every summer at Deer Isle had a local reputation as a complainer. One day she stopped at Ben Jordan's roadside vegetable stand and bought some tomatoes.

"These tomatoes are rather small, I must say," she commented as she handed over the money. Ben said nothing.

The next day the lady was back: "Mr. Jordan, those tomatoes you sold me yesterday were perfectly awful. They were dry and pulpy and tasteless."

"Ayuh," replied Ben agreeably. "Lucky they was small, ain't it?"

\* \* \*

Ira Richards of Bowdoinham up on Merrymeeting Bay raised retrievers to rent to vacationing duck and geese hunters. He was famous throughout the region for the quality and dependability of his dogs.

One bright autumn day a couple of sports from Massachusetts swung by Ira's place asking to rent a dog or two.

"Nope," said Ira. "They're all out."

One of the strangers, noticing a handsome Golden Retriever relaxing in the back yard, asked, "What about that one?"

"Old Barley? You wouldn't want him, mister. He's got awful peculiar ways."

"Does he retrieve?"

"Oh, he's dependable on that score, I suppose."

"Well, then, why can't we rent him?"

"Can if you like. But it'll cost you ten dollars cash. In advance."

The hunters paid and took the dog out to the marshes. The first duck they shot dropped a hundred feet off shore. Old Barley casually walked across the surface of the water and returned with the bird and casually dropped it at the feet of the flabbergasted hunters.

"My God, Jim, do you believe what I think I just saw happen?"

"No, I don't, but I'd like to see it again just to prove we're not crazy."

They shot more ducks and each time the dog walked out on the water and retrieved the game. When the hunters returned, the one named Jim blurted out: "Mister, that's the most unusual dog we ever hunted with. Do you know what you have here?"

Replied Ira defensively: "Now don't say I didn't warn you. Ain't my fault the son of a bitch can't swim."

\* \* \*

A summer theater company once came to Cundy's Harbor to present a melodrama, but on the day of the production one of the female performers fell suddenly ill. The director of the company decided to recruit a local stand-in rather than cancel the play. The prospects were slim, but he did manage to find a reasonably attractive native who was willing to step into the role. It was not a difficult part. There were only a few lines to be memorized and the script called for the woman to be murdered by a disappointed suitor at the conclusion of the first act.

Rehearsals went well and by the time the curtain rose that evening the Town Hall auditorium was satisfactorily filled with local playgoers. The atmosphere was one of high excitement.

The stand-in, though a bit nervous at first, was letter perfect in her role. Whenever she delivered a line there was an appreciative burst of applause, particularly from the male members of the audience. At the climactic moment of the act, the disappointed lover appeared on stage and fired a revolver at the lady. She delivered a piercing scream, clutched her breast and fell sprawling to the stage.

The lover's anger immediately dissolved into remorse. Falling to his knees he cried in horror, "My God, what have I done?"

From the back of the auditorium an indignant voice was heard: "I'll tell you what you done, you dang fool. You just shot the finest ho-ah in Cundy's Hah-bah!"

\* \* \*

Harry Balch was milking one of his cows in the barnyard one afternoon when a stranger drove up to get directions to Ellsworth. Harry told him. Then the stranger said, "By the way, do you happen to have the right time? My watch has stopped."

Harry reached under the cow's udder, lifted one of the nipples, studied it for a second or two and said, "It's twenty-two minutes past four."

The stranger gave a skeptical look and said, "You wouldn't be pulling my leg now would you?"

"Nope," said Harry. "That's the exact time, not a minute more, not a minute less."

"Okay, but tell me how you do that," said the stranger.

"Easy," said Harry. "Just sit down on this milkstool and I'll show ya." The stranger, curious, complied.

"Now with your right hand grab that left teat and raise it an inch-and-a-quarter." The stranger did.

"All right," Harry concluded, "if you bend down just so and look straight ahead you'll see the town clock over yonder."

\* \* \*

Fellow from Boston was driving through Orient on his way to a cabin he'd rented at East Grand Lake when he spotted an unusual

sight. An elderly man on the front porch of a country store was holding a fishpole with the line trailing into a bucket of water. Remem-
bering that he had some supplies to buy, the Bostonian stopped and

as he entered the store decided to have a little fun with the obviously
addled native.

"Hey, oldtimer," he said. "Catching any big ones?"

"Ayuh," replied the fisherman. "You're the third one I got today."

\* \* \*

A motorist stopped on the outskirts of North Pownal to ask directions of an elderly farmer working in a field with a horse-drawn
hand plow. The farmer appeared to be in his late sixties and the
stranger was impressed at the vigor with which he tackled the plow-
ing chore.

"Aren't you a little old to be doing heavy work like this?" he asked.

"Ain't so bad," the farmer replied. "My pa is an awful big help."

"Your father is alive?"

"Yup. That's him up by the barn there, pitching manure."

The stranger spotted the old gentleman in the distance. "But that's amazing. How old is he, anyway?"

"Pa's eighty-six."

"I can't believe it. A man his age ought not to be exerting himself like that."

"Well, ordinarily Grandpa is around to help him."

"You have a grandfather? Good heavens, how old would he be?"

"Hundred-and-three."

"This is astounding. Where is he now?"

"On his honeymoon."

"You mean to tell me he just got married? Why on earth would a man his age want to do that?"

"Didn't want to. Had to."

\* \* \*

A Texan passing through Aroostook County at the end of a successful potato harvest stopped overnight in Caribou. During dinner at the hotel he made the acquaintance of some locals and was invited to join them for their weekly poker game in one of the rooms.

As the game got underway, the Texan decided it would be to his advantage to make a strong impression upon the Mainers at the very outset. He pulled out a big roll of bills, slapped it down on the table and said, "I'll take a thousand dollars worth of chips."

So they gave him a blue chip.

\* \* \*

Harold and Herbert were walking down the Main Street of Freeport when a seagull flew over and made an unscheduled deposit square on top of Herbert's bald head.

"Gorry, Herbert, that's too bad," said Harold. "You wait right

here and I'll run across to the Rexall and get a Kleenex to take care of that."

"Don't bother," replied Herbert. "By the time you get back that seagull will be all the way to Kennebunkport."

* * *

Alton Greeley spent all of his life in the north woods, venturing only occasionally into town for provisions. He worked hard, lived frugally and moved through each day at a deliberate pace. On his 75th birthday, Greeley's boys, all of whom had left home years before, chipped in for a chain saw for the old man, hoping to make life a bit easier for him. When they explained to him that the machine would allow him to cut two or three cords in a single day, Greeley was skeptical but willing.

A couple of weeks later one of the boys came around to the cabin to see how the old man was making out. He found his father cutting wood by hand as usual, the new chain saw discarded in a far corner of the yard.

"Pa, what are you doing?" the son asked. "What's wrong with the chain saw?"

"Blamed thing don't work," replied Greeley. "Took me three days to get barely half a cord with it."

"That's strange," said the boy. "Art Walker over at Minot checked it out before he sold it to us and he said it was in tip-top shape. Let's have a look."

The son checked the gas and the oil, switched the starter button on and gave the rope a yank. The saw immediately started up, and old Greeley jumped in surprise.

"What's that god-awful noise?" he yelled.

\* \* \*

One particularly wet spring Arlo Benson of Magalloway missed seeing his neighbor, Seth Perkins, for several days and got worried. Arlo drove around to Seth's place and found him sitting in his pickup in the yard, mud up to the hubcaps.

"Howdy, Seth," said Arlo, "you all right?"

"Ayuh," said Seth.

There was a pause, then Arlo said, "You stuck?"

"I would be," replied Seth, "if I tried to move."

\* \* \*

A summer visitor drove up to Bill Putney's place and asked directions to the Rangeley Lodge.

"Oh, that's about five miles from here," Bill told him.

The fellow drove the specified distance without result and finally hailed a farmer in a field.

"Rangeley Lodge?" said the farmer. "Why you just go five miles down the road. Can't miss it."

Again the motorist followed directions but couldn't locate his destination. He pulled up to a country store and asked the way to the lodge.

"Just keep going the way you're headed," said the storekeeper. "You'll find Rangeley Lodge on the right side of the road, just about five miles."

"Look here," said the exasperated motorist. "I asked directions at a farmhouse and was told the lodge was five miles away. Then a fellow told me it was another five miles. Now you're saying it's still five miles. What am I to believe?"

"Well, look at it this way," replied the storekeeper, "at least you're not losing ground."

\* \* \*

# 2

# Beginnings — The 19th Century

# SEBA SMITH

*Seba Smith (1792-1868) is generally acknowledged as the father of that comic strain in American literature known as Yankee humor. He originated a device for political commentary — the unsophisticated "common man" naively and comically exposing the establishment — which endured as an element of American humorous writing for more than a century.*

*Smith founded Maine's first daily newspaper, the Portland Courier, in 1829 when the state capital was still located in Portland. The Courier was a politically independent newspaper in a day when journalistic partisanship was not only accepted but expected.*

*In 1830 the major political parties in the state were so evenly balanced that the legislature wasn't able to organize itself for several weeks. In an effort to pump some reader interest into his fledgling newspaper, Smith took advantage of the situation by creating the character of Jack Downing to comment in an amusing fashion upon the tangled political situation.*

*Downing was an innocent rustic who came to town peddling ax handles, hoop poles and other notions. During the slow sales season, he dropped by the legislature and recorded his observations on the strange goings-on (via the Courier's columns) in a series of comic letters home to his relatives in "Downingville."*

*The Downing letters proved an instant hit with readers. Within a short time they were being reproduced in Boston newspapers and eventually developed a national audience. In time "Major Jack Downing" moved to Washington, D. C., where he became a confidant and advisor of President Andrew Jackson. The democratic excesses of the Jackson administration proved an ideal target for deflation by the literal-minded rustic from Maine, and the Downing commentaries remained immensely popular for many years.*

*"Henceforth Americans would always regard their chief executives with a coldly skeptical eye,"* says Louis D. Rubin Jr. *in* The Comic Imagination in American Literature, *"and for that we may blame — or praise — Seba Smith, one of our first democratic 'levelers'."*

*Seba Smith developed an energetic band of imitators, who stole not only the character of Jack Downing but his name as well. One such imitator, Charles Augustus Davis, published a series of Downing letters in the New York Advertiser which exceeded in popularity those written by Smith himself. Another plagiarist was active as late as the Civil War, long after Smith had abandoned satirical writing. The imitator's pieces appeared in book form in 1864 under the title "The Letters of Major Jack Downing of the Downingville Militia."*

*Unfortunately, little of Seba Smith's political and social satire retains its flavor or interest today. Nevertheless the passages which follow provide an interesting historical example of a brand of humor which, initially parochial, provided a blueprint for American political humor which survives to this day.*

\* \* \*

## SKETCH OF MY EARLY LIFE

When we read about great men, we always want to know something about the place where they live; therefore I shall begin my history with a short account of Downingville, the place where I was born and brought up.

Downingville is a snug, tidy sort of a village, situated in a valley about two miles long, and a mile and a half wide, scooped out between two large rugged hills that lie to the east and west, having a thick forest of trees to the north, and a clear pond of water, with a sandy beach, to the south. It is about three miles from the main road, as you go back into the country, and is *jest about in the middle of Down East.* It contains by this time a pretty considerable number of inhabitants, though my grandfather Downing was the first person that settled there, jest after he got back from sogering in the Revolutionary war. It has a school-house and a tavern, and a minister, and a doctor, and a blacksmith, and a shoe-maker, and folks that work at most all sorts of trades. They haven't got any meeting house up yet, but the school-house is pretty large, and does very well to hold meetins in, and they have meetins very regular every Sunday — the men filling up all the seats on one side of the school-house and the women on the other.

They haven't got any lawyer in Downingville. There was one come once and sot out to settle there, and hired a room and put a sign up over the door with his name on it, and the word "office" in great large letters, so big you could read 'em clear across the road. A meeting of the inhabitants was called at the school-house the next day, and after chawing the matter over awhile it was unanimously agreed if the man wanted an office he should go somewhere else for it, for as for having an office-seeker in Downingville they never would. So they voted that he should leave the town in twenty-four hours, or they would take him down to the pond and duck him, and ride him out of town on a rail. A committee of twenty of the stoutest men in Downingville was appointed to carry the message to him, at which he prudently took the hint, and packed up and cleared out that afternoon. All the quarrels, and disputes and law-cases are always left out to Uncle Joshua Downing, and he settles them all, by and large, at two shillings a piece, except when they have come to blows, and then he charges two and sixpence a piece.

\* \* \*

Mother always said I was the smartest baby that she ever see. I don't speak of this by way of bragging, but as I am writing a history to go before the world, I'm bound to be impartial. She says before I was a week old I showed that I was real grit, and could kick and scream two hours upon the stretch, and not seem to be the least bit tired that ever was. But I don't remember anything about this.

We used to have a school in Downingville about three months in the winter season and two months in the summer, and I went to the winter school three winters, from the time I was twelve till I was fifteen. And I was called about the best scholar of my age that there was in school. But to be impartial, I must confess the praise didn't always belong to me, for I used sometimes to work headwork a little in order to get the name of being a smart scholar. One instance of it

was in reading. I got along in reading so well, that the master said I read better than some of the boys that were considerably older than I, and that had been to school a dozen winters. But the way I managed it was this. There was cousin Obediah was the best reader there was in school, and as clever a boy as one in a thousand, only his father hadn't got no orchard. So I used to carry a great apple to school in my pocket every day and give to him to get him to set behind me when I was reading, where he could peak into my book, and when I come to a hard word, have him whisper it to me, and then I read it out loud. Well, one day I was reading along so, pretty glib, and at last I come to a pesky great long crooked word, that I couldn't make head nor tail to it. So I waited for Obediah. But it proved to be a match for Obediah. He peaked, and squinted, and choked, and I was catching my breath and waiting for him to speak; and at last he found he could do nothing with it, and says he "skip it." The moment I heard the sound I bawled out, "*Skip it.*" "What's that?" said the master, looking at me as queer as though he had catched a weazel asleep. I stopt and looked at the word again, and poked my tongue out, and waited for Obediah. Well, Obediah give me a hunch, and whispered again, "skip it." Then I bawled out again, "*Skip it.*" At that the master and about one-half the scholars yaw-hawed right out. I couldn't stand that; and I dropt the book and streaked it out of school, and pulled foot for home as fast as I could go, and I never showed my head in school again from that day to this.

To come, then, right to the pint—I don't mean the pint of water-million seeds, but the pint in my life which seemed to be the turning pint. In the Fall of the year 1829, I took it into my head I'd go to Portland. So I tackled up the old horse, and packed in a load of ax-handles and a few notions, and mother fried me some dough-nuts and put 'em into a box along with some cheese and sassages, and ropped me up another shirt, for I told her I didn't know how long I should be gone; and after I got all rigged out I went round and bid all the neighbors good bye, and jumped in and drove off for Portland.

I hadn't been in Portland long before I happened to blunder into the Legislater; and I believe that was the beginning of my good luck. I see such queer kinds of carrying on there that I couldn't help setting down and writing to cousin Ephraim to tell uncle Joshua about it; because he always wanted to know everything that's going on in Politics. So I went to the editor of the Portland Courier and asked him if he would send it. So I let him have it, and fact, he went right to work and printed it in the Courier as large as life. He said he wouldn't let anybody else see it but cousin Ephraim; but somehow or other it leaked out, and was all over the Legislater the next morning, and everybody was inquiring for Mr. Downing. Well, this kind of got me right into public life at once; and I've been in public life ever since, and have been writing letters and rising up along gradually, one step after another, till I've got up along side of the President, and am talked of now pretty strong for President my-self, and have been nominated in a good many of the first papers of the country.

My public life will be found in my letters, one after another, jest as they come, from the time I first sent that letter in the Portland Courier to cousin Ephraim till this time.

MAJOR JACK DOWNING.

*Portland,* Me., 1834.

## Letter I

Portland, Monday, Jan. 18, 1830.

DEAR COUSIN EPHRAIM: — I've been here now a whole fortnight, and if I could tell ye one half I've seen, I guess you'd stare worse than if you'd seen a catamount. I've been to meeting, and to the museum, and to both Legislaters, the one they call the House, and the one they call the Sinnet.

Uncle Joshua may set his heart at rest about the bushel of corn that he bet 'long with the postmaster, that Mr. Ruggles would be Speaker of that Legislater they call the House; for he's lost it, slick as a whistle. As I hadn't much to do, I've been there every day since they've been a setting. A Mr. White, of Monmouth, was the Speaker the first two days; and I can't see why they didn't keep him in all the time; for he seemed to be a very clever, good-natured sort of man, and he had such a smooth, pleasant way with him, that I couldn't help feeling sorry when they turned him out and put in another.

They kept disputing most all the time the first two days about a poor Mr. Roberts, from Waterborough. Some said he shouldn't have a seat because he wasn't fairly elected. Others said it was

no such thing, and that he was elected as fairly as any of 'em. And Mr. Roberts himself said he was, and said he could bring men that would swear to it, and good men too. But, notwithstanding all this, when they came to vote, they got three or four majority that he shouldn't have a seat. And I thought it a needless piece of cruelty, for they wan't crowded, and there was a number of seats empty. But they would have it so, and the poor man had to go and stand up in the lobby.

Then they disputed awhile about a Mr. Fowler's having a seat. Some said he shouldn't have a seat, because when he was elected some of his votes were given for his father. But they were more kind to him than they were to Mr. Roberts, for they voted that he *should* have a seat; and I suppose it was because they thought he had a lawful right to inherit whatever was his father's. They all declared there was no party politics about it, and I don't think there was; for I noticed that all who voted that Mr. Roberts *should* have a seat, voted that Mr. Fowler should *not;* and all who voted that Mr. Roberts should *not* have a seat, voted that Mr. Fowler *should*. So, as they all voted *both* ways, they must have been conscientious, and I don't see how there could be any party about it.

It's a pity they couldn't be allowed to have two Speakers, for they seemed to be very anxious to choose Mr. Ruggles and Mr. Goodenow. They two had every vote except one, and if they had had *that,* I believe they would both have been chosen; as it was, however, they both came within a humbird's eye of it. I would have given half my load of ax handles, if they could both have been elected and set up there together, they would have been so happy. But as they can't have but one Speaker at a time, and as Mr. Goodenow appears to understand the business very well, it is not likely Mr. Ruggles will be Speaker any this winter. So Uncle Joshua will have to shell out his bushel of corn, and I hope it will learn him better than to bet about politics again.

\* \* \*

## Letter II

Portland, Jan. 22, 1830.

DEAR UNCLE JOSHUA:—I spose you learnt by my letter t'other day to cousin Ephraim, that you had lost the bushel of corn you bet about the Speaker in the Legislater—I mean that Legislater they call the House—for Mr. White got it first, and then Mr. Goodenow got it, and he's kept it ever since. And they say he'll be Speaker all winter, although he don't *speak* near so much as some of the rest of 'em.

They've disputed two days more about that poor Mr. Roberts having a seat. I can't see why they need to make such a fuss about it. As they've got seats enough, why don't they let him have one, and not keep him standing up for three weeks in the lobby and round the fire. It's a plaguey sight worse than being on a standing committee, for they say the standing committees have a chance to set most every day. But in the dispute about Mr. Roberts last Wednesday and Thursday, the difficulty seemed to be something or other about a *primy facy* case. I don't know what sort of a case 'twas, but that's what they called it. Some said he hadn't got any *primy facy* case, and he mustn't have a seat till he had one. The others stood to it that he *had* got one, and a very good one.

Oh dear, Uncle Joshua, these Legislaters have got the State into a dreadful pickle. I've been reading the Portland Argus and the Portland Advertiser, and it's enough to scare a Bunker Hill soger out of his seven senses to see what we are all coming to. The people are growing pretty mad at all this botheration, and I can't tell what'll be the end on't.

\* \* \*

## Letter XII

Portland, Tuesday, March 16, 1830.

DEAR UNCLE JOSHUA: — There's a hot time ahead. I almost dread to think of it. I'm afraid there's going to be a worse scrabble next summer to see who shall go to the State husking than there was last. The Huntonites and Smithites are determined to have each of 'em a Governor agin next year. They've sot up their candidates on both sides; and who in all the world should you guess they are? The Huntonites have sot up Mr. Hunton, and the Smithites have sot up Mr. Smith. You understand what it means, I s'pose, to set up a candidate. It means the same as it does at a shooting match to set up a goose or a turkey to be fired at. The rule of the game is, that the Smithites are to fire at Mr. Hunton, and the Huntonites are to fire at Mr. Smith. They think it will take a pretty hard battle to get them both in. But both parties say they've got the constitution on their side, so I think likely they'll both beat.

\* \* \*

### Letter XVI

Portland, March 30, 1830.

DEAR UNCLE JOSHUA: — In one of my letters, you know, I said newspapers were dreadful *smoky* things, and anybody couldn't read in 'em half an hour without having their eyes so full of smoke they couldn't tell a pig-sty from a meeting-house.

But I'm thinking, after all, they are more like *rum* than smoke. You know rum will sometimes set quite peaceable folks together by the ears, and make them *quarrel* like mad dogs — so do the newspapers. Rum makes folks act very *silly* — so do the newspapers. Rum makes folks *see double* — so do the newspapers. Sometimes rum gets folks so they can't see at all — so do the newspapers. Rum, if they take tu much of it, makes folks *sick to the stomach* — so do the newspapers. Rum makes folks go rather crooked, reeling from one side of the road to t'other — and the newspapers make one half the politicians *cross their path* as often as any drunkard you ever see. It was the newspapers, uncle Joshua, that made you bet about the Speaker last summer, and lose your bushel of corn.

Remember, that, uncle, and don't believe anything you see in the papers this summer, unless you see it in the Daily Courier.

I remain your loving neffu till death.

JACK DOWNING.

\* \* \*

# *ARTEMUS WARD*

**I was born in the State of Maine of parents. As an infant I abstracted a great deal of attention. The nabers would stand over my cradle for hours and say, "How bright that little face looks! How much it nose!"**

*Charles Farrar Browne (1834-1867) was the predominant figure in what E. B. White calls "the heyday of the crackerbarrel philosopher, sometimes wise, always wise-seeming, and nowadays rather dreary."*

*As Artemus Ward, Browne was the first Yankee humorist to develop a truly universal following. He combined all the principal characteristics of native American humor in the 19th century. Artemus Ward was the unschooled rustic employing laughable turns of speech, earthy metaphors and illiterate spelling to comment upon the political and social developments of the day.*

*Later, he and other humorists of the day — Josh Billings and Petroleum V. Nasby — would be put down as mere comic "misspellers" and vulgar "phunny phellows" whose wit was transitory. Mark Twain would assert that the humor of these writers, his own literary forebears, was in essence "merely an odd trick of speech and spelling." Yet, Artemus Ward and his imitators did much to establish a purely American style of humorous writing by incorporating into it the familiar dialectical patterns of their neighbors and friends with whom the ordinary reader could readily identify.*

*Born in 1834 in Waterford, Maine, Browne was the son of a farmer and surveyor who dabbled in politics. The father died when*

*Browne was 13, and the youngster began working as a typesetter and printer to help support the family. He joined the staff of "The Carpet Bag," a humorous Boston journal, and when that folded in 1852 the young Browne drifted west as a journeyman printer, eventually becoming a reporter and editor for the Cleveland Plain Dealer.*

*It was at the Plain Dealer that he developed his character of Artemus Ward. His articles became an instant success and his fame began to spread rapidly, enough so that in 1861 he began writing for Vanity Fair, the American version of the English comic periodical, Punch.*

*There developed two Artemus Wards. One was the literary character, the shrewd and vulgar wandering showman who travelled about displaying his "wax-figgers," commenting in semi-literate letters home about his adventures. This Artemus Ward was a favorite of Abraham Lincoln who, according to legend, delayed the signing of the Emancipation Proclamation to read aloud to his bemused Cabinet the latest Artemus Ward offering, "A High-handed Outrage at Utica."*

*The second Artemus Ward was a stage personality, a performer on the lecture circuit who proved more popular than Emerson, Longfellow, Whittier, Hawthorne and other contemporaries. Browne's stage performances burlesqued these popular lecturers, who traveled the country and dispensed wisdom and personal narratives in what was then the most popular form of American entertainment.*

*Bram Weber, in* "Native American Humor," *describes Browne's platform performance:* "Apparently spontaneous and haphazard, seemingly marred by forgetfulness, inappropriate pauses, verbal ineptitude, free-association rambling and other embarrassments, Ward's (program) was carefully planned and timed. The deadpan earnestness of his effort to communicate and the chaos that resulted were so beautifully intermingled that his audience often did not know whether to respond with pity, contempt or amusement."

*Browne's public career was brilliant, but short. He died, at age*

*33, of tuberculosis, while on a successful lecture tour in England. He is buried in his hometown of Waterford.*

*The following selections — including the piece Lincoln found so amusing — are representative of the brand of Yankee humor which kept America in stitches during an innocent but pivotal period of its literary development.*

\*   \*   \*

## HIGH-HANDED OUTRAGE AT UTICA

In the Faul of 1856, I showed my show in Utiky, a trooly grate sitty in the State of New York.

The people gave me a cordyal recepshun. The press was loud in her prases.

1 day as I was givin a descripshun of my Beests and Snaiks in

my usual flowry stile what was my skorn & disgust to see a big burly feller walk up to the cage containin my wax figgers of the Lord's Last Supper, and cease Judas Iscarrot by the feet and drag him out on the ground. He then commenced fur to pound him as hard as he cood.

"What under the son are you abowt?" cried I.

Sez he, "What did you bring this pussylanermus cuss here fur?" & he hit the wax figger another tremenjis blow on the hed.

Sez I, "You egrejus ass, that air's a wax figger — a representashun of the false 'Postle."

Sez he, "That's all very well fur you to say, but I tell you, old man, that Judas Iscarrot can't show hisself in Utiky with impunerty by a darn site!" with which observashun he kaved in Judassis hed. The young man belonged to 1 of the first famerlies in Utiky. I sood him, and the Joory brawt in a verdick of Arson in the 3d degree.

\* \* \*

## THE SHAKERS

The Shakers is the strangest religious sex I ever met. I'd hearn tell of 'em and I'd seen 'em, with their broad brim'd hats and long wastid coats; but I'd never cum into immejit contack with 'em, and I'd sot 'em down as lackin intelleck, as I'd never seen 'em to my show — leastways, if they cum they was disgised in white peple's close, so I didn't know 'em.

But in the Spring of 18—, I got swampt in the exterior of New York State, one dark and stormy night, when the winds blue pityusly, and I was forced to tie up with the Shakers.

I was toilin threw the mud, when in the dim vister of the futer I obsarved the gleams of a taller candle. Tiein a hornet's nest to my off hoss's tail to kinder encourage him, I soon reached the place. I knockt at the door, which it was opened unto me by a tall, slick-faced, solum lookin individooal, who turn'd out to be a Elder.

"Mr. Shaker," sed I, "you see before you a Babe in the Woods, so to speak, and he axes shelter of you."

"Yay," sed the Shaker, and he led the way into the house, another Shaker bein sent to put my hosses and waggin under kiver.

A solum female, lookin sumwhat like a last year's bean-pole stuck into a long meal bag, cum in and axed me was I athurst and did I hunger? to which I urbanely anserd "a few." She went orf and I endeverd to open a conversashun with the old man.

"Elder, I spect?" sed I.

"Yay," he sed.

"Helth's good, I reckon?"

"Yay."

"What's the wages of a Elder, when he understans his bizness — or do you devote your sarvices gratooitus?"

"Yay."

"Stormy night, sir."

"Yay."

"If the storm continners there'll be a mess underfoot, hay?"

"Yay."

"It's onpleasant when there's a mess underfoot?"

"Yay."

"If I may be so bold, kind sir, what's the price of that pecooler kind of weskit you wear, incloodin trimmins?"

"Yay!"

I pawsd a minit, and then, thinkin I'd be faseshus with him and see how that would go, I slapt him on the shoulder, bust into a harty larf, and told him that as a *yayer* he had no livin ekal.

He jumpt up as if bilin water had bin squirted into his ears, groaned, rolled his eyes up tords the sealin and sed: "You're a man of sin!" He then walkt out of the room.

Jest then the female in the meal bag stuck her hed into the room and statid that refreshments awaited the weary traveler, and I sed if it was vittles she ment, the weary travler was agreeable, and I follered her into the next room.

I sot down to the table and the female in the meal bag pored out sum tea. She sed nothin, and for five minutes the only live thing in that room was a old wooden clock, which tickt in a subdood and bashful manner in the corner. This dethly stillness made me oneasy, and I determined to talk to the female or bust. So sez I, "marrige is agin your rules, I bleeve, marm?"

"Yay."

"The sexes liv strickly apart, I spect?"

"Yay."

"It's kinder singler," sez I, puttin on my most sweetest look and speakin in a winnin voice, "that so fair a made as thou never got hitched to some likely feller." [N. B. — She was upards of 40 and homely as a stump fence, but I thawt I'd tickil her.]

"I don't like men!" she sed, very short.

"Wall, I dunno," sez I, "they're a rayther important part of the populashun. I don't scacely see how we could git along without 'em."

"Us poor wimin folks would git along a grate deal better if there was no men!"

"You'll excoos me, marm, but I don't think that air would work. It wouldn't be regler."

"I'm fraid of men!" she sed.

"That's onnecessary, marm. *You* ain't in no danger. Don't fret yourself on that pint."

"Here we're shot out from the sinful world. Here all is peas. Here we air brothers and sisters. We don't marry and consekently we hav no domestic difficulties. Husbans don't abooze their wives — wives don't worrit their husbans. There's no children here to worrit us. Nothin to worrit us here. No wicked matrimony here. Would thow like to be a Shaker?"

"No," sez I, "it ain't my stile."

I had now histed in as big a load of pervishuns as I could carry comfortable, and, leanin back in my cheer, commenst pickin my teeth with a fork. The female went out, leavin me all alone with the clock. I hadn't sot thar long before the Elder poked his hed in at the door. "You're a man of sin!" he sed, and groaned and went away.

Direckly thar cum in two young Shakeresses, as putty and slick lookin gals as I ever met. It is troo they was drest in meal bags like the old one I'd met previsly, and their shiny, silky har was hid from sight by long white caps, sich as I spose female josts wear; but their eyes sparkled like diminds, their cheeks was like roses, and they was charmin enuff to make a man throw stuns at his granmother, if they axed him to. They commenst clerin away the dishes, castin shy glances at me all the time. I got excited. I forgot Betsy Jane in my rapter, and sez I, "my pretty dears, how air you?"

"We air well," they solumly sed.

"Whar's the old man?" sed I, in a soft voice.

"Of whom dost thow speak — Brother Uriah?"

"I mean the gay and festiv cuss who calls me a man of sin. Shouldn't wonder if his name was Uriah."

"He has retired."

"Wall, my pretty dears," sez I, "let's hav sum fun. Let's play puss in the corner. What say?"

"Air you a Shaker, sir?" they axed.

"Wall, my pretty dears, I haven't arrayed my proud form in a long weskit yit, but if they was all like you perhaps I'd jine 'em. As it is, I'm a Shaker pro-temporary."

They was full of fun. I seed that at fust, only they was a leetle skeery. I tawt 'em puss in the corner and sich like plase, and we had a nice time, keepin quiet of course so the old man shouldn't hear. When we broke up, sez I, "my pretty dears, ear I go you hav no objections, hav you, to a innersent kiss at partin?"

"Yay," they sed, and I *yay'd*.

I went up stairs to bed. I spose I'd bin snoozin half a hour when I was woke up by a noise at the door. I sot up in bed, leanin on my elbers and rubbin my eyes, and I saw the follerin picter: The Elder stood in the doorway, with a taller candle in his hand. He hadn't no wearin appeerel on except his night close, which flutterd in the breeze like a Seseshun flag. He sed, "You're a man of sin!" then groaned and went away.

I went to sleep agin, and drempt of runnin orf with the pretty little Shakeresses . . . I was woke up arly by the Elder. He sed refreshments was reddy for me down stairs. Then sayin I was a man of sin, he went groanin away.

As I was goin threw the entry to the room where the vittles was, I cum across the Elder and the old female I'd met the night before, and what d'ye spose they was up to? Huggin and kissin like young lovers in their gushingist state. Sez I, "my Shaker frends, I reckon you'd better suspend the rules, and git marrid!"

"You must excoos Brother Uriah," sed the female; "he's subjeck to fits and hain't got no command over hisself when he's into 'em."

"Sartinly," sez I, "I've bin took that way myself frequent."

"You're a man of sin!" sed the Elder.

Arter breakfust my little Shaker frends cum in agin to clear away the dishes.

"My pretty dears," sez I, "shall we *yay* agin?"

"Nay," they sed, and I *nay'd*.

The Shakers axed me to go to their meetin, as they was to hav sarvices that mornin, so I put on a clean biled rag and went. The meetin house was as neat as a pin. The floor was white as chalk and smooth as glass. The Shakers was all on hand, in clean weskits and meal bags, ranged on the floor like milingtery companies, the mails on one side of the room and the females on tother. They commenst clappin their hands and singin and dancin. They danced kinder slow at fust, but as they got warmed up they shaved it down very brisk, I tell you. Elder Uriah, in particler, exhiberted a right smart chance of spryness in his legs, considerin his time of life, and as he cum a dubble shuffle near where I sot, I rewarded him with a approvin smile and sed: "Hunky boy! Go it, my gay and festiv cuss!"

"You're a man of sin!" he sed, continnerin his shuffle.

The Sperret, as they called it, then moved a short fat Shaker to say a few remarks. He sed they was Shakers and all was ekal. They was the purest and seleckest peple on the yearth. Other peple was sinful as they could be, but Shakers was all right. Shakers was all goin kerslap to the Promist Land, and nobody want goin to stand at the gate to bar 'em out, if they did they'd git run over.

The Shakers then danced and sung agin, and arter they was threw, one of 'em axed me what I thawt of it.

Sez I, "What duz it siggerfy?"

"What?" sez he.

"Why this jumpin up and singin? This long weskit bizniss, and this anty-matrimony idee? My frends, you air neat and tidy. Your lands is flowin with milk and honey. Your brooms is fine, and your apple sass is honest. When a man buys a kag of apple sass of you he won't find a grate many shavins under a few layers of sass — a little game I'm sorry to say sum of my New Englan ancesters used to practiss. Your garding seeds is fine, and if I should sow 'em on the rock of Gibralter probly I should raise a good mess of garding sass. You air honest in your dealins. You air quiet and don't distarb nobody. For all this I givs you credit. But your religion is small pertaters, I must say. You mope away your lives here in single retchidness, and as you air all by yourselves nothing ever conflicks with your pecooler idees, except when Human Nater busts out among you, as I understan she sumtimes do. [I giv Uriah a sly wink here, which made the old feller squirm like a speared eel.] You wear long weskits and long faces, and lead a gloomy life indeed. No children's prattle is ever hearn around your harthstuns — you air in a dreary fog all the time, and you treat the jolly sunshine of life as tho' it was a thief, drivin it from your doors by them weskits, and meal bags, and pecooler noshuns of yourn. The gals among you, sum of which air as slick pieces of caliker as I ever sot eyes on, air syin to place their heds agin weskits which kiver honest, manly harts, while you old heds fool yerselves with the idee that they air fulfillin their mishun here, and air contented. Here you air, all pend up by yerselves, talkin about the sins of a world you don't know nothin of. Meanwhile said world continners to resolve round on her own axeltree onct in every 24 hours, subjeck to the Constitution of the United States, and is a very plesant place of residence. It's a unnatral, onreasonable and dismal life you're leadin here. So it strikes me. My Shaker frends, I now bid you a welcome adoo. You hav treated me exceedin well. Thank you kindy, one and all."

"A base exhibiter of depraved monkeys and onprincipled wax works!" sed Uriah.

"Hello, Uriah," sez I, "I'd most forgot you. Wall, look out for them fits of yourn, and don't catch cold and die in the flour of your youth and beauty."

And I resoomed my jerney.

\* \* \*

## AGRICULTURE

My farm is in the interior of Maine. Unfortunately my lands are eleven miles from the railroad. Eleven miles is quite a distance to haul immense quantities of wheat, corn, rye, and oats; but as I hav'n't any to haul, I do not, after all, suffer much on that account.

My farm is more especially a grass farm.

My neighbors told me so at first, and as an evidence that they were sincere in that opinion, they turned their cows on to it the moment I went off "lecturing."

These cows are now quite fat. I take pride in these cows, in fact, and am glad I own a grass farm.

Two years ago I tried sheep-raising.

I bought fifty lambs, and turned them loose on my broad and beautiful acres.

It was pleasant on bright mornings to stroll leisurely out on to the farm in my dressing-gown, with a cigar in my mouth, and watch those innocent little lambs as they danced gaily o'er the hillside. Watching their saucy capers reminded me of caper sauce, and it occurred to me I should have some very fine eating when they grew up to be "muttons."

My gentle shepherd, Mr. Eli Perkins, said, "We must have some shepherd dogs."

I had no very precise idea as to what shepherd dogs were, but I assumed a rather profound look, and said:

"We must, Eli. I spoke to you about this some time ago!"

I wrote to my old friend, Mr. Dexter H. Follett, of Boston, for

two shepherd dogs. Mr. F. is not an honest old farmer himself, but
I thought he knew about shepherd dogs. He kindly forsook far more
important business to accommodate, and the dogs came forthwith.
They were splendid creatures — snuff-colored, hazel-eyed, long-
tailed, and shapely-jawed.

We led them proudly to the fields.

"Turn them in, Eli," I said.

Eli turned them in.

They went in at once, and killed twenty of my best lambs in about four minutes and a half.

My friend had made a trifling mistake in the breed of these dogs. These dogs were not partial to sheep.

Eli Perkins was astonished, and observed:

"Waal! *did* you ever?"

I certainly never had.

There were pools of blood on the greensward, and fragments of wool and raw lamb chops lay round in confused heaps.

The dogs would have been sent to Boston that night, had they not rather suddenly died that afternoon of a throat-distemper. It wasn't a swelling of the throat. It wasn't diphtheria. It was a violent opening of the throat, extending from ear to ear.

Thus closed their life-stories. Thus ended their interesting tails.

I failed as a raiser of lambs. As a sheepist, I was not a success.

\* \* \*

## SURRENDER OF CORNWALLIS

It was customary in many of the inland towns of New England, some thirty years ago, to celebrate the anniversary of the surrender of Lord Cornwallis, by a sham representation of that important event in the history of the Revolutionary War. A town meeting would be called, at which a company of men would be detailed as British, and a company as Americans — two leading citizens being selected to represent Washington and Cornwallis in the mimic surrender.

The pleasant little town of W——, in whose schools the writer has been repeatedly "corrected," upon whose ponds he has often skated; upon whose richest orchards he has, with other juvenile bandits, many times dashed in the silent midnight; the town of W——, where it was popularly believed these bandits would "come to a bad end," resolved to celebrate the surrender. Rival towns had celebrated, and W—— determined to eclipse them in the most signal manner. It is my privilege to tell how W—— succeeded in this determination.

The great day came. It was ushered in by the roar of musketry, the ringing of the village church bell, the squeaking of fifes, and the rattling of drums.

People poured into the village from all over the county. Never had W—— experienced such a jam. Never had there been such an onslaught upon gingerbread carts. Never had New England rum (for this was before Neal Dow's day) flowed so freely. And W——'s fair daughters, who mounted the house-tops to see the surrender, had never looked fairer. The old folks came, too, and among them were several war-scarred heroes, who had fought gallantly at Monmouth and Yorktown. These brave sons of '76 took no part in the demonstration, but an honored bench was set apart for their exclusive use on the piazza of Sile Smith's store. When they were dry, all they had to do was to sing out to Sile's boy, Jerry, "a leetle New Englan' this way, if *you* please." It was brought forthwith.

At precisely 9 o'clock, by the schoolmaster's new watch, the American and British forces marched on to the village green and placed themselves in battle array, reminding the spectator of the time when

> "Brave Wolfe drew up his men
> In a style most pretty,
> On the Plains of Abraham
> Before the city."

The character of Washington had been assigned to 'Squire Wood, a well-to-do and influential farmer, while that of Cornwallis had been given to the village lawyer, a kind-hearted but rather pompous person, whose name was Caleb Jones.

'Squire Wood, the Washington of the occasion, had met with many unexpected difficulties in preparing his forces, and in his perplexity he had emptied not only his own canteen but those of most of his aides. The consequence was — mortifying as it must be to all true Americans — blushing as I do to tell it, Washington at the commencement of the mimic struggle was most unqualifiedly drunk.

The sham fight commenced. Bang! bang! bang! from the Americans — bang! bang! bang! from the British. The bangs were kept hotly up until the powder gave out, and then came the order to charge. Hundreds of wooden bayonets flashed fiercely in the sunlight, each soldier taking very good care not to hit any body.

"Thaz (hic) right," shouted Washington, who during the shooting had been racing his horse wildly up and down the line, "thaz right! *Gin* it to 'em! Cut their tarnal heads off!"

"On, Romans!" shrieked Cornwallis, who had once seen a theatrical performance and remembered the heroic appeals of the Thespian belligerents, "On to the fray! No sleep till mornin'."

"Let out all their bowels," yelled Washington, "and down with taxation on tea!"

The fighting now ceased, the opposing forces were properly arranged, and Cornwallis, dismounting, prepared to present his sword to Washington according to programme. As he walked slowly towards the Father of His Country he rehearsed the little speech he had committed for the occasion, while the illustrious being who was to hear it was making desperate efforts to keep in his saddle. Now he would wildly brandish his sword and narrowly escape cutting off his horse's ears, and then he would fall suddenly forward on to the steed's neck grasping the mane as drowning men seize hold of straws. He was giving an inimitable representation of Toodles on horseback. All idea of the magnitude of the occasion had left him, and when he saw Cornwallis approaching, with slow and stately step, and sword-hilt extended toward him he inquired,

"What-'n devil *you* want, any (hic) how!"

"General Washington," said Cornwallis, in dignified and impressive tones, "I tender you my sword. I need not inform you, Sir, how deeply —

The speech was here cut suddenly short by Washington who, driving the spurs into his horse, playfully attempted to run over the commander of the British forces. He was not permitted to do this, for his aides, seeing his unfortunate condition, seized the horse by the bridle, straightened Washington up in his saddle, and requested Cornwallis to proceed with his remarks.

"General Washington," said Cornwallis, "the British Lion prostrates himself at the feet of the American Eagle!"

"*Eagle?* EAGLE!" yelled the infuriated Washington, rolling off his horse and hitting Cornwallis a frightful blow on the head with the flat of his sword, "do you call me a *Eagle,* you mean sneakin' cuss?" He struck him again, sending him to the ground, and said, "I'll learn you to call me a Eagle, you infernal scoundrel!"

Cornwallis remained upon the ground only a moment. Smarting from the blows he had received, he arose with an entirely unlooked-for recuperation on the part of the fallen, and in direct defiance of historical example; in spite of the men of both nations, indeed, he whipped the Immortal Washington until he roared for mercy.

The Americans, at first mortified and indignant at the conduct of their chief, now began to sympathize with him and resolved to whip their mock foes in earnest. They rushed fiercely upon them, but the British were really the stronger party and drove the Americans back. Not content with this they charged madly upon them and drove them from the field — from the village, in fact. There were many heads damaged, eyes draped in mourning, noses fractured and legs lamed — it is a wonder that no one was killed outright.

Washington was confined to his house for several weeks, but he recovered at last. For a time there was a coolness between himself and Cornwallis, but they finally concluded to join the whole county in laughing about the surrender.

They live now. Time, the "artist," has thoroughly white-washed their heads, but they are very jolly still. On town meeting days the old 'Squire always rides down to the village. In the hind part of his venerable yellow wagon is always a bunch of hay, ostensibly for the old white horse, but really to hide a glass bottle from the vulgar gaze. This bottle has on one side a likeness of Lafayette, and upon the other may be seen the Goddess of Liberty. What the bottle contains inside I cannot positively say, but it is true that 'Squire Wood and Lawyer Jones visit that bottle very frequently on town meeting days and come back looking quite red in the face. When this redness in the face becomes of the blazing kind, as it generally does by the time the polls close, a short dialogue like this may be heard:

"We shall never play surrender again, Lawyer Jones!"

"Them days is over, 'Squire Wood!"

And then they laugh and jocosely punch each other in the ribs.

\* \* \*

# BILL NYE

*Edgar Wilson "Bill" Nye (1850-1896) transformed the native American humorous literature of the 19th century by abandoning the comical and illiterate dialect popularized by Artemus Ward and others. He was the first humorist successfully to employ good grammar and perfect spelling.*

*Strictly speaking, Nye was not a downeast humorist, although his writing is marked by the same spare, understated qualities of the genre. Born August 25, 1850 at Shirley Mills in Piscataquis County, he moved west with his family at age two. Years later, after he had achieved international fame, he recalled meeting a native of his hometown while on a lecture tour in England. The Shirley Mills man informed Nye that the town had erected a sign at the old Nye homestead.*

*"Really, what does it say?" inquired the flattered author.*

*"It says, 'Eight miles to Greenville'," his friend replied.*

*Nye grew up in Wyoming where he studied for the law, but upon discovering that his clients "found they would be hanged just as well without a lawyer" he turned to newspaper writing.*

*He worked for a number of publications before founding the* Laramie Boomerang, *a paper named for his mule. Although initially not a successful enterprise — Laramie boasted only 3,000 residents and there were two rival newspapers — Nye's humerous style of writing soon attracted a national circulation. Subscriptions began to pour in from all over the United States and several foreign countries as well.*

*Eventually he left Wyoming and began publishing a series of books, mostly collections of his funnier newspaper pieces. During the last two decades of the 19th century Nye's books, now largely forgotten, were popular bestsellers.*

*Nye also took to the lecture circuit, often crossing paths with Mark Twain, who also found the stage a reliable source of income.*

*Nye appeared throughout the United States and Europe in tandem with James Whitcomb Riley, the Hoosier Poet. Nye would be first on stage to introduce the dual performance: "I will talk to you in my inimitable way until I get tired, whereupon Mr. Riley will entertain you until you get tired."*

*Also during these years Nye wrote a column for the* New York World *which became enormously popular in households across America. The largest circulation daily in the nation, the* World *paid him $60,000 a year, the highest salary ever paid a newspaper writer to that time. It remains something of a record to this day.*

*Nye contracted a spinal infection in his Laramie days and was troubled by ill health throughout his career. His most successful books, comic histories of the United States and Europe, were completed during the last two years of his life. He died Feb. 22, 1896 at the age of 45.*

* * *

## WHERE HE FIRST MET HIS PARENTS

Last week I visited my birthplace in the State of Maine. I waited thirty years for the public to visit it, and as there didn't seem to be much of a rush this spring, I thought I would go and visit it myself. I was telling a friend the other day that the public did not seem to manifest the interest in my birthplace that I thought it ought to, and he said I ought not to mind that. "Just wait," said he, "till the people of the United States have an opportunity to visit your tomb, and you will be surprised to see how they will run excursion trains up there to Moosehead Lake, or wherever you plant yourself. It will be a perfect picnic. Your hold on the American people, William, is wonderful, but your death would seem to assure it, and kind of crystallize the affection now existing, but still in a nebulous and gummy state."

A man ought not to criticise his birthplace, I presume, and yet, if I were to do it all over again, I do not know whether I would select that particular spot or not. Sometimes I think I would not. And yet, what memories cluster about that old house! There was the place where I first met my parents. It was at that time that an acquaintance sprang up which has ripened in later years into mutual respect and esteem. It was there that what might be termed a casual meeting took place, that has, under the alchemy of resistless years, turned to golden links, forming a pleasant but powerful bond of union between my parents and myself. For that reason, I hope that I may be spared to my parents for many years to come.

Many memories now cluster about that old home, as I have said. There is, also, other bric-a-brac which has accumulated since I was born there. I took a small stone from the front yard as a kind of memento of the occasion and the place. I do not think it has been detected yet. There was another stone in the yard, so it may be weeks before any one finds out that I took one of them.

How humble the home, and yet what a lesson it should teach the boys of America! Here, amid the barren and inhospitable waste of rocks and cold, the last place in the world that a great man would naturally select to be born in, began the life of one who, by his own unaided effort, in after years rose to the proud height of postmaster at Laramie City, Wy. T., and with an estimate of the future that seemed almost prophetic resigned before he could be characterized as an offensive partisan.

Here on the banks of the raging Piscataquis, where winter lingers in the lap of spring till it occasions a good deal of talk, there began a career which has been the wonder and admiration of every vigilance committee west of the turbulent Missouri.

There on that spot, with no inheritance but a predisposition to baldness and a bitter hatred of rum; with no personal property but a misfit suspender and a stone-bruise, began a life history which has never ceased to be a warning to people who have sold goods on credit.

It should teach the youth of our great, broad land what glorious possibilities may lie concealed in the rough and tough bosom of the reluctant present. It shows how steady perseverance and a good appetite will always win in the end. It teaches us that wealth is not indispensable, and that if we live as we should, draw out of politics at the proper time, and die a few days before the public absolutely demand it, the matter of our birthplace will not be considered.

Still, my birthplace is all right as a birthplace. It was a good, quiet place in which to be born. All the old neighbors said that Shirley was a very quiet place up to the time I was born there, and when I took my parents by the hand and gently led them away in the spring of '53, saying, "Parents, this is no place for us," it again became quiet.

It is the only birthplace I have, however, and I hope that all the readers of this sketch will feel perfectly free to go there any time and visit it and carry their dinner as I did. Extravagant cordiality and overflowing hospitality have always kept my birthplace back.

\* \* \*

## FARMING IN MAINE

The State of Maine is a good place in which to experiment with prohibition, but it is not a good place to farm in very largely.

In the first place, the season is generally a little reluctant. When I was up near Moosehead Lake, a short time ago, people were driving across that body of water on the ice with perfect impunity. That is one thing that interferes with the farming business in Maine. If a young man is sleighriding every night till midnight, he don't feel like hoeing corn the following day. Any man who has ever had his feet frost-bitten while bugging potatoes, will agree with me that it takes away the charm of pastoral pursuits. It is this desire to amalgamate dog days and Santa Claus, that has injured Maine as an agricultural hot-bed.

Another reason that might be assigned for refraining from agricul-

tural pursuits in Maine is that the agitator of the soil finds when it is too late that soil itself, which is essential to the successful propagation of crops, has not been in use in Maine for years. While all over the State there is a magnificent stone foundation on which a farm might safely rest, the superstructure, or farm proper, has not been secured.

If I had known when I passed through Minnesota and Illinois what a soil famine there was in Maine, I would have brought some with me. The stone crop this year in Maine will be very great. If they do not crack open during the dry weather, there will be a great many. The stone bruise is also looking unusually well for this season of the year, and chilblains were in full bloom when I was there.

In the neighborhood of Pittsfield, the country seems to run largely to cold water and chattel mortgages. Some think that rum has always kept Maine back, but I claim that it has been wet feet. In another article I refer to the matter of rum in Maine more fully.

The agricultural resources of Pittsfield and vicinity are not great, the principal exports being spruce gum and Christmas trees. Here also the huckleberry hath her home. But the country seems to run largely to Christmas trees. They were not yet in bloom when I visited the State, so it was too early to gather popcorn balls and Christmas presents.

Here, near Pittsfield, is the birthplace of the only original wormless dried apple pie, with which we generally insult our gastric economy when we lunch along the railroad. These pies, when properly kiln-dried and rivetted, with German silver monogram on top, if fitted out with Yale time lock, make the best fire and burglar-proof wormless pies of commerce. They take the place of civil war, and as a promoter of intestine strife they have no equal.

The farms in Maine are fenced in with stone walls. I do not know why this is done, for I did not see anything on these farms that anyone would naturally yearn to carry away with him.

I saw some sheep in one of these enclosures. Their steel-pointed bills were lying on the wall near them, and they were resting their jaws in the crisp, frosty morning air. In another enclosure a farmer was planting clover seed with a hypodermic syringe, and covering it with a mustard plaster. He said that last year his clover was a complete failure because his mustard plasters were no good. He had tried to save money by using second-hand mustard plasters, and of course the clover seed, missing the warm stimulus, neglected to rally, and the crop was a failure.

Here may be noticed the canvas-back moose and a strong antipathy to good rum. I do not wonder that the people of Maine are hostile to rum — if they judge all rum by Maine rum. The moose is one of the most gamey of the finny tribe. He is caught in the fall of the year with a double-barrel shotgun and a pair of snow-shoes. He does not bite unless irritated, but little boys should not go near the female moose while she is on her nest. The masculine moose wears a hare-lip, and a hat rack on his head to which is attached a placard on which is printed:

PLEASE KEEP OFF THE GRASS

This shows that the moose is a humorist.

\* \* \*

### DOWN EAST RUM

Rum has always been a curse to the State of Maine. The steady fight that Maine has made, for a century past, against decent rum, has been worthy of a better cause.

Who hath woe? Who hath sorrow and some more things of that kind? He that monkeyeth with Maine rum; he that goeth to seek emigrant rum.

In passing through Maine the tourist is struck with the ever-varying styles of mystery connected with the consumption of rum.

In Denver your friend says: "Will you come with me and shed a tear?" or "Come and eat a clove with me."

In Salt Lake City a man once said to me: "William, which would you rather do, take a dose of Gentile damnation down here on the corner, or go over across the street and pizen yourself with some real old Mormon Valley tan, made last week from ground feed and prussic acid?" I told him that I had just been to dinner, and the doctor had forbidden my drinking any more, and that I had promised several people on their death beds never to touch liquor, and besides, I had just taken a large drink, so he would have to excuse me.

But in Maine none of these common styles of invitation prevail. It is all shrouded in mystery. You give the sign of distress to any member in good standing, pound three times on the outer gate, give two hard kicks and one soft one on the inner door, give the pass-word, "Rutherford B. Hayes," turn to the left through a dark passage, turn the thumbscrew of a mysterious gas fixture 90 deg. to the right,

holding the goblet of the encampment under the gas fixture, then reverse the thumbscrew, shut your eyes, insult your digester, leave twenty-five cents near the gas fixture, and hunt up the nearest cemetery, so that you will not have to be carried very far.

If a man really wants to drink himself into a drunkard's grave, he can certainly save time by going to Maine. Those desiring the most prompt and vigorous style of jim-jams at cut rates will do well to examine Maine goods before going elsewhere. Let a man spend a week in Boston, where the Maine liquor law, I understand, is not in force, and then, with no warning whatever, be taken into the heart of Maine; let him land there a stranger and a partial orphan, with no knowledge of the underground methods of securing a drink, and to him the world seems very gloomy, very sad, and extremely arid.

At the Bangor depot a woman came up to me and addressed me. She was rather past middle age, a perfect lady in her manners, but a little full.

I said: "Madam, I guess you will have to excuse me. You have the advantage. I can't just speak your name at this moment. It has been now thirty years since I left Maine, a child two years old. So people have changed. You've no idea how people have grown out of my knowledge. I don't see but you look just as young as you did when I went away, but I'm a poor hand to remember names, so I can't just call you to mind."

She was perfectly ladylike in her manner, but a little bit drunk. It is singular how drunken people will come hundreds of miles to converse with me. I have often been alluded to as the "drunkard's friend." Men have been known to get intoxicated and come a long distance to talk with me on some subject, and then they would lean up against me and converse by the hour. A drunken man never seems to get tired of talking with me. As long as I am willing to hold such a man up and listen to him, he will stand and tell me about himself with the utmost confidence, and, no matter who goes by, he does not seem to be ashamed to have people see him talking with me.

I once had a friend who was very much liked by every one, so he drifted into politics. For seven years he tried to live on free whiskey and popular approval, but it wrecked him at last. Finally he formed the habit of meeting me every day and explaining it to me, and giving me free exhibitions of a breath that he had acquired at great expense. After he got so feeble that he could not walk any more, this breath of his used to pull him out of bed and drag him all over town. It don't seem hardly possible, but it is so. I can show you the town yet.

He used to take me by the buttonhole when he conversed with me.

If I had a son I would warn him against trying to subsist solely on popular approval and free whiskey. It may do for a man engaged solely in sedentary pursuits, but it is not sufficient in cases of great muscular exhaustion. Free whiskey and popular approval on an empty stomach are highly injurious.

* * *

# 3

# *Humor in Politics*

"The trouble with political jokes," someone once said, "is that often they get elected." Politics is a fertile field for humor principally because the thin line between rhetoric and bombast, between dignity and pomposity is so often unintentionally crossed.

Former Gov. John H. Reed had a special proneness to the malapropism. As a political reporter I can remember covering a Reed re-election rally at Monmouth where the governor's syntax proved as ornate as the filigree on Cumston Hall, the site of the exercise.

Reed listed every known accomplishment of his reign from holding a lid on government spending to installing air dryers in the State-house rest rooms. Buoyed by the wild applause which frequently punctuated this recital, Reed — whose style of delivery had a hearty, booming quality — wound up his speech with a promise of even mightier deeds to follow:

"You see, my friends, I'm not satisfied with this record although I am mighty proud of it. No, not satisfied, because there is still much to be done. There are new horizons to conquer; there are new goals to be met; there are new platitudes to be reached."

It wasn't true. Reed had reached them all earlier in his speech.

Jim Erwin, a Republican who made a number of unsuccessful runs for the governorship, was a bright and articulate campaigner but occasionally could serve up a metaphoric mixture which defied the imagination. He once complained to reporters that "the Democrats have sent out their hatchetmen to pour garbage all over me." Someone commented drily that Erwin should have been grateful the Democrats hadn't sent out their garbagemen.

Since wit and humor bubbles in the genes, it is not surprising that many Maine political figures have deliberately cultivated it as a

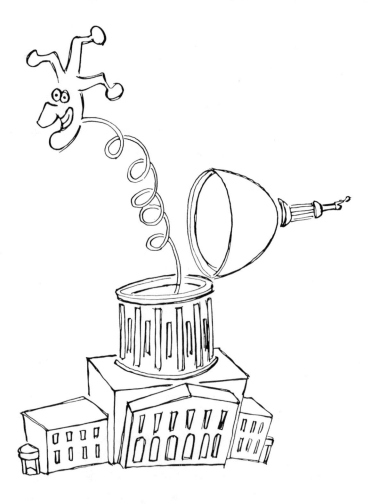

basic forensic tool. Even as Seba Smith was establishing a literary tradition of humorous political commentary in the earliest days of Maine statehood, public officeholders were introducing a tart, taciturn style of debate which flourished effectively through much of the 19th century and marked the Maine man as no one to tangle with verbally.

John Holmes of Alfred, who went to the U.S. Senate in 1820, the year Maine became a state, was a sharp debater with a special feel for pointed sarcasm and irony. His opponents engaged him in a battle of wits at their peril, as one colleague found out one day in the Senate. Alluding to some now-forgotten political liaison, the fellow asked during debate: "And what has become of that famous political firm of James Madison, Felix Grundy, John Holmes and the Devil?"

Holmes was instantly on his feet with a reply: "The first is dead, the second is in retirement, the third now addresses the Senate, and the fourth is electioneering among the gentleman's constituents."

Holmes himself was on the receiving end of a similar, though considerably more ham-fisted rejoinder from Hannibal Hamlin, Lincoln's first vice president, when Holmes and Hamlin served together in the Maine Legislature in 1835. The two were locked in a strong rivalry for leadership on the floor of the House, when Holmes made a rude and ill-considered remark about Hamlin's swarthy countenance.

"If the gentleman chooses to find fault with me on account of my complexion," replied Hamlin, "what has he to say for himself? I take my complexion from nature; he gets his from the brandy bottle."

Well, those were rougher times, after all, when the bludgeon often served as usefully as the stiletto. The history books tell us Hamlin's retort convulsed the House and was appreciatively repeated in the halls of the Statehouse for days afterward.

The quality of wit in legislative debate improved in time and was perhaps most deftly handled when William R. Pattangall served in the Maine House in the early part of this century. Once, during a debate on a bill relating to a closed time in a fish and game law, the sponsor of the measure gave a lengthy dissertation on the question of time, asking, "What is time anyway?"

Pattangall rose to reply: "The gentleman asks 'what is time?' I will tell him. Time is that which has occurred since the morning stars first sang together. Time is what the gentleman wastes whenever he attempts to enter into a debate in this House."

On the national level Maine political wit was brought to its apogee by Thomas B. Reed, a Portland man political historians rank among the top half dozen speakers of the U.S. House of Representatives.

In his time he was the most powerful figure in either branch of Congress. When James G. Blaine passed from the scene, it was Reed who inherited the mantle as national leader of the Republican Party.

He was a big man, even in those corpulent days, weighing in at about 300 pounds. But his great bulk was probably the least impressive thing about him. A political strong man, his imprint was felt on virtually every major piece of legislation to come before Congress in the final quarter of the 19th century. As speaker, he ruled the House with such iron-fisted discipline that he became known as "Czar Reed."

He was a persuasive extemporaneous speechmaker, some said the match of William Jennings Bryan in floor debates. Like his friend, Mark Twain, he had an acid wit which he used often to lacerate a hapless opponent.

When another congressman solemnly declared that he would rather be right than president, Reed quickly shot back, "Don't worry, you'll never be either."

Referring to a couple of his colleagues, he once said, "They never open their mouths without subtracting from the sum of human knowledge."

When he first became speaker he shattered a longstanding policy of obstruction which for years had allowed a minority in the House to paralyze the flow of legislation. Reed rewrote the rules and revolutionized House behavior in the process.

Because the partisan makeup of the House was quite close in those days, members of the minority party often prevented a quorum simply by refusing to answer roll calls even though they were actually present in the House chamber. Reed soon put a stop to the dilatory practice. He simply started counting in every congressman in sight, regardless of whether there was a response when the clerk called the roll.

The first time this happened, infuriated Democrats dashed toward the rostrum and shouted at Speaker Reed that he had no right to count them as present. Reed managed to break his gavel during the

uproar, but eventually he brought the sputtering throng under control by thundering, "Will the gentlemen who say they are not here please take their seats?"

In the end they did. Reed's new rules were reluctantly accepted and the logjam of legislation finally broken. "The best system is to have one party govern and the other party watch," pronounced the Czar. "The rights of the minority consist of answering a roll call and drawing a salary."

In one sense he was a brilliant politician, for he knew how to seize power and to use it. He knew how to make the art of politics work for what he believed to be the good of the American people.

On the other hand he had little feel for the common touch of politics. He often angered constituents back home by refusing to carry out the little chores expected of all elected representatives.

A ladies group from Brunswick once sought his help in obtaining a second-hand cannon for the village green. He responded with a brusque note to the society's secretary: "Dear Madam, I am not running a junk store. Yours respectfully, Thomas B. Reed."

It was Reed, not Harry Truman, who said, "A statesman is a successful politician who is dead." And it was Reed, not any of a dozen others credited with the line, who first listed the three classifications of lies: "Lies, damned lies and statistics."

According to local legend, Reed once sent a telegram to the president of Maine Central Railroad asking that a special train be dispatched to the Poland Spring House to pick up a large party. The train was sent, but when it arrived the conductor found only Reed standing at the platform.

"Where's the large party?" inquired the conductor.

"Isn't this a large enough party for you?" asked the beefy congressman, stepping aboard.

Maine political humor can be as self-effacing as it is pungent. In 1936, when Maine was one of only two states to vote for Alf Landon in the Roosevelt landslide of that year — prompting Jim Farley to quip, "As Maine goes, so goes Vermont" — a sign was erected at the border in Kittery the day after the election: "You are now leaving the United States and entering Maine."

Margaret Chase Smith, the first woman elected to the U.S. Senate, was frequently mentioned as a presidential possibility throughout her long and distinguished political career. In the early 1950s CBS reporter Robert Trout interviewed her on the subject: "Suppose you woke up some morning and found yourself in the White House. What would you do?"

"I'd go straight to Mrs. Truman and apologize," she said. "Then I'd go home."

And when Ray Rideout, a two-term state representative from Manchester, failed to win a primary contest for renomination to the House of Representatives he told reporters his defeat was "the result of illness and fatigue — the voters were sick and tired of me."

Until 1964 Maine was a rock-bound bastion of rock-ribbed Republicanism. But that was the year the presidential candidacy of Barry Goldwater frightened the pants off the electorate and the Democrats took control of the Maine Legislature for the first time in 50 years. Many of them were genuinely surprised by their own election day victories including Ed Stern, a successful Bangor lawyer, who had allowed his name to be placed on the ballot in token opposition to the local GOP senatorial incumbent. When a reporter telephoned Stern to inform him he'd won and to ask for his reaction, the flabbergasted victor exclaimed, "I want a recount."

The quality of debate in the Maine Legislature in this century has not been of the highest, due particularly to the decline of the simple declarative sentence and generally to the abandonment by its members of the old Maine principle that one does not get up to speak unless he can improve upon silence. Fifty years ago the Legislative Record — a verbatim account of debates and proceedings of the House and Senate — ran to less than a thousand pages and was contained in a single volume. Today it fills three thick books with upwards of 4,000 pages.

With verbosity, however, has not come any upsurge in the degree of wit with which lawmakers conduct their arguments. These days legislative humor is more likely to be accidental rather than intentional. The bon mot has been wrestled to the floor by the malapropism.

An Aroostook representative, testifying in behalf of a bill before a legislative committee, listed all the different interest groups which would benefit from its provisions. He concluded: "This bill will be good for everyone but the people."

Another representative, warning against the perils of DDT, told of

watching the accidental spraying of a bird with the stuff. "That bird," he said, "fell into a stupidity and died before my eyes."

I once stopped a senator in the hallway to ask him about a legislative study which had just been issued under his name. He went on at some length in a vague, general way, but eventually slowed down and finally petered out in the middle of his explanation. Following an awkward pause he said, "Frankly, uh, I haven't read the report."

Another time a Kennebec County senator rose in indignation to denounce some gubernatorial outrage or other: "The dead corpse of sincerity died sometime this week in the governor's office, and it stinks." Political writer Donald C. Hansen duly reported this charge, commenting that it was "the very least one could expect from a dying, dead corpse."

But while there are any number of examples of this sort of unconscious humor in Maine politics, you can find similar stories in any state capital in America. It is still the story of deliberate wit — stoic, understated, economical — which represents the most telling character of Downeast political humor. It is at its best when it deflates pomposity with the most innocent of thrusts. Don Hansen tells the following story about politicians who find it easier to talk than to listen:

Louis J. Brann, a two-term Maine governor during the 1930s, was a gregarious chief executive who turned the handshake and the backslap into a political art form.

Once, while handshaking his way through a Democratic reception, he clasped the hand of the son of a man he knew casually. "Hello, Jim," said Brann, pumping away. "How's your father?"

"He died last week," said Jim sadly.

But Brann had already grabbed another hand to massage. As the governor worked his way around the hall he eventually made his way back to the disconsolate Jim. He grabbed the hand again, shook it warmly and asked, "Well, Jim, how's your father?"

"He's still dead, Governor," Jim replied.

\* \* \*

# 4

## The Man Who Ate Republicans For Breakfast

# WILLIAM R. PATTANGALL

*William Robinson Pattangall (1865-1942) was Maine's Renaissance Man. At one time or another he was a sailor, teacher, banker, newspaper editor (Machias Union, Waterville Sentinel), state legislator, mayor of Waterville, state attorney general, two-time candidate for governor and Chief Justice of the Maine Supreme Judicial Court.*

*Pattangall began his long political career as a Republican, representing Machias in the Maine Legislature. In time he switched allegiances to the Democratic Party and embarked on a literary crusade aimed at breaking the GOP stranglehold on the state, an endeavor which proved wildly successful. It is in his role as political satirist that Pattangall is best remembered.*

*His campaign began with publication in the Machias Union of "The Meddybemps Letters," a series of satirical pieces ostensibly written by a traveling plow salesman named Stephen A. Douglas Smith. This naive character, in the style of Seba Smith's Jack Downing, wandered around the state blithely exposing Republican sins with wide-eyed, devastating insouciance.*

*Later, Pattangall refined his techniques with publication of the "Hall of Fame" portraits, sketches which ridiculed prominent Republicans with such lethal effectiveness they were generally credited with sparking a popular revolt within the GOP and enhancing Democratic fortunes at the polls.*

*Much of Pattangall's material is as fresh and funny today as when it first appeared around the turn of the century.*

*"Byron Boyd's career in politics is worthy of study," he wrote about a long-time secretary of state. "He is a living refutation of*

*the generally accepted theory that there is no money in politics in Maine."*

*Of U.S. Sen. William P. Frye he commented, "Forty years in Congress is a long time, twice as long as James G. Blaine served there. During that time a man of Sen. Frye's talent ought to have accomplished something for public good. If he has done so, the matter has been kept profoundly secret."*

*Commenting about a GOP gubernatorial candidate, he said, "I like a man who believes in himself. That is what attracts me toward William T. Haines. His feeling toward himself cannot be called egotism. It is worship."*

*As a public debater, Pattangall had no peer. His speech was as literate and well-formed as his writing, and he could bring sarcasm into devastating play when the need arose.*

*Sometimes Pattangall's wit took a back seat to the practical joker in him. Once, as a young lawyer, he arrived in a small town for a court session and discovered the local hotel full. He had to spend the night in the vestry of the local church. Upon awakening in the morning, he began frantically ringing the church bell, arousing the countryside and summoning the local fire brigade. "I was just ringing for room service," he explained to the astonished natives who answered the call.*

*Maine Democrats in those days were no friends of the state prohibitory law, which antedated National Prohibition by nearly seven decades. Pattangall enjoyed more than just an occasional nip of the grape, although it did nothing to inhibit his sense of humor.*

*Once, on a rollicking train trip between Bangor and Machias, he accidentally broke a window in the smoking car. The conductor came by and informed the ructious attorney that it would cost him $5 to cover the damages. Pattangall fished a $10 bill out of his pocket, but the conductor protested that he didn't have the correct change.*

*"Well, I'll fix it," replied Pattangall, and picking up an empty*

*whiskey bottle from the floor he promptly shattered a second window.*

*On another occasion he turned up in Farmington to represent a client and again discovered overnight accommodations were lacking. The only available shelter was the hotel's livery stable which, after some pointed grumbling, the attorney accepted. Next day, Pattangall appeared at the hotel office to pay his bill. He deposited a well used barn shovel on the desk and remarked, "Here's my key, I'm checking out."*

*As a judge, Pattangall enjoyed quoting the advice of an old attorney to a young trial lawyer: "Young man, if the law in your case is strong for you, dwell on the law. If, on the other hand, the facts constitute your strength, dwell on them. But if neither the law nor the facts are with you, just roar."*

*Although he did as much or more than any Maine politician to promote the fortunes of the Democratic Party during one of the most rock-ribbed periods of Republican domination, his appointment to the Supreme Judicial Court in 1926 and his designation as Chief Justice in 1930 were made by Republican governors, a measure of his stature as a public figure in the state.*

*He did not remain faithful to the Democratic cause, however. Disillusioned with the New Deal policies of Franklin D. Roosevelt, he proclaimed loftily that "the Democratic Party has left me," and reverted to his original GOP affiliation. He died a Republican in 1942.*

\* \* \*

## THE MEDDYBEMPS LETTERS

### MR. SMITH AT AUGUSTA

Hotel North, Augusta, Me.,
November 19, 1903.

Dear UNION:

Left home last Friday and been going ever since.

Augusta ain't changed much since I was here to the legislature twenty years ago. That is, it ain't changed enough so that I couldn't get round all right.

I stopped here at the Hotel Friday night and in the morning went over to the State House.

Most everything was changed around there except the office holders, they were the same old lot.

The only change I could see in them was there was more of them and some of them had changed places.

They believe in rotation in office in Augusta and they've got it down fine.

They start a man in office and keep him there until some one kicks and wants a change, then they shift him into the next office and keep right on until he gets back to the old place again.

In that way they keep up the good old Jeffersonian plan of rotation in office without any of them ever getting out of a job.

Of course besides the old crowd, I saw lots of new faces there. In twenty years they have created lots of new offices and given each one an assistant, a clerk and a stenographer and these were mostly strangers to me.

The way they do, they create an office, appoint an official and give him a salary. Then the next year they give him an assistant and raise the salary. Then they add a clerk and raise the salary again. The last thing is a stenographer and some more salary and then they give him a contingent fund.

The contingent fund follows the stenographer closer than the constitution ever followed the flag.

In the old days when men wrote by hand, contingent funds were scarce but now a state official who didn't have a Smith Premier typewriter, a lady stenographer and a contingent fund would be as much out of place as one of Congressman Burleigh's relations would if he didn't hold any public office.

I saw Governor Hill at the State House.

He's a fine looking man and they say that he shaves every morning.

I was glad the Republicans elected him Governor.

He's a bright man. He's rich and he made his money by his brains.

I used to take his paper, the "Fireside Companion," I think it was called and if ever the UNION gets to be a paper like that you may expect to be Governor.

We took it one year and they gave me four chromos, a double barrelled shotgun and a boy's sled for premiums. All for a dollar, too. It was worth it if you didn't try to read the paper, and of course we wasn't foolish enough to do that.

There was a column or so of advertisements in it, something like these:

"Send twenty-five cents and get a machine for killing potato bugs." Address Vickery & Hill, Augusta.

"Send ten cents and your middle name in full to Vickery & Hill, Augusta, Maine, and get a full description of your future wife," and so forth.

Well, John Bridges was over to our house reading the paper one night.

John had a horse that winter that he thought was pretty near the best that come down the Meddybemps road. He could go some and John used to take the girls out riding a good deal with him. He had just one fault. He kind of foamed at the mouth and being a black horse the foam would fly all over him and make him look like sin.

John had tried every way to stop him and couldn't and as he was reading he struck this column I was speaking of and he see a place where it read, "Send ten cents to Vickery & Hill, Augusta, Me., and get a receipt for stopping a horse drooling."

John went right home and wrote a letter forwarding the ten cents.

In a few days the reply came back.

"Teach him to spit."

John got mad and he wrote on the back of the letter:

"Go to the devil," and sent it to Vickery & Hill.

By return mail he received a letter from them. It read like this:

"Send money for traveling expenses and hotel bills. We can't travel round on your business at our own expense."

I made up my mind then that if there was ever anything I could do to help one of that firm get in the way of making an honest living I'd do it and I was glad when they made Hill Governor.

Well, I've written too much though I haven't told you half I wanted to.

Yours truly,

S. A. D. SMITH.

\* \* \*

## MR. SMITH AT BANGOR

Bangor, Me., Nov. 27, 1903.
Windsor Hotel.

Dear UNION:

This town is drier than Meddybemps — under foot.

The streets are paved.

I have met a whole lot of good people here.

Dan Rawlins who used to teach school down our way is practicing law here now and he took me round and introduced me.

I want to say right here that the man I was most impressed with was Mayor Beal.

He's been Mayor so much that most of the people here have forgotten his first name and just call him Mayor.

He is a splendid man.

I met him in his office at City Hall and I took to him right off.

He has the widest and the kindest smile and the biggest diamond in his shirt front, that I've seen since they stopped those fellows working the shell game on the Pembroke Fair ground.

Somehow he made me think of those people, he was so gentlemanly and polite.

Of course he knew me, as soon as I told him what my name was, and when I told him I wrote for newspapers, he went right to talking.

He said he didn't know why it was but there was something

about a newspaper man that made him want to talk the minute he met one.

Said he often had talked a column and a half of fine print to Bangor News reporters and still not said much of anything.

This being interviewed habit gets the best of lots of men. I saw that your Mr. Pattangall had it in the Bangor Commercial the other day when he admitted that he was a Democrat. I thought just as much of him for owning up, although ordinarily I think it is just as well for a man to keep his bad habits to himself. The public will find them out soon enough.

The Mayor had a stack of letters on his desk asking about the late decision of the Supreme Court in the Brewer bridge case, and he was busy answering them until I interrupted him.

He explained the whole case to me.

It seemed that the main question was, whether Bangor should pay for this bridge or not.

Mayor Beal said not and the court said that he was wrong.

Probably without really realizing the responsibility they were taking.

He said that he had letters from a whole lot of people asking him to overrule the decision of the court but that he didn't feel like doing it.

He said that many of the judges were personal friends of his and had stopped at his hotel and he didn't like to hurt their feelings, or drive away trade, and that they were fairly intelligent men and in the main, honest, so that he felt that in a case of this kind where the wrong that they had done was only due to ignorance of law, he ought not to be too hard on them and by overruling their decision subject them to ridicule, on the part of thoughtless men, who might not know all of the facts.

I asked him, if he was sure they were wrong, and he said:

"Oh! yes, there can be no doubt about that, I looked it up myself and besides that I asked Tabor Bailey and he said so too. If you doubt it I'll telephone him."

I had no doubt about it. I only wondered why the Judges hadn't asked Mayor Beal what the law was before they decided the case.

It's no use talking, it won't do for the Judges of our Supreme Court to go around this way deciding cases without taking advice.

Especially important cases.

They little realize how many good men there are standing ready and willing to tell them how to decide any case if they would only apply to them for counsel.

Mayor Beal told me that he had always been and still was a Republican.

He said he had never deserted the party since 1865, with the exception of the years that they failed to nominate him for office, and never would unless they made the same foolish mistake again.

He said that in the next campaign there were important public questions to be settled, which must be settled right.

When I asked him what they were, he paused and smiled and turned around, until that big diamond in his shirt front shone just like a jack light in the eyes of a deer in the Wesley woods, and he says:

First — The Panama Canal must be dug.

Second — No more rumsellers must go to jail.

Third — Lew Barker cannot rent offices in City Hall.

And then he says, "Of course . . . they may add a few items to the national platform about the tariff and the currency and such trifling things, but these are the issues upon which the people will divide and I stand on them."

"On which side?" says I; because where he hadn't told me, I was anxious to know.

He sighed.

"That's a thing," he said at last, "That nobody ever knows about me until afterwards."

I felt that I was in the presence of a great man.

\* \* \*

This Simpson is a great man. Not so great a man as Beal is but still a great man.

It beats all how many great men there are in Bangor. I'll bet there are more men there who are fit to go to Congress to the square acre than you can grow potatoes on any farm in Washington County.

I met at least twenty that were candidates and I know they were all fit to go, because they told me so themselves and they didn't look like men who would try to deceive any one.

Simpson don't want to go to Congress.

He told me that being State Assessor and Treasurer of the American Realty Company and Chairman of the Republican State Committee was really all he could attend to.

He said the first two required most of his attention and he only carried the party jobs round as sort of a side line, although it came in handy enough Presidential years when the campaign fund was more substantial.

He said he was in a trying position, assessing the value of wild lands and acting as Treasurer of the Company that owned more of them than anyone else in the State, and that when he took the place some of his friends told him that they were afraid it might hurt the party.

He said he told them he was sure it wouldn't hurt the Realty Company and that one or two more small loads like that for the Republican party to carry ought not to make much difference.

Then he said really the hardest position and the one that required the most judgment was to assess the value of a township just at the time when his company was dickering to buy it.

I could see that that might strain a man's mind some and I told him so.

"Yes," he said, "Mr. Smith it does. I tell you," he says, "When you look out over a township of virgin spruce worth at present prices of pulp about twenty-five dollars an acre, that our poor struggling corporation has offered three dollars for in cash, being willing to take on itself the interest charges and the awful risk of fire, besides the enormous tax of two and three-fourths mills on the dollar which the State puts on it, almost equal to one-eighth the average rate of taxes on good prosperous farms and thriving saw mills, and the grasping land owner holds out for three dollars and a half, it is a great temptation to me to assess that property at its real value and see the owner drop dead, when we could perhaps make a better trade with his administrator."

"He might have heirs," says I.

"Very rarely," he said. "Timberland owners usually outlive their heirs. There is nothing like a whole lot of nice green land for a man's health."

"I am an honest man," says he.

"You don't look it," I says.

"I know it," says he, "Lots of people have told me that, but I am.

"That look I've got came from holding office under Republican Administration so long.

"As I was saying, I'm honest and this mixed up position of mine is telling on me. It's knocking my conscience all out of gear and sometimes I wish I was a young man back in the store in old Carmel giving fourteen ounces of sugar to the pound and never selling less than thirty-four inches of calico for a yard.

"Why, my conscience got in such shape last month that I went to Dr. Robinson about it. He said it was atrophied.

"I don't know what that meant, but I suppose it meant over-worked."

Yours truly,<br>Stephen A. Douglas Smith.

P.S. — Kindly send Mayor Beal a copy of this issue so that he can see I used him all right.

S. A. D. S.

* * *

## MR. SMITH AT HOULTON

Snell House, Houlton, Maine, Dec. 18, 1903.

Dear UNION:

I came up here on the cars, of course, and from Bangor up I rode with Elliot Benson of Bar Harbor, who is President of the Maine Resubmission Club.

He's a pleasant man and we got good friends right off quick. He explained the club to me and asked me to join it.

I asked him if there was any initiation to it, or oath, or regalia, or any of them things like there is in the Sons of Temperance, and Loyal Legion and Elks and such orders.

He said there wasn't. All you had to do was to sign your name and pay five dollars and if you didn't like to sign your name, that that

part could be omitted but the five dollars was important and must be insisted on.

"What is the five dollars for?" I asked.

"For expenses," he says.

"Whose expenses?" says I.

"Mine," says he. Travelling is good for my health, but it's quite expensive. The scenery of Maine as viewed from the window of a parlor car is striking and picturesque, but I can't live on scenery and I have a family."

"Besides," he went on, "There are other expenses. We are going to collect ten thousand dollars for the club."

"What will become of all that money?" I asked again, because that is more money than I am used to hear spoken of in a careless and disrespectful way.

"You can search me," says he.

And I made up my mind that that would be the right way to hunt up the heft of it.

I met a young man named Briggs in the evening.

He said he was Register of Probate. He was an Elk and when I told him what a good time Barker gave me in Bangor, he took me over to the Elks club here where he introduced me to Don Powers and several others.

The last time I saw Don was at the convention in Bangor in 1892 when John Robinson counted him in as the Democratic candidate for Congress.

That was the year when we had six hundred delegates and nine hundred and eighty-four votes.

Don is a Republican now.

I often think that the Democratic party is not grateful enough for the blessings which it enjoys.

Yours truly,

S. A. D. SMITH.

* * *

## MR. SMITH AT ELLSWORTH

Hancock House, Ellsworth, Me.,
December 23, 1904.

Dear UNION:

I took a little walk around town . . . and ran into a young man named Burrill who was in the last legislature and didn't seem to realize that it was anything to be ashamed of, because he spoke of it openly.

I asked him to show me the way to Senator Hale's house. I had heard Hale was in town and I wanted to call on him.

As we walked along, I asked him how he liked legislative work.

"Fine," says he. "Especially the five step."

"The what?" says I.

"The five step," says he. "It's a dance. I learned it at Augusta last winter, and I tell you what, Mr. Smith, when you dance it in the Augusta House dining room in the evening with the windows all closed and the radiators working, you are having a hot time."

"I shouldn't wonder," says I. "But I'm more interested in the political side of life there than the social. How does that strike you?"

"I don't know anything about it," says he. "Those things I left to Arthur Littlefield and voted as he suggested. I had no time for public matters. Socially I was a great hit. As a politician I am not so much of a success, but in my own line, I can step some."

At that he began to sing softly to himself a song that went like this:

"I'd like to be a legislative lady
And travel with my husband on a pass."

I didn't catch the rest of it and was glad of it. Indeed I was pleased when I saw Senator Hale's door-plate for while Burrill was kind and good to me, he was almost too gay to fit my style.

I found Senator Hale at home all right.

I sent my card in by the hired man who came to the door. I have just had some printed and I like to use them.

They read like this:

"STEPHEN A. DOUGLAS SMITH,
Meddybemps, Maine.
Agent for Chicago Plow Co., and Correspondent of the
MACHIAS UNION."

Hale greeted me kindly but with dignity.

I hadn't seen him since 1868 when I was a Pike delegate to the convention which nominated him for Congress the first time.

I was a Republican then, a regular Lincoln Republican but I flopped over in 1872 and haven't seen any reason to go back since.

I didn't expect to sell Hale any plows so I wasted no time talking agricultural machinery. I opened right up on politics and I says,

"Mr. Hale, what do you think of Roosevelt?"

"Is this an interview?" says he looking at my card, which he held in his hand.

"Not exactly," says I, diplomatically, "Any conversation which we may have will be considered confidential until mail time. After that I may telephone it to the Machias UNION."

"I would like what I say to remain private and not to be talked about among the people," he went on, "And if you'll agree not to print it in anything but the Machias UNION, that is private enough for practical purposes. If that is understood, I'll talk.

"Answering your question, I like Roosevelt very much. I always was fond of children. It is true they are cuter and sweeter and more lovable in their early infancy than when they reach the noisy, boisterous, athletic, imitation-cowboy age, but even then there is something about a good, pure boy, just budding into early manhood that strongly appeals to me."

"Will he be nominated?" I asked.

"He probably will be," says he, thoughtfully, "We are in favor of it, if there isn't any way to prevent it and I guess there ain't.

"He will be re-elected also I should think, in spite of the large Republican majority in the Senate.

"It would be well, I think in the event of his re-election to amend the constitution so as to provide for a Regency to run the government during his minority.

"Aldrich or Allison or I would take the job, or perhaps we could act jointly.

"He will make a good President when he grows up."

He thought a minute and then he added, "If he ever does."

I was kind of bothered to get his drift, and I said, "You don't mean to say that Teddy isn't twenty-one yet, do you, Senator?"

"Measuring age by birthdays, he is," he said, "And considerable to spare, but measuring by his late speeches and acts, I should place him somewhere between seven and eleven for a rough guess.

"Speaking, however, strictly for publication, I'm for him, first, last and all of the time."

Yours truly,

S. A. D. SMITH.


## MR. SMITH AT PORTLAND

New Years Day, 1904.

Portland, Me.

Dear UNION:

Have been for three days stopping at the West End Hotel. I came to this house first because it was nearest to the depot and then I stayed because I got acquainted with Harry Castner and I liked him and his house so well that I didn't want to leave. Castner is a good fellow and knows how to run a hotel.

Day before yesterday he introduced me to a Mr. Drew who was in the last legislature and who wants to be speaker of the next house. I told Drew that I had met Barker in Bangor and that, so far as a Democrat could go in such matters, I was pledged to support him but I explained to him that it had always been my custom to pledge myself to several candidates so as to have a chance, if one or more of them dropped out.

He said he thought that that was a good scheme and that, to some extent, he had practiced it himself.

He told me that his early life had been spent in the Aroostook where it was customary to promise everyone anything they wanted and then take it yourself if you could get hold of it.

He said that, so far in his speakership campaign, he had promised the chairmanship of the Judiciary committee to four men and that of Railroads to seven but that if he was once elected he thought he could straighten those things out all right.

"What did you do in the last legislature?" says I.

"Nothing," says he, "And that qualified the last four speakers."

Historically speaking I could see that he had good grounds to base his fight on and a member of the last legislature who didn't do anything was way ahead of the average, besides that, Mr. Drew appeared like a man who could keep it up and not make much of an effort.

Yours truly,

S. A. D. SMITH

\* \* \*

## "MAINE'S HALL OF FAME"

### EDWIN CHICK BURLEIGH

Edwin Chick Burleigh was born in 1843, in the town of Linneus in Aroostook County.

He has lived 66 years, has held office 38 years of that time and bids fair to continue to draw a public salary for the rest of his life but he has not been dependent upon an official position for his livelihood.

Maine once owned large tracts of timberland. Maine does not own any timberland now. Mr. Burleigh was once without any timberland. He owns considerable timberland now. Maine sold its timberland at a low price, a very low price indeed. It has since become very valuable. The men who bought it have prospered. It was sold, in part, through the land agent's office. Mr. Burleigh and his father had charge of that office for 11 years. Some of the land which Maine once owned and sold so cheap was afterwards owned by Mr. Burleigh.

These are mere isolated, disconnected facts which probably have no relation to each other, which, indeed, may have no more to do, one with the other, than the tariff has to do with prosperity. We merely mention them in passing, draw no inferences from them and ask our readers to draw none.

In one of Mr. Burleigh's biographies, evidently dictated by some one very near to him, it is stated "that he never drank nor smoked, that he was a man of great natural ability and an editorial writer of facility and vigor." We are willing to accept the first part of that statement as true and incorporate it herein as a fact, the balance of the quotation we simply give for what it is worth. If the subject of this sketch is a man of great natural abilities, he exhausted them in accumulating timberlands and offices, for he never has exhibited them in any other line. If he has written facile and vigorous editorials, he has carefully suppressed them for none of them have ever appeared in the newspaper which he controls.

Perhaps no man with a slighter equipment for public life has ever travelled faster or farther on the road of political success than has Mr. Burleigh. In all of his long public career he has never attempted to convey a single thought to his constituents, by word of mouth, but twice. The first time was when he returned to Augusta in 1888 after having received the Republican nomination for governor at Bangor. A great reception awaited him. The city which had welcomed Blaine a hundred times and hung breathless on every word he uttered in response to its welcome, turned out en masse to welcome the man who was destined to succeed Blaine in Congress. It was an occasion calculated to warm the coldest heart, to thaw the chilliest reserve, to almost make a statue speak.

He spoke. Fearing that he might say something inappropriate he had reduced his remarks to writing and had placed the manuscript in his pocket. In the same pocket he had placed a letter recently received. Amidst tremendous applause he rose to address the great crowd. Pausing a moment to gain the attention of the audience he reached in his pocket for his speech, took out the wrong paper, started to read it in a ringing voice not entriely free from emotion, got as far as "My dear Cousin —" and sat down. The rest of the contents of the letter have never been made public and the facile and vigorous speech which he had composed for the occasion was never delivered.

The only other time that he essayed the role of an orator was at Waterville. That time he did not even claim relationship with the crowds. He looked it over with considerable care and some anxiety. The people waited for him to begin. They are still waiting. He never began. As Tom Reed once said of a brother congressman, "He was dumb, mute, silent, and besides that he wasn't saying a word."

It was fortunate that time that he had projected his speech from a car platform, otherwise, he and his Waterville admirers might still be standing gazing at one another, in solemn and respectful silence. As it was the train moved on after a while, carrying Mr. Burleigh and his unuttered thoughts away with it and the crowd went home.

* * *

## JOHN P. SWASEY

Mr. Swasey is an earnest believer in prohibition. Over and over again has he firmly repressed a yearning on the part of some of his young neighbors to escape from the narrow bounds of Republicanism and wander in the free fields of Democracy by asking them "Who fought the war?" and by telling them that the Democratic party is the rum party. That last part is his strong point. He can convulse an audience with laughter by repeating to it one of those mossgrown anecdotes of the vintage of 1856 about the man who saw the other man drinking out of a large, black bottle and offered to bet him a peck of apples that he was a Democrat and when the other man asked him in astonishment how he guessed it, said that "if he wasn't a Democrat, he had all the symptoms." Men laugh at that story when John P. tells it, not so much because it is funny as out of respect to their fathers and grandfathers who used to laugh at it, years ago, when he had only told it a couple of thousand times or so.

\* \* \*

## FRANK EDWARD GUERNSEY

A true census of the candidates for Congress in Maine's eastern district 1908 would have included every able-bodied man in the district excepting Fred Powers who wanted to go to the Senate and such wise people as preferred to be delegates rather than candidates, thinking that the market was better to sell than to buy on.

This time Mr. Guernsey was lucky. He was opposed by very weak men. Very weak men indeed. Men less fitted to go to Congress than he. It would be unkind to name them. This is a series of biographical sketches, not an obituary column. Suffice it to say that Mr. Guernsey was nominated.

Of course he was elected. If Thomas Jefferson, Andrew Jackson and Grover Cleveland should all come back to earth as one man and run for Congress on the Democratic ticket in the fourth district, the combination would be beaten because Aroostook has the votes to do the trick and Aroostook firmly believes that Democracy is fatal to the potato crop.

So far (that is, up to the time of his receiving his nomination for Congress), Mr. Guernsey's career had been one to cause his friends to rejoice and his enemies to shudder but in a fatal hour be consented to take the stump and then conditions were reversed.

As a stump speaker the congressman from the fourth district is not a success. That is putting the cause mildly. Very, very mildly indeed. He is not as tiresome a speaker as Senator Hale because he couldn't be. The audience would not let him. It would leave. He is not as unreliable in his statements of alleged fact as Senator Frye. He hasn't Frye's imagination. He is not grotesque like Swasey nor venerably platitudinous like Allen. Nor is he reduced to making signs like Burleigh. But he is not much of a speaker.

It is too bad. He is by a long way the best looking man in Maine's Republican politics excepting former Governor Hill. We say Republican politics advisedly. That adjective will save the feelings of our sensitive Democratic friends. He looks so good that an audience expects something from him. But the expectation is not realized.

He makes as poor a fist of public speaking as State Auditor Hatch does of trying to keep office holders from stealing.

\* \* \*

## HERBERT MILTON HEATH

Herbert Milton Heath was born in Gardiner, Maine, August 27, 1853. It is related that there was a total eclipse of the sun on the next day. Whether the two events bore the relation of cause and effect or were merely coincidences has never been decided. Probably the latter, because Mr. Heath has never objected to the sun shining whenever it wanted to do so ever since then so long as it did not interfere with his shining too.

He attended Gardiner High School, and the Dirigo Business College in his earlier youth, and gave instructions to the faculty at Bowdoin for four years. He was admitted to the Maine Bar in 1876.

Mr. Heath is one of the greatest men, perhaps the greatest man, which this country or any other has ever produced; a greater lawyer than Choate, either Rufus or Joseph, a finer orator than Webster or Ingersoll, surpassing Gladstone in statesmanship, Disraeli in diplomacy or Bismarck in ability to mould men to his thinking. Aside from the ice trust and possibly the Lewiston Journal, he is Maine's most remarkable production and he created the ice trust.

In one of those petty moments which come to the greatest men, when from the heights they live on, they feel like reaching down to pick a pebble from the beach, a flower from the vale, he announced himself a candidate for the United States Senate. No one took it seriously. All knew the mood would pass. It was as though Blaine had idly said that he wished he were an alderman, as though Lincoln had expressed a desire to become a Justice of the Peace.

Herbert Milton Heath in the United States Senate! Thank Heavens, the people of Maine have a better sense of the fitness of things than that. As well send Jupiter to join the village ball team or Demosthenes to take part in the debates of the district lyceum. Senators look small enough now. Think how they would look with **Mr. Heath** among them! In such a case debate would cease. There would be nothing but a monologue. Would Bailey talk law, would LaFollette attempt oratory, would Aldrich essay constructive legislation with Herbert M. Heath personally present at the time? The question answers itself. It presents a patent absurdity. No. The constitution guarantees to each state equal representation in the Senate. It would be unconstitutional for Maine to send one man there who so plainly more than equals all the rest. Besides it would be unfair and, in his more thoughtful moments, Mr. Heath himself would see the injustice of it.

\* \* \*

# 5

# The World
# of John Gould

# JOHN GOULD

*"Maine folks just don't accept the obvious," says John Gould. "They've got to find something that's not so obvious or they're not happy. When I start to write anecdotes about Maine people, or tell stories about them, there are some here who don't believe things are the way I see them and they think I'm trying to overact the part. That's the old mocassin stitch again."*

*The "mocassin stitch" derives from the exaggerated movements of Maine cobblers as they work. The sewer draws the rawhide out to arm's length with each stitch, making a lot of work out of a small task and adding a comic touch to an otherwise commonplace endeavor. It is just this ironic juxtaposition of elements, the understated exaggeration, which is the essence of Gould's art — indeed of Maine humor itself.*

*John Thomas Gould had the great bad fortune to be born on foreign soil — Brighton, Massachusetts in 1908. But the Gould family roots in Maine run back to the early 17th century. And because John was raised in Freeport, educated at Bowdoin and has spent all his life diligently applying the mocassin stitch to chronicles of Maine life as reporter, editor, author, lecturer, storyteller and columnist, he is more or less cheerfully accorded native status.*

*He began his writing career as a country correspondent at the age of 15. Later, upon graduation from Bowdoin in 1931 he joined the staff of the* Brunswick Record, *covering the area for several urban dailies as well. He left to start his own newspaper, the* Yarmouth Town Times, *to do some freelance reporting for metropolitan newspapers and magazines, and to begin writing books. "Farmer Takes a Wife," his third book, produced a national audience which has grown more avid with each of the dozen-and-a-half books which have followed.*

*For several years Gould edited the* Lisbon Falls Enterprise, *a Maine weekly newspaper "so intensely local that it achieves universality." His humorous "Dispatch From the Farm" columns have appeared each week for the past three decades in the* Christian Science Monitor, *and he has also written a regular column for the* Baltimore Sun *which appeared in the hallowed space once reserved for H. L. Mencken.*

*Despite his prodigious literary output Gould still lists his occupation as farmer and professional guide. He is also regarded as a passable fisherman, sailor, maple sugarer, furniture maker and, by his own estimation, champion horseshoe thrower.*

\* \* \*

## MAINE WEATHER

It has long been customary for Maine people to invent prodigious weather, but in recent years the development of four-seasons recreation has put a crimp in the tradition. To a ski resort, snow is worth thousands of dollars an acre, and what was once considered a miserable winter day is now a valuable asset. Our official state publicists have actually suggested that the old-time tall tales of rugged Maine weather are bad for business, and as loyal citizens we should make things sound as lovely as we can. The real old claims may thus become only collectors' items, and the day of bragging about unbearable storms, as intellectual pastime, is gone forever.

The town of Pittsfield once had a poor farm and, for some reason nobody has ever explained, there were three thermometers on the porch. Now, three thermometers make excessive equipment, and that this opulence was lavished on a poor farm is interesting. But there they were, and when one of them said it was thirty below zero you could go and look at the other two, and they would corroborate the testimony. At length this gave somebody an idea, and for a number of years whenever there was a cold spell the aggregate temperature of Pittsfield, namely ninety below zero, would be announced. The Associated Press got sucked in on this a few times, mostly when they had a change in managers and a new man took over.

This was in keeping with the old way — to make weather sound as bad as possible, and embellish the cold facts until they became amusing.

"Snowed? I guess it snowed. It took me two days to sweep out what blew through the keyhole."

"Snowed? Well, I guess . . . Why, I started for the barn with two empty milkpails, and it was snowing so hard I had to dump 'em out three times on the way!"

"We had a lot of snow that winter. Power failed, and the electric light company sent a crew to shovel out the line. They dug down and found a row of apple trees, so they knew they were in the wrong place."

"I shoveled the path for the first two-three storms, but after that I had no place to put more snow, so I tread 'er down."

"I took snowshoes come March and went around and tapped some maple trees. Then came a warm spell and the snow melted, and we had to collect sap with ladders."

"See out the windows? We coudn't even see out the one in the attic."

Thermometers that burst from the cold were frequently reported, and if somebody demurred that cooling mercury will never expand, the answer was, "Well, it was so cold it did that time!" This objection was also countered by stories that the mercury was hanging six inches below the glass. Another favorite was to go look at the thermometer on the side of the house and report that it was six clapboards below zero. Farmers woud tell how the mercury had gone to the bottom of the glass and two feet down a hoe handle leaning against the wall. And a 33-degree Mason dropped to just four above.

"Mild winter. Fairly mild. Only went down to minus forty-five twice, and then only a week at a time. Shot up to thirty-eight in February, and we had a heat wave."

"There was one night we had a teakittle of water boiling on the stove, and it was froze solid."

This was the tendency, but now we merely say there is an adequate base, with six inches of new powder, and all areas are in operation. The clear, bright, snappy morning is just fine, and gone are the old-time observations that "I wouldn't want to hazard a guess as to how cold it was, but my cow wouldn't let me milk her without mittens on."

A Maine fog gets tiresome after a couple of weeks, but one or two days at a time is bearable. The poet R. P. T. Coffin rose to magnificence with his line about a Maine fog: "And cows in pasture fade away to bells." But a more typical reaction goes like this:

"We was shingling the fish house when it came in to fog, and I'm telling you I never see just such a mull as that one. We had to hang our heads right down to the roof to see the nails at all, and the only way I knew Charley was still on the roof with me was, I could hear his hammer going. But we had the job most done so we stuck with it to finish up, and you know what happened — we shingled right off onto that fog bank and laid the roof seventeen feet out beyond the boards. Nailed her right down to the fog. Next morning the fog lifted, and carried my fish house out to sea — just left a chimney hole standing there, and I don't mind saying I was some put out. Worst fog I ever saw."

Often told about Seguin Light, but equally at home with any other mariner's beacon, is the story of the twenty-seven days' fog. It closed in the last week of July and hung on almost through August, a thick blanket of fog that shut out all the world and left the Maine coast mildewed and despondent. When it moved in, Leslie Bridges, the keeper of the lighthouse on Seguin Island, started up his compressor engine and set the foghorn a-going. Every minute, for ten seconds, the foghorn would blat out its warning, and such is the power of "Old Seguin" that landlubbers twenty miles inland can hear the thing. Can you imagine sleeping out on the island with the thing, and having it go off every minute for twenty-seven days?

Well, it wasn't twenty-seven days, really. It was on the twenty-third day, about half-past two in the morning, that the belt on the compressor snapped, and all at once there was no air for the horn. So at the end of the next minute the horn didn't blow, and Leslie jumped out of bed and said, "What was that?"

The allegation that Maine lobstermen have a sixth sense and navigate in bedtick fogs without compasses is gratuitous. They can get lost just as fast as anybody, and do, but being knowledgeable on the water they recover quickly, and being smart they try not to get lost in the first place. It's about like the woodsmen inland; ask a guide if he ever really got lost in the woods, honest-injun, now, and he'll have some answer like, "Well, not above a day or two at a time." It's like Reuel Hanscomb, who got lost in the snowstorm. He'd been to town, and he started the two-mile walk home just as it began to snow. It got dark, and all at once Reuel realized that he had wandered off the road, wading hip-deep in snow, that he couldn't see his own mittens, and that he was lost. He exhausted himself trying to get back on the road, and he finally leaned against a tree and felt himself slowly fading away. He knew that he was freezing to death, and this is the way it went: numb, but comfortable. A great peace settled over him, and cark and care eased away. He thought vaguely about how long it would take them to find his body. Just then a great-horned owl that had been perching out the snowstorm on a limb of that same tree gave off his whooping who-who-who right into Reuel's ear.

It scared Reuel so that he roused up and went home.

Fishermen who get lost usually finish the experience by coming home, and there is some bravado that overplays the true concern that prevailed when they were still out. Novelists have tried several times to portray the anxiety of a small Maine fishing harbor when, for a short time, somebody is missing. True, the anxiety on occasion is prologue to tragedy, but far more often it passes when off in the harbor fog a familiar exhaust is heard, and everybody says "He's in." Then come the bravado, and when Shorty Walpole appeared from a fog-mull a good five hours late, Henry Weston jibed at him with, "What happened — you didn't get lost, did you?"

"Hell, no! How could I get lost — I didn't know where I was, anyway."

Another time Russ Balfour guessed wrong and struck out toward Spain when he thought he was heading for Chicago, and as soon as he found his mistake he turned around and came home. Meantime the whole town was sure he was lost, and it was a wonderful moment when they finally heard his engine coming. But on the dock, when he arrived, the conversation gave no hint of the municipal concern and public apprehension:

"Couldn't see too well out there, could you, Russ?"

"No, I got to get my glasses changed."

Then comes a Maine day such as no other place in the world ever sees. Sky so high and so blue, and fair breezes. An April morning with geese wedging in, or a bright September afternoon. There never was, and you can't find, any hyperbole or deprecation of good Maine weather. The state stands mute when the good days come. It was on just such a fine day that the Massachusetts motorist drove in at Tyler Brigham's filling station in Cornville, and found Tyler sitting in the sun, his chair tilted back against the building and his hat balanced over his eyes. Tyler made no move, and the Massachusetts motorist tooted his horn. Tyler paid no never-mind, and the Massachusetts motorist tooted again. Then the Massachusetts motorist called at him in the manner of the tourist, and he said, "Hey, there!"

He finally had to get out of his automobile and walk over and shake Tyler by the shoulder, and Tyler pushed his hat back and looked up at him.

"Well," said the Massachusetts motorist. "Don't you want to fill my tank?"

"Nope."

"Aren't you open for business?"

"Nope."

"Don't you sell gasoline?"

"Yes."

"Well — Can I buy some?"

"Not today."

"Why not today?"

"Because," said Tyler, "it's too good a day. I woke up and I took one look at it, and I decided I was going to sit here and enjoy it. And that's what I'm doing, and that's all I'm going to do. No, it's too good a day to pump gas."

The Massachusetts motorist didn't seem to believe what he heard. Tyler said, "But I was sitting here half expecting you."

"Expecting me?"

"Eyah, more or less. I bet my wife ten cents I'd no more'n get comfortable when some goddam Massachusetts driver'd show up."

\* \* \*

## WATER WITCHING

Walter Maybury needed a well. Many a Maine farm had gone along for generations with water supplies provided in colonial days, but times changed. A well which had adequately watered the farm stock, and by the bucketful had supplied the household needs, couldn't keep up with modern plumbing after an electric pump was installed. Walter was in this fix. His old well had seemed fine, and it was excellent water, but lately he had refurbished his home. The upstairs bathroom, the downstairs half bathroom, the laundry, the dishwasher — these simply used more water than the farm had previously required. Now Walter had to find a new supply, and he consulted a well driller. The well driller came and looked the situation over. And he said something which all honest well drillers should say here in Maine, where dowsing is common. It went like this: "Now, if you leave it to me, I'd drill right here; but if you believe in witching and want to do it some place else, it's all one with me and I'll go down wherever you say."

At this time Mr. Maybury was open-minded. He neither believed nor disbelieved in dowsing. He just hadn't thought about it. That is to say, he was aware that dowsing existed, but it didn't occur to him to turn to it even when he was considering a well. So he smiled and was a moment amused at the obvious disclaimer of the well driller, and then he decided that since drilling a well is a sizable expense he might as well cover all angles. So he went over on the back road and called on Ronald Sanborn, who was a reputable water witch, and Ronnie came over with his stick the next day and dowsed.

This is truly something to see if you never have. The two ends of a limber crotch from a tree or bush are held in the hands, leaving the singular end free to dip down when the magic moment comes.

What causes it to dip is what all the fighting is about, and for some people who lack the gift it never will dip. With Ronnie it dipped finally, and he made several passes to confirm his spot. "Right here!" he said, and he stuck down a little stick. "Fourteen feet down, you'll get all the water you want."

The amusement with which Mr. Maybury first approached the suggestion of a dowser had by now nurtured a little curiosity, and being a thoughtful man he decided on some insurance. He drove over to the next town to see a Mrs. Ruth Goodwell, who was also a reputable dowser, and without telling her that Ronnie Sanborn had already dowsed the field he inquired if she would favor him. Before she came, Mr. Maybury removed Ronnie's little stick, but triangulated the spot so he could find it exactly again. When Mrs. Goodwell came she did about as Ronnie had done, and coursed back and forth as in a trance, waiting for the stick to tell her something. When she got a response, it was where Ronnie had got his, and after several passes she said, "Right here! Down about fifteen feet, I'd say." When she set her little stick in the ground Mr. Maybury knew it was close, but after she left he triangulated the spot and her stick was precisely where Ron's had been.

Mr. Maybury was not a little caught up with the whole thing, and it was hard for him to believe that these two dowsers could have found the same spot without collusion. He accordingly drove some thirty miles in another direction and inquired if any dowsers lived about, and he found a man who guaranteed to find him water or there would be no charge. The man came, and he was such a total stranger that he kept calling Mr. Maybury "Mr. Bradbury," and after he paddled back and forth a half hour or so he said, "Right here! Can't say how far down for sure, but it's a good vein, and not over twenty feet." Mr. Maybury first noticed and afterwards proved that the dowser had set down his little stick exactly where Ronald Sanborn and Mrs. Goodwell had put theirs. Dowsing never had better proof.

"I think I'll have you drill right here," said Mr. Maybury to the well driller, and he indicated the spot on which the three dowsers had independently agreed. "Anywhere you say," said the well driller, and he set up and went down seven hundred and eighty feet without finding a drop of water.

* * *

## CAUSE AND EFFECT

Captain Clarence Meservey of Brooklin tells of a neighbor of his who began to detect a fault in his well water. He immediately sent to the State Department of Health and Welfare in Augusta for one of the glass bottles. This department, free of charge, will analyze well water, and if something is believed wrong, make suggestions as to a correction. The bottle came promptly, so the Brooklin farmer filled it and mailed it back, and the statehouse laboratory ran a test.

The results were so pronounced that they didn't wait to get a letter off — they called the farmer right up, and they said not to touch that water. It was in bad shape. They said it was so bad they were sending an inspector down the next day, and not to use the water until he got there.

The inspector came, and after a quick look around he surmised that the family cesspool was in such a location that seepage was possible, and he said, "I think you'd better stop using that cesspool, and relocate another off in that direction."

So they stopped using the cesspool, and the well dried up.

* * *

## HOME TO ROOST

In the long ago the United States mails were handled mostly by the Railway Post Offices, and a whole grid of RPO's operated the length and breadth of Maine. Most of them were short runs with but one or two clerks riding in the car to sort mail in transit and to take in and put off bags when the train stopped. Those trains were work trains, handling freight, mail, baggage, and passengers, and stopping at every small town on the line. But each mail car was in fact a rolling post office and had all the status of any municipal mail center — it sold stamps and money orders, kept a cancellation stamp, and had a slot on the side for dropping letters. The big post office in Portland was no more a post office than the mail car that rolled up to Rumford and was called the Rumford & Portland RPO — distilled in the lingo of the railway postal clerks to **Rum & Port.**

But the major RPO in Maine was on the through line, and of all the mail cars on the Vanceboro & Boston RPO the elite were the sixty-footers that howled through the night on the Maritime Express. This was one of the continent's great trains, and for a long time maintained the fastest over-the-route speed of all. It made up more or less simultaneously on each end, and as the eastbound pulled out of North Station in Boston, its westbound counterpart would leave Halifax. Boston has always had close affinity with the Maritimes, and as relatives visited back and forth the Maritime Express accommodated them and showed a profit for the Boston & Maine, the Maine Central, the Canadian Pacific, and the Canadian National — all joining in the operation. Many a night the train would run in two sections — mail and express cars first, and the sleepers and coaches following close behind. Even in the early days of its run the train averaged something like eighty miles an hour, and on the level stretches of Maine's Sebasticook Valley it would throttle up and clock off an even hundred for mile after mile. It was a friendly train, where folks from "down east" socialized and shared sandwiches. Those who didn't take a sleeper would curl up on a seat, and if their overcoat coverlet slipped off, a brakeman would smooth it back. To those leaving Boston for the Maritime homeland, the first stop of consequence was MacAdam Junction for breakfast — a thirty-minute pause just after daybreak. Here the Canadian National took over. For those coming to Boston the night was a rolling, jolting charge down the wilderness corridors of Maine to arrive at North Station about seven o'clock — just before the morning rush of suburban commuter trains. Clearly, to be a railway postal clerk on the Maritime Express was top-hole.

For people asleep, the few stops across Maine were only silent pauses in the roar of the wheels, but to the postal clerks, Biddeford,

Portland, Waterville, and Bangor were busy spots. Here they exchanged incoming for outgoing pouches, rearranged their stacks of bags, and closed the doors to make ready for the next town. And that meant the next town, because the Maritime Express pouched whether it stopped or not. As the train roared through a sleeping community a bag would be kicked from the mail car door into the night, to be picked up by a waiting mail messenger, and then a hook would be pulled up to snag a bag hanging on a trackside yardarm. Throwing and catching was a delicate maneuver, and a new clerk, or one who wasn't paying attention, could sometimes heave a bag into the river, or a greenhouse, and then see the hanging pouch rush by before he got the hook up.

Newport was in the Sebasticook Valley, and still is. When the engineer advanced the throttle up to an even century, the great train of fifteen or eighteen cars would go through Newport like a bullet going past a knothole. Throwing and catching at Newport would have been fraught with continuing surprises, except that the engineer always hit his precise hundred, and held it. This gave the postal clerks a delicate advantage. The pouch was supposed to land on a patch of green grass, or in winter in the snowbank that covered it, between the water tank and the freight shed. Too soon, or too late — disaster. They would lay the pouch in the car door and listen for the click of a certain yard switch. Then, instantly, a switchman's shanty lantern would flick past. Taking the count from there a clerk would tell off nine seconds on his watch, and at nine they would place-kick the pouch into the Newport night. It would land exactly on the little patch of green grass. If the engineer hadn't been in cahoots and the train hadn't sustained its speed, the pouch could have ended up in many an interesting place.

Now, during World War I butter was hard to come by. It was on ration stamps if you could find any, and the price was high. But one of the postal clerks in the crew on the Maritime Express lived near Newport, and his daily "run" started from that station. He would work down to Portland on a day train, join the Maritime Express as far as Bangor, and then work back to Newport on a local. That was his day's work. And one night he said, "Hell, I can get you all the butter you want. The station agent at Newport has a brother who keeps cows — they make butter all the time. How much do you want?"

So this man took two pounds, and another took five, and when they added up the total demand it came to thirty-three pounds. "Sure," he said. "I'll pick up thirty-three pounds and bring it on the next trip."

So he did. He came on the train at Portland with a big bundle done up in brown paper, and after the pouches were hung and the work under way he undid the brown wrapper and began to give each clerk his requested amount. But the mail car was inundated with a loud and smothering stench. The butter was more than strong — it was rancid. It had the appearance of being rancid a long time. He quickly wrapped up the bundle again and tied the string with a double knot. He kicked the thirty-three pounds of butter under a sorting case, which is a poor place for butter. Mail cars always rode in the position of honor, next behind the locomotive, and this gave them first crack at the steam heat. As the Maritime Express hurtled through the Maine night the butter thus became more rugged, although softer, and the stench was unbearable even to the clerk in the far end of the car who was sorting mail for Prince Edward Island. Many a sharp opinion was expressed about the parentage of the station agent at Newport and his brother who kept a few cows.

And then one of the clerks who had been watching the time said, "Get ready for Newport," and they opened the car door. They listened for the switch, and they saw the fleeting flash of the switchman's shanty lantern. They counted off nine seconds — and then they counted ten, eleven, and twelve. At twelve, they placed-kicked the thirty-three pounds of butter from the threshold. And they closed the door.

The brown paper bundle hit the side of the Newport depot at a westbound, or ricochet, spot, and the station agent who had a brother who kept cows was providentially positioned on the platform, watch in hand, to see the train go by. He got most of it, but thirty-three pounds is a lot of butter and when strong and rancid, butter will go much farther. Newport was largely a mess.

The moral is that when you butter somebody up, it's a lot more fun at 100 mph.

\* \* \*

# 6

# *Scrapbook—*
# *A Miscellany*

In the course of the day all the returns were accounted for except for five or six towns, among them the town of Lyman, in which six only were in favor and one hundred and seventy-nine votes against separation. The return was traced into two or three hands and lost in the fog . . . The returns from Eliot and Frankfort were traced to A, from A to B, and B to C, and were probably tried by fire and lost.

*— Contemporary account of 1816 balloting on Maine statehood*

\* \* \*

Captain Britton from Otisfield was at Uncle Richard's today. Not long ago Uncle brought here from Salem a new kind of potatoes called Long Reds. Captain Britton had some for seed and Uncle asked how he liked them. He answered, "They yield well, grow very long; one end is very poor and the other good for nothing." I laughed about it after he was gone, but Uncle looked sour, and said there was no wit to his answer and the saying was stale. It was new to me and his way of saying it very funny.

*— Diary entry by young Nathaniel Hawthorne, whose uncle kept a general store near Sebago Lake.*

\* \* \*

A gentlemanly friend of mine came one day with tears in his eyes. I said, "Why those weeps?"

He said he had a mortgage on his farm and wanted to borrow two hundred dollars.

I lent him the money, and he went away.

Some time after, he returned with more tears. He said he must leave me forever. I ventured to remind him of the two hundred dollars he borrowed. He was much cut up. I thought I would not be hard upon him, so told him I would throw off one hundred dollars. He brightened up, shook my hand and said:

"Old friend, I won't allow you to outdo me in liberality; I'll throw off the other hundred."

And thus he discharged the debt.

— *Artemus Ward, quoted in a 19th century joke book.*

\* \* \*

Maine people dearly love stories concerning out-of-state visitors. Such a story, for example, as that of the stranger being shown around town who remarked to his guide on the extraordinary number of elderly people in the place.

"Seems as if everybody we meet is old," he said.

"Yes, the town has lots of old folks," the guide admitted.

"I see you have a cemetery over there," remarked the stranger.

"Yes," was the laconic answer, "we had to kill a man to start it."

— *"It's an Old State of Maine Custom"*
*Edwin Valentine Mitchell*

\* \* \*

Two commercial tourists from the Pine Tree State happened to meet the other day.

"Hello, Charlie!" cried No. 1; "I haven't seen you in an age. What are you doing now?"

"Oh, I am in the same old line," responded No. 2.

"With the same house?"

"Yes, same old concern, but situated a little differently."

"How is that?"

"Well, I've got an interest."

"Is that so. How long since?"

"Since the first of the month."

"Let me congratulate you."

"Yes, the old man told me I'd got to take an interest in the business this year, or quit. So I took the interest."

— *From a 1903 joke book.*

\* \* \*

At one term of Court held by Judge Pattangall in an eastern county, a juryman presented himself to the judge asking to be excused. When asked his reason he said, "My wife is about to become pregnant, 'er, I mean confined." Judge Pattangall said, "You are excused because you should be there in either event."

Judge Pattangall told of a doctor who was testifying in a case before him in which the attorney asked the doctor: "Doctor, in language as nearly popular as subject will permit, will you please tell the jury just what the cause of this man's death was?"

Doctor: "Do you mean the proxima causa mortis?"

Attorney: "I don't know, Doctor, I will have to leave that to you."

Doctor: "Well, in plain language he died of an oedema of the brain that followed, in turn, an arteriosclerosis combined with the effect of a gangrenous cholecystitis."

A juror: "Well I'll be God damned."

The Judge: "Ordinarily I would fine a juror for saying anything like that in court, but I cannot in this instance impose a penalty upon you sir, because the Court was thinking exactly the same thing."

\* \* \*

Judge Pattangall told the following story as happening in Pembroke, Maine.

An old lady who was about to die told her niece to bury her in her black silk dress, but to cut the back out and make herself a dress.

"Oh, Aunt Mary," said the niece, "I don't want to do that. When you and Uncle Charlie walk up the golden stairs, I don't want people to see you without any back to your dress."

To which the old lady replied, "They won't be looking at me. I buried your Uncle Charlie without his pants."

\* \* \*

When the railroad was new, a man plainly under the influence of liquor was riding through Washington County. In the seat in front of him sat one, who from his clothes, was evidently a minister.

The drunk had been looking out the car window at the blueberry "barrens." He tapped the man in front.

"Excuse me, but are you a member of the Cloth?"

"I am," was the reply.

"Is it true, Reverend, that the Good Book says that God made the world in six days?"

"Absolutely true."

Then the intoxicated individual, waving an unsteady hand towards the out of doors, said, "Don't you think, Parson, He could have put in another day to advantage in Washington County?"

*From "William R. Pattangall of Maine"*
*by Raymond Fellows, Chief Justice,*
*Maine Supreme Judicial Court, 1954*

\* \* \*

The town of Rangeley was voting to build a bridge across a stream, and after someone had moved that the town raise the sum of $2,000 to build the structure, an old gentleman got slowly up from his seat, and without addressing the moderator, roared out over the room.

"I protest! Two thousand dollars is too much money to build that bridge. Why, I could spit half way across that stream!"

The moderator impatiently banged the table with his gavel.

"Sit down, sit down!" he said sternly, "You're out of order."

"I know I'm out of order," the old man said defiantly. "If I weren't, I could spit *all* the way across!"

— *"Tales of the Rangeley Lakes"*
  *LeRoy Nile*

\* \* \*

Theodore Roosevelt, who liked to fish in Maine, was fond of telling of the wet spring he was there. While proceeding along a rocky road he said to his guide, "How do you tell the roads from the river?"

"No beaver dams in the roads," was the prompt reply.

— *"It's an Old State of Maine Custom"*
  *Edwin Valentine Mitchell*

\* \* \*

On one leg of this junket, Moore and I were somewhere in Maine riding a caboose, the only way to reach a remote cement plant. It was a warm spring day and Moore sat by an open window. The benches in the caboose, as usual, ran along each side of the car. Moore sat with one leg under him and *The New York Times* held by his two hands in front of him. He was absorbed in reading when the brakeman, sitting opposite, let go a wad of tobacco juice that passed between Moore's face and the newspaper and went smack out the window. Moore ruffled his paper and muttered something in-audible and returned to his reading. In a few moments the brakeman let go another wad of tobacco juice, and it also passed between Moore's face and the paper, neatly clearing the open window. Moore, flushed with anger, turned to the brakeman and shouted, "What

goes on here?" The brakeman rose to his feet, cleared his throat, and said, "I'm sorry, sir, if I upset you. But I think you must admit it was some spitting." I could no longer contain myself and broke into loud laughter, to which first the brakeman and then Moore succumbed.

— *"Go East, Young Man"*
*Justice William O. Douglas*

\* \* \*

**Ayuh.** *Adv.* A general purpose term which is considered THE WORD.

"Ayuh" is the truest touchstone of genuine Yankee speech. While its pronunciation may vary throughout the region ("eeyuh," "ehyuh"), a Mainer and a Vermonter using it know they're cut out of the same cloth. But let some rusticator from Yonkers try to render it, and the result will be as apparent as a beached whale.

Listen to "The Word" a few hundred times before you try it. The most common mistake outlanders make is to render it with the same inflection, no matter what the circumstances. The Word has infinite shades of meaning. To attempt duplication in cold print would be useless; suffice to say that according to rendition, it can preface an extended observation or abruptly conclude one. It is comforting and it is sarcastic. Listen often to The Word in its sundry applications before you attempt it, and then begin very tentatively, low key — *ayuh*.

> — *"How to Talk Yankee"*
> *Gerald E. Lewis*

\* \* \*

In the annals of Bar Harbor no native is deserving of a higher place than the late Chet Sprague. The owner of a local paint shop, Sprague was also the owner of a mongrel dog — a male. A Bar Harbor *grande dame* owned a pedigreed *Pekingese* — a bitch. One

summer, despite careful supervision, the Pekingese was unfortunately compromised by Sprague's mongrel. Immediately the Bar Harbor lady sent for Sprague. Arriving, he was ushered by the maid into an elaborate marble foyer. He stood there, cap in hand. The lady, in a high state of distress, appeared at the head of the stairs. Without any preliminaries she began an unmerciful tirade against Sprague, the worthlessness of his mongrel, the shame that had fallen to her beloved Pekingese and the general sensual degeneracy of the modern generation. On and on she went — until finally she paused for breath. Sprague, who had not said a word, turned around. At this the lady was completely infuriated.

"I'm not through talking to you yet," she screamed. "Where are you going?" Sprague turned back.

"Ma'am," he said quietly, "I was just going home to ask my dog if he'll marry your dog."

> — *"The Last Resorts"*
> *Cleveland Amory*

\* \* \*

Monday visited John Allen, the smith of Sargentville, to get my pole ax drawed out. Mr. Allen is around and about again after an appendectomy. Been coming on him for twenty years — then all of a sudden she exploded. He had plenty of chance to just lie there and think about things when he was in the Bluehill Hospital, and although he had formerly been opposed to the Automobile, because it had driven out the horses and spoiled a smith's trade, he remembered that it was an automobile that got him to Dr. Bliss in time to save his life. Has changed his mind about motor cars. I pointed out, however, that automobiles were killing people awful fast, too. "By gorry," he said, "I hadn't thought about that. Now I'll have to think it all out again."

> *E. B. White*
> *1937 letter to his wife.*
> — *From "Letters of E. B. White"*

\* \* \*

How Clem got the idea, the Lord only knows, but somehow he got the notion he could make quite a bit of change by selling rabbit sandwiches. Anyhow he put a stock out in front the house and started selling them like hot cakes to the autos what come through with out-of-state folks in them.

He went along pretty good for a couple of months cutting bread and spreading on rabbit meat, and then one day the pure-food officer come down from Bangor and dropped in on him. He says to Clem, "How in Sam Hill do you git enough rabbit meat to put in all them sandwiches?"

"Oh, I git it," says Clem.

"Is it all rabbit meat you use?" says the feller.

"Every bit of it's rabbit meat," says Clem, "that is, all but just a mite."

"Then you do use a little other meat?"

"Just a mite now and then," says Clem.

"What other kind of meat do you use?"

"Sometimes I just put in a pinch of horse meat to give it foundation."

"I don't see how you have enough rabbit meat even then," says the feller. "What proportion do you use?"

"Fifty-fifty," says Clem.

"Fifty-fifty, eh? Seems to me that's quite a 'pinch.' How do you measure to be sure it's fifty-fifty?"

"There ain't no trouble to that," says Clem. "I take one rabbit and one horse."

*— From "Seth Parker's Album"*
*By Seth Parker of Jonesport, Maine*

\* \* \*

In another community, well known to me, there was a large Baptist meeting house with pew doors opening into the aisle. There came a powerful revival in this community and two brothers who had been rather wild blades were converted — Jeremiah and Joseph.

One evening Jeremiah was conducting the prayer meeting and was engaged in reading the Scripture lesson, when Joseph came in late with his friend Elisha.

Elisha was "splay-footed" which means that he "toed-out." As they came up the aisle Elisha's foot first on one side and then again on the other, hit the open pew-doors and slammed them shut with a bang.

Jeremiah stopped his reading and called out: "Joe, take 'Lish out and back him in."

*— From "Rufus Jones' Selected Stories*
*of Native Maine Humor" — Clark*
*University Library, Worcester, 1945*

\* \* \*

Last week, a local resident went to Biddeford to seek out a thermometer. At the department store he discovered that each of the dozen or so on display registered a different temperature. Accordingly, he bought two — one with a lower reading for summer and one with a higher reading for winter.

*— From "County Commeni 'ry" by Ed Mayo,*
*Portland Press Herald, May 30, 1979*

\* \* \*

# 7

## Tales of
## Cedar River

# WILLIAM M. CLARK

*"In Maine," says John Gould, "we don't write books. "We live 'em."*

*William M. Clark, columnist, author and upriver philosopher, fits the mold. His writing is an outgrowth of his experience rather than a literary endeavor per se, yet the result is always literate, perceptive and entertaining. Clark describes himself, unpretentiously, as "a country boy with country leanings," and his style has never betrayed the integrity of that characterization.*

*Cedar River is a composite of nine Maine communities where Clark lived variously as a logger, master electrician, teacher, restaurant operator, woodworker and bulldozer operator. Its characters — Jeb Seekings, Francis Gage, Burleigh and Jane Anson, the Uncles Waldron, Jake and Oscar — are as real as Clark's prismatic memory of their flesh-and-blood progenitors.*

*Cedar River is inland Maine's Everytown. Gladys Hasty Carroll explained it this way: "I am here to say that every small Maine community whose center is five miles or more from the center of any other is a Cedar River, often obscured from the rest of the world — sometimes, it seems, at will — by mists on which all manner of things, beautiful and terrible, ugly and tender, credible and incredible, ride; and by which such things are forever hidden from passersby along the glaring strip of the Maine Turnpike."*

*Bill Clark now lives in a converted schoolhouse in Caratunk with his wife Betty, where he continues to turn out regular columns of native wit and wisdom for the Guy Gannett newspapers of Maine.*

## TALES OF CEDAR RIVER

Jeb Seekings was a homely man. He had lost three of his upper front teeth in evenly spaced locations. He had one ear joined to his head by a mass of scar tissue, the results of a misunderstanding with a biting brother. Because of these irregularities he was handsomest when he scowled and kept his ear lappers down. He wasn't very handsome even then.

Jeb Seekings was a pretty good citizen. He paid his taxes without any more than a normal amount of growling at the assessors. He worked at this and that, and he rarely ran afoul of the law, even though he was a crony of men who did. Whenever Jeb felt that the fun was getting to a point where there might soon be trouble, he went home and went to bed. He explained this to Uncle Jake one night.

"Men who have nice, clean, honest faces can get away with murder," he said. "Men who look like me get twenty years the first time they step out of line. If a man's planning a career of crime, he better get born with a good honest face. That way he can be the world's worst thief and swindler, but he'll still have a chance to stay out of the pokey."

Despite his propensity for a crimeless life, Jeb had to eat just like other citizens of Cedar River, and once in a while he let temptation overcome his fear of retribution, and he took a preseason shot at a grazing deer that was flaunting its charms with too much boldness. This happened one still September night in his lower meadow. He watched a big buck wandering around in the half moonlight for about two hours, and finally he decided that the thing was pushing its luck and might better be taught a lesson.

Jeb had a tough break. The deer had just dropped when a car came down the road, brakes slammed, the game warden jumped out, and that was that.

Jeb put up bail and waited for trial. He thought about his situa-

tion. He thought about the impression he was going to make on any judge or jury. He knew he looked like a cross between Simon Girty and Al Capone. He knew that men who look like him have a fair chance of being incarcerated for life just for appearing on the street when there are ladies present.

He took twenty-five dollars from the bank and he sent to Boston for a lawyer. He had heard there were men over there who could get Jack the Ripper acquitted by a jury made up of the mothers of his victims. He figured that was the kind of a man he needed.

He hit the jack pot. The law firm sent him a young trainee who was William Jennings Bryan and Clarence Darrow all in one. He was Daniel Webster and Abraham Lincoln and Patrick Henry. He pleaded his client not guilty, called for a jury, and went to work with the full force of his eager rhetoric. He waved the flag. He quoted Homer. He told of the minute men. He glorified Jeb's struggle for survival in a world beset by alien forces.

All the game warden had was facts. Jeb Seekings had the greatest speaker since Chauncey Depew. After he got finished talking, the judge didn't know whether he was in court or at Antietam, and the jury were convinced that Jeb had been defending his home against a mass invasion by the animal world.

Jeb was found not guilty, of course. The jury almost voted him a pension.

Jeb shook hands with his fiery defender. He paid him another twenty-five dollars to settle the bill. Then he took him by the arm and led him over to the other side of the room.

"I got a little mixed up back there," he said. "After the British landed and we all started shooting, who in hell do you suppose knocked off that deer?"

The lawyer assured him that the deer had probably died of heart failure. Jeb never was sure after that if he had killed it or not.

* * *

City people come to the country in the fall and they stand outside of their heated cars just long enough to buy a bushel of apples and they say, "It must be wonderful to work outdoors on a crisp, cool day like this."

Crisp, cool days are all right if you're looking forward to a winter in a steam-heated office. If you're planning on taking the hardwood out of the pasture woodlot, crisp, cool days are the forerunner of a lot of pain. I never felt like rhapsodizing when it was twenty below zero and the tractor kept running up on snow-buried stumps while I was singling out logs or cabin poles, and the snow kept bunching up in the sprockets and finally the tread spun right off the idler and there I was. I was not poetic at all on days like that. I spoke harshly of the beautiful, crisp air. I didn't care whether my lungs were being cleaned or not. I was only interested in their not being seared.

You have to put in days like that, days when every kick sends tingles through your half-dead feet, days when you try to shrink up inside your clothes in the forlorn hope that you may feel warmer, before you can appreciate the automatic response of Deak Trembley to the story of a friend whose wife had been the victim of a heart attack.

The only thing that keeps a man going in the last hour of numbed misery in the woods with the trees cracking and the snow squeaking as the coming of night makes the air grow colder is the thought of the coffee pot on the stove when he steps into his kitchen. His wife knows this, and she has the coffee ready. She times it to be just right, five minutes before she expects him. He might run all the way home.

Deak's friend was telling about how he found his wife.

"I opened the door and all I could smell was coffee. I went out into the kitchen. The pot was chugging away like mad. Lottie was lying on the floor. She must have just managed to get that coffeepot on before she keeled over. I set it back away from the heat and I called the doctor. He came right off and he worked on her for an hour. She's going to be all right. She's just got to take things a little easier."

"By gorry," commented Deak, "I'll bet that coffee was awfully black."

\* \* \*

Country people have a couple of very interesting points of view in regard to the various laws by which our land is governed. One of these is a complete horror of the disregard of city people for law and order. Newspaper stories of robberies and murders and various misdeeds have made the country dweller very suspicious about there being any law-abiding folks down in the cities at all.

On the other hand, laws which have a limiting effect on their own behavior are considered by many country dwellers as being made for somebody else, rather than for them. They go about opening the deer season in September and setting a few trot lines as nonchalantly as a gangster strolls into a bank and demands the available assets.

My uncle Waldron was one of the more law-abiding citizens of Cedar River. He had this one little failing, however. Whenever he was particularly incensed at some of the actions of his wife, my aunt Margie, he would take out his resentment in a little illegal netting of fish.

Uncle Waldron was really a little afraid of Aunt Margie. She was a little afraid of him, too. Some of their battles were classics of their time, and their idea of domestic bliss was for neither one of them to raise a club of some kind to the other for a couple of days straight. They achieved tranquillity by not talking to each other, but the balance was always precarious. Aunt Margie liked to talk. She especially liked to talk about the failings of Uncle Waldron. She didn't do this behind his back. She did it while he was right there and could hear her and thus get the benefit of her criticism. She wasn't above being an educator as well as a critic.

He didn't appreciate this. Sometimes he would strike back with a soup plate or a helping of mashed potatoes. Sometimes, however, he would just get up and go fishing.

Aunt Margie hated fish, but she was a frugal woman. She didn't like to see food wasted. When Uncle Waldron brought home fish, she kept them and she cooked them. She resented having them around but she was a disciple of thrift. Uncle Waldron knew this and it gave him a great deal of satisfaction to see her struggling against her conscience. It was one of the only ways that he could put her on the spot.

He also eased his resentment toward my aunt Margie by taking these fish with an extremely illegal trawl. For the benefit of the un-

initiated, a trawl is just any kind of big net on a frame that a man drags behind his boat, picking up lake trout, sunfish, old rubber boots, rocks, and various odds and ends. Uncle Waldron had a little old outboard motor that he used in this operation. He would simply get out on the river, pull to the middle where he could keep both banks in view, drop his net, and start violating the laws of the state of Maine.

It would take a psychologist to determine just why violating laws satisfied Uncle Waldron's anger against his wife, but it did. He took out his hate against the forces of society at the same time that he gathered in a stock of fish that would make Aunt Margie squirm when he brought them home.

One day, after a particularly vigorous session in which his faults were brought out and catalogued one by one, Uncle Waldron stomped down to the shore with brimstone in his heart. He was resolved to bring home the biggest catch of hard-to-cook fish that his boat would hold. He loaded his boat, put on his motor, got out to midstream, and commenced operations. He was so angry at Aunt Margie and so intent on making her a sad woman that he didn't spot the game warden taking off from the opposite bank. He got within hailing distance before he became aware of his danger.

He reached for his ax. All he had to do was to cut the trawl lines and let the thing drop to the bottom. Unfortunately, he was in too much of a hurry. He took a hefty slash at the left-hand line, missed it completely, cut down through the transom, split the board, and had to look on aghast as his outboard motor broke away the other side of the transom and dropped into the deepest part of the channel. He had a chain on the motor for emergencies, but the chain was fastened to the transom too.

He got the lines cut just before the warden pulled up to him. The warden checked his fishing license. He noted the newly split board on the back of the boat.

"Have some trouble?" he asked, grinning. He was just astute enough to guess exactly what had happened.

"No trouble," said Uncle Waldron, "no trouble at all. I just lost my domestic weapon, my transportation, my food supply, and my confidence in my ability as an axman. No, I haven't had a bit of trouble. I've had what you might call a very pleasant day. That is, you might call it that if you were a complete damn fool. Why don't you go and catch some kid taking undersized perch?"

Aunt Margie had a field day that night. Uncle Waldron was too downhearted even to look longingly at a club-sized chunk of beech in the woodbox.

* * *

In the old days in Cedar River we didn't have any idle chatter about being free from class distinctions. We had them and we honored them.

We had an upper class that was composed of people such as Postmaster Clint Reynolds and the Reverend Mr. Adams. They had white collars and clean hands. They had it made. They didn't have to work.

We had a middle class. These people worked. They were farmers and mechanics and teamsters and guides and loggers. They earned the bread they ate. Mostly they had a pretty good time. We boys strove to attain this level when we grew up since there could be only one postmaster, and since being a minister called for more restraint in regard to the fringe benefits of life than we were prepared to exhibit.

Below the middle class there were the lost sheep such as the Gages and Uncle Oscar. They worked only when there was no other way to get whisky. Mostly they found other ways. Work took up too much time from their real careers.

Folks in Cedar River weren't worldly enough to admire this bohemianism. They had little sympathy with the struggles of free souls against the conventions. My Uncle Oscar was tolerated by the family in public, for the most part, but in private he was condemned in every detail. Uncle Jake defended his brother for years, both publicly and privately, and then he, too, became convinced that he was a scoundrel. From then on, he was Oscar's loudest critic.

This change of heart on the part of Uncle Jake was due to a difference of opinion about the causes of an unfortunate affair in a pasture wood lot back in the days before Uncle Oscar had visions of grandeur to go big time and set up his still. He was at the stage where he brewed strange concoctions in a ten-gallon crock with yeast cakes and molasses and prunes. Uncle Jake accepted an invitation to sample one of these brews, but when he partook of the proffered cup of nectar, he swallowed a live wasp. It stung him about four times. It stung him all the way down.

Uncle Jake had a painful few days, and when he got well, he crossed Uncle Oscar off his list of acceptable people. He said the wasp was no accident but pure malice toward humanity. He said that anyone who had the ingenuity to put together a beverage strong enough to make a stinging wasp unnoticeable until after you had drunk him down was also smart enough to invent a way to keep wasps at a distance. Uncle Oscar said that if Uncle Jake hadn't been in such an all-fired hurry to quaff the convivial cup, the wasp would have been dead and dissolved and would have done no damage.

Uncle Oscar said he had been drinking wasps for years. He said they were fragile and that if a man just took time enough to raise his filled dipper in a salute to his host, the detached wings would be floating in the foam. He said Uncle Jake drank as though he feared the fate of Sisyphus and that was why he got stung.

Whoever was right, there was a coolness between them from then on. Uncle Oscar lost his family defender, and Uncle Jake lost his source of supply. It wasn't until years later, when I got back to town, that they made up.

This pariah status never seemed to bother Uncle Oscar, though. He could get along without friends as long as he had whisky.

Of course he wasn't without friends altogether. He almost got Joe Caruthers permanently.

Nobody was ever able to figure out just how Joe Caruthers nailed himself into a trap by wrapping his arm around a two-by-four brace on the new storeroom back of Turner's store. Joe did it, though. He got his hand between the new block and the old stud and he drove the nails home and the block squeezed over just enough so that his elbow wouldn't pull back through.

He couldn't get enough leverage to pull the nails, and he couldn't beat the thing back because he would have broken his wrist. Not even a Caruthers can use his arm as a driving block.

Joe stood there a few minutes and considered his plight. He was right within calling distance of Mr. Turner, but he hated to let anyone know what a stupid thing he had done, especially a man who was paying him top wages as a carpenter.

He tried to squeeze his hammer in below his elbow and pry a bit, but a sharp pain in his upper arm made him realize that he wasn't

prying on the right thing. He was a pretty mad builder, and he was telling himself just what he thought of such stupidity, when my Uncle Oscar came sauntering down the road, spotted him, and came over to talk.

If there was one person in the world that Joe Caruthers didn't want to get help from, that person was my Uncle Oscar. Every time Uncle Oscar helped anyone do anything he levied a lasting tribute for all the nonessentials of life. He believed people when they said they'd like to do something for him in return. He found things for them to do.

Joe looked up and down the street to see if there wasn't some other helper within call aside from Mr. Turner. There wasn't. He told Uncle Oscar what had happened. Uncle Oscar picked up a saw and drew blood only three or four times before he had cut Joe loose. Then he stood back and admired himself. Joe cut him short.

"Oscar," he said. "I guess you don't know what you've done."

"I do, too," said Oscar. "I've kept you from being pointed at as the stupidest man in town."

"More than that," said Joe. "I wouldn't have called anybody. I'd have starved to death right here. I figure you've saved my life."

"Is that right?"

"Yes, it is. Do you know what that means? It means that you're reseponsible for me from now on. I am in your hands. It is your obligation from this time on to feed me, shelter me, and buy me cigarettes."

"What are you, crazy?" yelled Uncle Oscar.

"No, I'm partly Chinese. All we Chinese believe that a saved man is the lifelong responsibility of his saver."

"Chinese, my neck. Your father was an Irishman and your mother was an old-line Yankee. I knew them both"

"Everybody thinks that, but it isn't true. My mother was the daughter of a Chinese merchant smuggled into the States during the Boxer Rebellion. Oscar, what are we having for supper and what are you smoking these days?"

"No, you don't by golly," said my Uncle Oscar. "As far as I'm concerned, I haven't even seen you this afternoon. I don't know what you're talking about, but I'm not going to be tricked into feeding the biggest eater in town. You nail yourself back in there and try to catch somebody else."

He took off toward home on a dead run. He needed to soothe his nerves.

When Mr. Turner came out a few minutes later, Joe was working away at a pretty good clip.

"How are you coming along?" asked Mr. Turner.

"Just fine," said Joe Caruthers, "just fine."

\* \* \*

One day Joe Hanrahan and Francis Gage were shingling a roof. It was a large roof and there was plenty of room for both of them to work but Joe kept crowding Francis, nailing right up beside him most of the time. Francis got a little worried about this, especially when he found Joe eager even to drive the last nails in a strip that Francis had started.

Francis kept moving over. Joe kept crowding him. Francis got tired of it. He waited until Joe had squatted down on his hunkers, right next to him, and he reached into his pocket and found an eightpenny nail, of no use at all in roofing but good enough for what he had in mind. He looked at Joe. Joe wasn't paying any attention,

Francis took that nail and he nailed Joe's shoe right down to the roof. This is easier than anybody might think it is because a man shingling a roof usually pays little attention to his feet until he wants to move them. Francis put that nail neatly into the outer sole. He never bothered Joe a single bit.

Then Joe started to squidge over a bit to reach some more shingles. His foot didn't come. He tugged a bit. The foot stayed still.

Now what Francis didn't know was that Joe had had a few recent twinges from the direction of his heart and, although Doc Yates had assured him that these twinges were only the result of not being able to refuse a third helping of baked beans when it was offered, Joe was convinced that he had heart trouble and was liable to get a stroke any minute.

The inability of his mind to move his foot was enough evidence to Joe that the worst had happened. He started thinking in terms of paralysis and shock and such horrible items. He became completely panicked. He never even looked at his shoe. He just started hollering bloody murder.

The plumber came running. So did the electrician. So did all their helpers. Two trucks stopped along the road and the drivers poured out. Francis Gage had to clip Joe Hanrahan over the head with a hammer in order to shut him up enough to get pried loose from the roof and lowered to the ground.

When Joe came to they tried to tell him what had happened, but he refused to believe. He thought they were just cheering him up. He stayed on the ground after that. He said he was getting too old to shingle roofs.

As a result, fewer people in Cedar River had falling plaster when it rained.

\* \* \*

Uncle Oscar would have been a happy man if it hadn't been for the terrible tendencies of his creditors to renew their hopes of payment every time he got hold of a little cash money. He resented this unsporting attitude on their part. It made him morose and unhappy. He had no intentions of playing any honorable part as regards past debts, and he couldn't see why his creditors couldn't just accept their defeat with good grace.

He thought that after he had held off the payment of a bill for three years or so the payee should wipe it off his mental books and come around and shake hands. He was disgusted with the complex provisions of the laws of limitations. He thought the game should have a clear-cut ending.

Some of his creditors did acknowledge defeat and stop yammering for payment. Uncle Oscar honored them for this. He said they had the right attitude, and he would have done more business with them if they had not forbidden this type of reconcilement. They were will-

ing to be bitten once in the name of education, but they were not willing to be renipped.

There were other creditors, however, who did not recognize any
rules about time. Even four or five years after the event they still
acted as if Uncle Oscar owed them money, and this narrow-minded-
ness on their part made him despair, sometimes, of the inherent fair-
ness of mankind.

He was particularly despairing of Clint Reynolds. He owed Clint
two dollars and forty cents that Clint, in absent-minded neglect of
the post-office regulations, had allowed to accumulate as box rent.

Nobody had any idea of why Uncle Oscar had rented a post-office
box in the first place. He didn't know himself. The rent was sixty
cents a quarter, and Uncle Oscar had a lot of uses for sixty cents, but
of course he never paid the sixty cents anyway, so there was no harm
done until Clint got doing a little scheming in an underhanded way.
He told Uncle Oscar that he would have to pay the first sixty cents
or else keep renting the box with the money being added to his account. He said that the Government would stand for only so much,
or it would slap Oscar in the pokey.

The box rent got up to two dollars and forty cents before Clint
closed the box. Clint had to pay the money himself, of course, because he had no business charging such a thing, box rents being due
strictly in advance.

He tried to collect. Again he threatened Uncle Oscar with Alcatraz
or Atlanta, but Uncle Oscar knew the Government wasn't going to
transport him all that distance for any such paltry sum, so he smiled
and smiled, and promised and promised, and never paid.

Then there came the deluge of coupons that featured 1933. Desperate manufacturers, trying to sell their wares, printed coupons galore
and sent them out to the hinterlands, promising cash discounts for
merchandise when they were presented.

It came to Uncle Oscar's ears in some way that there was a merchant down in Cranston who would redeem these papers for half

their value in cash without the owner having to burden himself with soap or dog food or tooth paste or anything else. He was interested in this offer. He was always interested in anything that promised a reward for no effort.

Uncle Oscar went down to the post office to get his share of the gift.

Clint refused to give him any of the coupons. Clint said that the coupons came addressed to "Box Holder" and that Uncle Oscar didn't have a box. He said Uncle Oscar got his mail general delivery and there were no coupons for such forlorn individuals. He said Uncle Oscar was out of luck.

He hinted, though, that for two dollars and forty cents Uncle Oscar might get converted into a general-delivery box-holder and be entitled to share the wealth.

Uncle Oscar screamed. He accused poor thirty-five-dollar-a-week Clint of being a bloated plutocrat who didn't understand the problems of the common people. He threatened to write to the Post Office Department, but Clint told him that he had forfeited his civil rights when he refused to pay his box rent and that the post office would refuse to take his mail for delivery.

They argued back and forth for quite a while, but finally Uncle Oscar saw that Clint Reynolds meant what he said. So he went out and wrapped up his left hand in about fifteen old dish towels, and he told Jeb Seekings that he needed two-fifty to buy medicine for blood poisoning. Jeb fell for it. Uncle Oscar got his coupons. He hit out for Cranston.

When he got there he found out that the whole thing about the redeeming merchant was a snare, a hoax, a delusion. There wasn't any such person. Clint Reynolds had fostered the tale from beginning to end and was back home laughing all over town about how he had finally fixed Oscar.

Uncle Oscar was pretty mad, but Jeb Seekings was madder. When he heard the details of the swindle, he went in and punched Clint

Reynolds right in the nose. He said there was such a thing as being too eager to collect your bills. He said he resented being a transfer creditor.

He hounded Uncle Oscar halfheartedly for a while to see if he could get some of his money back, but then he got discouraged, and he took his place at the end of the line.

* * *

Big John Hammond came to Cedar River from the last intervale farm on the other side of Baxter's Ridge. He wanted a touch of city life. Baxter's Ridge had begun to pall on him. He wanted to walk on a sidewalk and sit around for an evening in a store where the stock in trade was more than flour and molasses and salt and tea. He wanted to eat a box of crackers and some cheese that his mother hadn't pressed and seasoned for herself.

John could have done things up right and gone on down to Cranston, the county seat. He didn't want that much city, however. He said that there was so much going on in Cranston that a man's head got to aching from being swiveled around so much. He said that Cedar River was just right –– one street, four stores, a hotel, a post office, a small bank, two churches, and a schoolhouse.

He sat on the porch of the store and he watched the street. He saw the mail stage come in and he saw it leave. He saw the bread truck stop and he saw the meat delivery made at the side door. He ate his lunch with four pulp haulers from Bennett Brook. When evening came, he won three games of checkers at the store, ate a can of peaches and a box of fig newtons, thanked everyone for the good time he'd had, and turned to leave. Jubal Dean, the game warden, stopped him.

"John," he said, "you know Baxter's Ridge is in my district. I don't get much chance to get over there but I'm responsible for it, just the same. Do you suppose that if I came to see you later on this summer that I'd have a chance to find a few night hunters or jack-lighters? It would do me a lot of good down at the main office if I could."

"Why, yes," said John, "I guess I could show you quite a lot of them. Seems there's always a little night hunting over home and I guess there's quite a lot of early-season shooting going on, too. I don't think you'd have any trouble finding all the jack-lighters you'd want to find."

"That's fine," said Jubal, "that's just fine. I'd sure appreciate that, John. I sure would."

John stood for a minute considering.

"I guess maybe I could do something else for you, too," he ventured. "I'm not sure, but I think I could."

"What's that? What else could you do?"

"Well, I'm neighbor to those fellows and I get along with them pretty well. I think that when I tell them what good treatment I got over here, in the post office and in the store and all, they'd agree to just whomping you over the head with something instead of shooting you. Then I could carry you back over here."

Jubal jumped to his feet. "Hit me over the head?" he roared. "I'm, an officer of the law. You can't do that."

"Yes, I think I can. Like I said, I get along with them pretty good. Of course there's a couple that might argue about it, but you've been real friendly, and I think I could fix things up. I'd just as soon, too. It'll give me a chance to watch that mail stage come in again. You come any time you like. I'll have everything fixed up. I'll have them whomp you real easy. You'd be kind of like my guest, you know. I wouldn't like for them to shoot my guest. They know that. They'll go along with what I say."

Jubal Dean never did get to Baxter's Ridge. Every time he planned to, something more important came up. After a while he stopped planning. He said he had enough work right in town.

\* \* \*

Burleigh Anson was an ox of a man who could knock over a small sapling with a blow of his fist. He had the build of a gorilla and the heart of a quail. He could be cowed, shamed, and put to flight by his wife, Jane, for any and every minor misdemeanor against the rules in her handbook for husbands.

Jane Anson was a belligerent lady. She stated opinions when others might have hushed, either in deference to the company or in fear of the consequences. Jane had no fear. She would just as soon have tangled with a panther as to shell out a pan of peas.

Burleigh had a yoke of oxen that he kept long after oxen ceased to be an asset to any mountain farm. In days gone by a farmer with a good yoke could put them into the woods for the company come winter and make them earn a good deal more than their keep. As the Lombards began to take over the tougher hauls and the shorter skidding began to be done solely by horses, oxen became a luxury. Jane knew this and so did Burleigh.

Jane did her best to shame her husband and then to bully him to make him get rid of his oxen. She called them lazy beasts who just stood around eating their heads off and taking the dresses off her back and the food from the table. These arguments weren't strictly true. Burleigh Anson was a good provider. He had a good farm and he worked it hard. He didn't have any real problem about putting up a little extra fodder for those oxen and, since they were about the only source of enjoyment he had in life, any reasonable woman would have left them alone. Jane wasn't a reasonable woman. She kept harping about them. For once in her life it didn't do her any good. Burleigh was defiant about the oxen. He liked them. He vowed that he was going to keep them, Jane or no Jane.

Now it happened one night in the late weeks of August that the oxen broke through the pasture fence and made some rather fancy inroads on the cornfields, not only of Burleigh but of his neighbors, the Swansons. The Swansons were argumentative, anyway. Burleigh knew, when he discovered the damage the next morning and shooed the oxen back into the pasture, that there was going to be trouble. Jane was going to have her say and so were the neighbors. Burleigh was a man of peace. He hoped he could get out of all this ruckus somehow.

He came into the house after chore time to get his breakfast, and he didn't tell Jane anything about the oxen. Unbeknown to him, however, she had gone down to the barn to call him, seen his activities, followed him in the pursuit of the oxen, and then gone back to put the meal on the table. She was cunning. She held back her knowledge to see what would happen. When he said nothing, she let on that she knew the oxen had gotten out of the pasture.

"Shoot," said Burleigh, "they didn't do no damage to speak of."

Jane knew better. "Burleigh Anson," she said, "there ain't so much truth in you as there is in a big Newfoundland dog. They ate a clean swath through the cornfield—"

She was interrupted by a knock on the door. Without a pause the door opened. In came the Swanson brothers with meanness in their eyes.

Jane took in the scene. She wasn't above laying out her own husband but she wasn't going to have anyone else doing it for her.

"What do you want this time in the morning?" she demanded.

"Burleigh knows what we want," said the elder Swanson, flexing his hands. "Them oxen of his had a field day in our corn last night. We want to know what he's going to do about it."

Jane advanced on the Swansons with her left hand held in front of her like John L. Sullivan, her right hand cocked back with a spider full of fried potatoes.

Burleigh jumped from his place at the table over to a position immediately behind her.

"Up with your guard a little higher, Jane," he said, "up with your guard a little higher, or one of them will get over it sure. If you have to let go with that spider, you'll be off guard and the other one can get right in. Bring up your guard, Jane."

He reached behind him in the woodbox and he prepared to defend himself if anything should happen to his wife. The Swansons took the hint. They were willing to face Burleigh Anson but they weren't willing to have to get past Jane in order to do it. They muttered and they departed.

The minute the door closed on their backs, Jane swung the spider around and laid poor Burleigh out among a splattering of fried potatoes. Then she walked over to the telephone, cranked, got her number, and said to the newspaper editor on the other end, "I want to advertise a yoke of seven-year-old steers. Say they're strong, willing, well fed, and docile. Say ill-health of the owner is the reason for selling."

Most people in Cedar River weren't broken of their stubbornness quite so easily as Burleigh Anson, however. For instance, anyone with any brains could have predicted what was going to happen when Vernon Faulkner's father chained the back bumper of the family car to the front porch to keep Vernon from stealing it after the rest of the family had gone to bed. Vernon was too strong to be thwarted and too weak to scheme. He took direct action.

He simply lurched the car into a running start, hoping to snap the chain. The chain held but the porch post yanked free, and that was good enough. Vernon was off into the night.

The family car had an attraction for Vernon that overcame his moral scruples, his fear of punishment, and his early training in obedience. He loved it.

Nobody taught Vernon to drive. He was born with the ability. From the time he was ten years old he was a master. His father issued warnings, then threats, then beatings. Vernon was untouched by either. At the age of thirteen he had driven as many miles as the average man of forty.

Vernon didn't care where he went. He just drove. He wheeled

around back roads and main roads and mountain roads until the gas tank was close to empty and then he came home, took his beating, and waited until there was more gas so he could take off again.

He was fourteen when he took the porch post off and he was fifteen when he bulldozed his way out of a chained barn door with the splinters flying in all directions. The barn door was the last straw. Vernon's father turned him over to the juvenile authorities. He admitted that he was frustrated in his attempts to keep Vernon off the roads.

The next thing we heard about Vernon Faulkner was that he had won state-wide fame as the object of a five-day chase through the wildlands in which he outdistanced state troopers on hopped-up motorcycles while he was making a clean get-away with a pickup truck. They finally found the truck. Vernon, however, had disappeared.

When Vernon's father heard of the escape and the chase, he built a log ramp and he winched his car up through the horse-fork doors of the lower barn. Then he tore down the ramp. He took the tires off the wheels and he chained the steering wheel to a rafter.

When he climbed into bed, he half-expected to hear screams of frustration in the night, but the night was quiet.

The next morning there were tire tracks in the driveway and the old car was gone. They never did find it again. They heard rumors and they checked them out, but they were either false or the checking was too late.

\* \* \*

In Cedar River most of us walked the thin edge. We have always felt that life was meant to be lived rather than played with. Besides, we found that some of those among us who stayed aloof from our normal, ordinary pleasures sometimes ended up just as sad in their own minds as we did in the minds of everyone else.

\* \* \*

# 8

## *Over to Home*

# R. E. GOULD

*Ralph E. Gould ran country stores in the Somerset County towns of Harmony and Anson for forty years.*

*He was a wily trader, marketing innovator, community benefactor and all-round country philosopher. He also doubled as Harmony's "leading mortician," that is, the only one. His preparation consisted of a weekend course in a Boston school for undertakers and a cheeky self-confidence.*

*In 1946 Gould set down his experiences in a book of reminiscences, "Yankee Storekeeper," in which he outlined the trading arts of backwoods Maine in the early part of the century.*

*Probably the most amusing parts of the book were not Gould's adventures as a flinty merchant, but his boyhood recollections of life on his father's farm in Lisbon Falls.*

\* \* \*

## MY PARENTAL INHERITANCE

I know what it is to skin skunks actually. When I was a boy on the farm Aunt Eunice would occasionally step to the door and sniff. She'd come in and say, "Lizzie, there's an essence peddler around tonight."

She didn't refer to the traveling man who sold extracts, essences, and hair oil by the ten cents' worth, but to a brighteyed, black-and-white animal the Indians named skunk and meant it. In those days skunk skins were worth from ten to fifty cents, depending on the amount of white on them — the more white the less worth. The ten-cent one predominated, but their power of offensive action was a constant power.

A farm boy could often earn a neat amount of pin money with a string of traps. They were easy to catch. I've heard it said that if anyone sets a trap in the middle of a twenty-acre field, a skunk would find some way to get in it. It was always easy in school to tell which boys tended their traps before classes. A teacher in the Ridge school, in those days, was a martyr to her sense of smell. I always smelled nice, comparatively speaking, because I never had money enough to buy a few traps to get started.

Then the beneficent Providence that watches over us and grants our reasonable desires noted my plight. The Lisbon Fox Club, composed of the mill agent, a hotel man, the jeweler, the boss of the corn shop, the meat man, and a few others, used to go out in the woods on fall days and hunt foxes in front of a hound, Rover. Rover was a plodding old dog, just about the right speed for these sports. Ladies of the community made slighting remarks about the Fox Club, commenting on the quantity of beverages the members were supposed to consume, but as far as I know none of them died an inebriate's death but prospered and were happy. Happy, that is, until one day Rover died.

One of the members shortly thereafter saw a hound dog advertised in a sporting magazine, and he wrote and inquired the price. The price of $75 struck them as somewhat high, but they were resourceful. They enlarged the club and took in everyone who had a dollar, and when they had 75 new members they wrote and bought Saul's Upland Champion. The new dog arrived and was a beauty. A hunt was organized for the next Saturday.

Old Rover used to move about two miles an hour, and kept the fox curious about that howling thing that chased him so intently and so slowly. The hunters, guided by Rover's bugling voice, would head across lots and surprise the fox as he dodged about looking back over his shoulder at Rover. But the new dog was trained for riding to hounds, and when they set him on a scent he gave one yipe, two barks, a howl and a yelp and was clear over to Witcher's pasture before the Fox Club knew he was gone.

The fox, his tongue hanging out, couldn't keep up the pace, and he holed up in the sandy hill on the back end of our farm. The dog brought up at the hole, his head underground, and the members of the club found his stern sticking up in the air and his tail wagging gaily. His muffled outcry clearly indicated the fox was just ahead of him.

The club prepared to dig out the fox, and members came up to our house to borrow shovels, axes, picks, lanterns, and other implements. They would shove a stick in the hole and feel out its direction, then sink a shaft and feel with the stick again. Then the dog leaped into one of the shafts and started barking. He plunged in beyond his forward shoulders, then stopped and wagged his tail in an ingratiating manner and attempted to back out. One of the hunters became disgusted at such half-hearted attempts on the part of a $75 dog, and presented the dog with a swift kick in his eastern elevation. The effect was marvelous. The dog gave a muffled yelp and sprang ahead and in an instant was out among the members of the Fox Club holding in his jaws the largest skunk ever seen in captivity. He shook him savagely and the skunk responded nobly. He distributed his favors upon the just and the unjust. Scott covered the situation well when he wrote:

> ". . . and the grim lord of Colonsay
> hath turned him on the ground
> and laughed in death pang that his blade
> the mortal thrust so well repaid."

The skunk was dead, but he exacted a fearful retribution. The hunters finally got the skunk away from the dog and threw him down the gully. The dog, however, returned to his hole. If they wanted skunks he knew where they could be found. He brought out another

and another. He brought out nine. Each time the hunters felt sure the fox would be next, but the fox was never found, and the dog's nose was never any good again for the fox. Around two in the morning I smelled the hunters bringing back the tools. My father got up and gave them some good suggestions about removing skunk stink from clothing, and they told him to go to hell.

The next morning, directed by something a little stronger than a sense of direction, I rushed to the scene of the massacre and skinned nine skunks which later brought me $1.35. I stretched the skins and nailed them to the shed, and intended to keep my good fortune a secret, but somehow mother got wind of it. She wouldn't let me in the house until I rinsed my hands in vinegar and changed my clothes in the barn. I tried to explain to mother that in time she would get used to it, but I gathered from her remarks that she had no intention of getting used to it. I have observed that women are like that — not waiting to consider that all great enterprises have some slight drawbacks. From that time on she spoke less sincerely of my fitness for the ministry, especially since I bought traps with my $1.35 and subsequently smelled just like the other boys when I went to school.

* * *

One of my earliest memories is of a religious experience. Just what it did for me has never been openly manifest, but it was an experience calling for much faith — and I was let down. Father left me to saw wood while he went away on business, and made it understood that I was not to dillydally by sliding on the hills with worthless friends who had nothing better to do.

I sawed a while, but the boys and girls on the hill joyfully called amongst themselves and seemed to be having such a fine time that I was tempted. I reflected on what father would do to me when he came home if the pile wasn't sawed, and then I would hear the boys and girls, and I finally succumbed. I got out our old pung, pulled it over to the hill, and invited everyone to ride. I sat on a sled between the shafts and steered the pung down the hill.

The boys and girls pronounced this a great improvement, and we had several rides. Then one of the girls wanted to steer, and again I succumbed. She got flustered and dropped the shafts just when the speed was most fun. One of them snapped off.

I never felt that way before. Doom, without the slightest question, was about to descend on me. Father would lick me for not sawing wood. He would lick me for going sliding. Then the pung! He had bought it at an auction for thirty-five cents and was most proud of it. He would lick me for breaking the pung. There was no pleasure within me. I was undone.

We sneaked the pung back in the barn and then the boys and girls went home and left me to my sorrow. I climbed up into the mow, walked out on the big beam, and dangled my legs into a space that was shallow compared to the depts of my despair. I reflected to learn if any remedy might prevail. I appealed to the Providence of whom my mother had taught. And Providence, at this point, aided me.

Father was working with his wood team — six cattle in three yokes in a string. He had two yokes of two or three years, and an old team on the tongue. The old team was a bull and an ox. The ox was bigger, but the bull was so much more powerful that the clevis in his yoke was set off-center an inch and a half. He was a frightening bull for all the world but father. Mother worried herself sick, but father worked with the snorting and headshaking bull as if he were another docile ox. That morning, when father walked the six cattle out of the yard, the bull had put on an exhibition. Mother watched from the door and said, "Sure as you're born, that bull will kill your father some day."

I had been taught to pray for help if I needed it. If the bull was going to kill father, I felt now was the time. I climbed down off

the beams, slid down the mow, discreetly, went in behind the mowing machine and knelt down. Very earnestly I prayed that the bull would kill father before he got home. I cast my burden on the Lord, and as soon as I stood up I felt much better.

I went back to sawing wood, and kept one eye on the road. Far off on the rim of the world I saw the team appear at last — and father was teaming the cattle along in his usual good health. The team came down Hall's Hill and disappeared behind Frazier's Hill. I sawed some more wood. It would happen, I figure, behind Frazier's Hill. But then the team came up over Frazier's Hill and father was still teaming them. I watched the load crawl nearer and nearer. The Lord was unnecessarily slow, I thought. He had still withheld His hand when father turned the load into the yard and stopped the steers by the woodpile.

"You'll have to unyoke the oxen," he said. "My head aches so I can hardly see." Then I saw that God moves in a mysterious way His wonders to perform. If He thought it best to kill father with a headache instead of by means of the bull — the matter was out of my hands now. I was reconciled, and no longer feared for my hide.

But this powerful religious experience soured on me when I discovered that the real solution took exceedingly small help from divine power. My uncle came home that night after long years in the West, and everyone was so glad to see him. Father never thought about my woodpile. The next day Uncle wanted to use the pung, and when he found a broken shaft he made a new one with a maple sapling and a drawshave — and in a matter of minutes he was off behind the mare to get his trunk at the Falls. No one has asked me to this day how the shaft got broken.

The incident, however, has been recalled many times since, and while I am frequently ashamed that I had too little sense to think of making a new shaft myself, I have also reflected that the Creator has more brains than I have anyway — and I'm willing to leave everything to Him. It seems to me that if a little boy's plight requires heavenly interference, it isn't necessary for the little boy to bother reminding Him about it. Spiritually, I have since followed such a belief, partly because my observations have never suggested a better.

* * *

# ED MAYO

*Edward Mayo was another latecomer to humorous writing. A successful watercolorist and seascape artist, Mayo for years ran a gallery out of his home in Kennebunkport. In the 1960s he founded the Kennebunkport Dump Association, a serio-comic organization aimed in part at drawing attention to growing solid waste disposal problems in the state but mostly to satisfy his own wonderfully developed sense of the absurd. Mayo's grand joke has generated considerable publicity for the town. The association once applied for a $100 million federal grant to build a combination university-museum dedicated to the study of dumpology. "It'll be the only museum in the world which will let you take the exhibits home," explained Mayo.*

*His whimsical columns began appearing regularly in the Portland Press Herald in the 1970s. Mayo now makes his home in Arundel. Although the town is real enough, Mayo's chronicles of the community are more or less purely fictional.*

\* \* \*

## LOPSTER? AYUH

This is a supplemental glossary of expressions thought to be indigenous to Maine.

It is commonly believed that we all say "ayuh" but this word occurs mostly in writings about our state and is used mainly in season by natives who seek to impress summer people.

Many of us display an alarming degree of erudition by simply saying "yes."

Immigrants who have settled here and brought with them their own form of verbal delicacy often pronounce "yes" as if it has two syllables. Competition is intense between members of the "I can talk lower than you" cults as they labor to broaden their newly found Maine "A's."

Accordingly, our speech is rapidly deteriorating into a composite of native and foreign vernacular and bilingual tourist's dictionaries become out of date faster than they are printed.

North of Brunswick, the name of the town is pronounced "Brumswick" and lobster is "lopster." If you are lost, listen carefully to the sound of these two words and you may establish whether you are going north or south so it will be unnecessary to ask directions of another person who is certain to be a fellow visitor.

"Finest kind" is never used with reference to the lobstering business which is always terrible. More useful is the phrase "pretty good" which says almost nothing. Since anyone can remember, lobstermen have caught very few lobsters but would do nothing else for a living even though they confess to being "farmers without a brain."

Lobster catching is a love-hate relationship between sturdy Maine men and the hostile sea.

There is frequent mention of "the man." Outsiders assume this means a hateful individual such as the tax man who is engaged and very unhappy to think of "shack money" being lavished on post-fishing enjoyment or an imbecile who is responsible for oppressive insanities in business or government.

It is neither of these. Because of a running feud with God, He is designated as "the man" in lower case letters. If a strong unfavorable wind develops just when the hauling is at its best, boat operation is extremely difficult and "the man is at it again."

"Why doesn't he take the day off?" is said when there are so many opportunities elsewhere for creation of genuine chaos that it seems inappropriate for the man to devote so much of his time to the ruination of the fishing occupation. "He took the day off" refers to a profitable day when the sea yielded its bounty, bait was delivered on time, preparations for the next day went well and the beer was cold and available.

Mention of the man is generally exchanged between commiserating men of the sea but occasionally clenched fists are raised and imprecations are shouted directly toward the sky with uncomplimentary personal remarks. Because fishermen are continually subjected to persecution in an unfair world, the man is blamed as a convenient scapegoat.

If you are at the wharf and hear "ping pong" mentioned, you should not conclude that the men are talking about recreation. Neither should you believe that foreigners who at one time tried to wipe out our fish population have returned for a friendly game of table tennis with erstwhile fishing adversaries.

Ping pongs are small haddock caught by draggers and although the fish are of market value, many believe the practice to be detrimental to conservation.

"Hate month" begins around the middle of June and lasts into July. At this time lobsters become listless as they shed their shells and will not seek out baited traps. Sparse catches will not compensate lobstermen for the expense of bait and fuel so they say the hell with it and haul their boats for maintenance. Thus they gather to labor and trade friendly insults at the boat yard. Learned and salty speech is heard as funds are depleted, paint refuses to dry between showers and tools are mislaid. However, work is eventually completed and, one by one, boats return to the ocean.

Then, as lobstering resumes, further additions are made to our extensive Maine vocabulary.

\* \* \*

## DUMP IMPERILED

The insidious manner in which progress erodes American institutions should have been apparent to us long ago when opaque trash bags were introduced at the Kennebunkport dump.

Although the bags disguised contents and provided a measure of comfort to dumpers embarrassed by the poor quality of their rubbish, dump picking was inhibited and a training program designed to refine techniques had to be curtailed.

Today the dump's existence is imperiled by the insidious effects of bureaucracy as, from the sterility of their offices, minions of the government have decreed that it be converted to sanitary landfill — a sandwich of garbage and dirt.

It is feared that most of the good stuff will be buried, possibly lost forever, and casualties may result as avid pickers attempt to compete with the implacable bulldozer.

Consequently a first aid station must be installed at the dump, an added expense that confirms what every taxpayer knows — progress instituted by governments is always costly and does not necessarily benefit the individual.

Built-in mediocrity makes what we throw away more expensive than ever and denial of reclamation cannot but boost the zooming rate of inflation.

Sanitary landfill is a social as well as an economic disaster. The leisurely atmosphere prevalent at the town dump is replaced by hasty deposits and departures and prolonged and friendly visits become things of the past as citizens retreat to the post office, the gas station and the drug store where facilities are already over-taxed.

It may no longer be recognized that, should a man take his wife to the dump he must allow her to get out of the car at once so she may have first pick.

Grandiose plans for the future of our beloved trash pile may be abandoned. A plexiglass dome over the site, funded by a federal grant of $100 million, was to have created a mall-like ambience for year 'round dumping comfort. The dump easily handled a flood of waste as it had been redesigned in the shape of a pentagon.

Memorabilia and artifacts were stored under the west wall of trash for eventual inclusion in the many exhibition halls of the proposed dump museum. In order to take advantage of the cultural values of the museum a university, Dump U, was planned.

The complex was originally to be housed in a 32-story condominium-type building. In conformity with zoning restrictions that allowed but one-story structures, plans were revised to erect one story above ground and bury the remaining 31.

The top floor would house the museum and the next immediately underground would be made up of classrooms. The other 30 subterranean floors would be devoted to administration, an arrangement consistent with the best in American education today.

The Kennebunkport Dump Association was built around a town dump that was made America's Number One by the efforts of its president and 39 executive vice presidents. Seventy-two working committees and 23 subcommittees were constantly planning for the future and drive-in dumping was scheduled for 1979 as part of a continuing program of improvement.

It now appears that the future of the dump and the association is uncertain.

In the midst of gloom there is a cheerful note, however. One important mind believes that because of our profligate use of resources we may soon be in short supply of many strategic materials while we struggle nearly up to our necks in trash. Thus the town dump may become a mining site and assume a new and opposite role in history.

So we traditional dumpers may take comfort and put bitterness behind us as we are reminded that nothing stays the same. Many things we cherish and revere are bound to perish but may be resurrected in another form.

\* \* \*

## ARUNDEL DIARY

Now that I am a citizen of Arundel, some long forgotten talents of mine have been rediscovered — deception, for instance.

It all started when I remembered someone's saying that the surest way to conquer a country is to declare war on it one day and surrender the next. Consequently the victor would become obliged to care for and support the vanquished, and in these inflationary times the winner would soon go bankrupt and the loser would own everything.

Because Arundel could perform more effectively as a republic, I recommend secession not only from the State of Maine, by which we are bounded, but also from the United States.

Then the war and peace procedure would result in much bountiful largesse flowing in from Washington, a prospect that delighted the hangers-on at Jerry's Market. The enthusiastic suggestions came rolling in.

Immediate nominations were made to the Privy Council, a governing body most essential to a rural community like ours. Some folk applied for ambassadorial posts to other towns, and one bilingual smarty insisted on his qualifications as emissary to Biddeford.

To decrease our dependence on Kennebunk someone believed we might produce our own libations through building a chain of stills. This seemed logical until it was remembered that this same citizen claimed at one time to have been actually clobbered by cats and dogs during a heavy rainstorm and was famous for his unlikely ventures such as frog farms in drier parts of town.

Another, noted for his weekly sighting of UFO's, volunteered to marshal a task force to survey the possibility of poisonous truffles being introduced into Arundel. This proposal was seriously considered until someone said that a visiting nurse association in Lyman has been studying the problem for years, and in any case nobody locally knew what a truffle was.

The only cogent action to date is the issuance of under the counter passports to disillusioned folk fleeing to Arundel from other towns.

Here we have a splendid social and economic climate for the intellectual and the self-employed as well as for gentle folk who are more knowledgeable than they realize and those who must leave our boundaries five days a week to labor on foreign soil.

Like the rest of the worried world we hang suspended between the benefits of technology and the consequences of its errors, and as much as we would like to believe that we are unique we secretly know that it is not so.

If the establishment of a republic would put the rug back under us we would all be happy.

\* \* \*

Arundel jokes do not proliferate like the snide stories told about Old Orchard Beach, Biddeford and the Kennebunks.

Arundel does not have a bank, and although there is no possibility of a bank robbery here it is likely that fleeing miscreants would appreciate our remote back roads for their escape route.

Arundel has neither post office nor zip code of its own. This effects a saving in postal operations but is not reflected in the price of stamps, which cost 15 cents here — the same as in the outside world.

Arundel does not have a liquor store, but we are amply supplied by manufacturing up on the ridge. When inventory is low or variety is sought, natives travel to Kennebunk where they complain bitterly about the prices.

Arundel selectmen meet regularly for friendly quarreling.

Unlike Old Orchard Beach, our budget is not lost and we are certain that there is one somewhere in town. Because we have no beach we are neither plagued nor blessed by nude bathers. We have no equivalent to a Bikini Tavern although a gentleman up on the ridge vaguely remembers that what he calls a "biniki" is not worn when the chill factor is 40 below.

There is no Arundel news column in the local paper, and we are spared semi-literate musings of little consequence.

The town dump is obscurely located and residents searching for it become hopelessly lost. Thus they are accustomed to using out of town facilities.

Arundel does not have a downtown district to maintain for boarding up of store fronts. Its most turbulent region is Route 1 at the Arundel Market, especially at 5 p.m. when worried natives and others purchase comestibles and libations sufficient to last the evening.

It is bounded in part by Biddeford and natives have been known to cross the boundary inadvertently, immediately to return in terror. Fortunately, many travelers who arrive are lost but soon escape to less desirable places.

The most cherished aspect of Arundel is its anonymity.

\* \* \*

One of the reasons that Arundel is such a pleasant place to live is, of course, the size of our government: it is small.

For some years now, the inhabitants have existed in harmony except for occasional town meetings when irate folk reveal their knowledge of what words to use when they are angry.

We suffer from a lack of psychologists and counselors in tandem and have no recreation programs designed for people who would rather be sitting down.

It is feared that, if we were invaded by Biddeford or the Kennebunks, they would bring these so-called amenities with them, much to the dismay of sedentary citizens who wish to be left alone.

Because they were alarmed at the possible encroachment of the outside world, they have recruited a militia up on the ridge.

The start of the organizational meeting was delayed when someone discovered there were no paper cups. Once the cups were supplied and several infusions of ridge power dispensed, a snappy drill session followed. It was immediately decided to eliminate the command "right dress" because most of the ridge folk are left-handed.

After the auxiliary voted to form a squad of camp followers everybody got down to the important business of eating a sumptuous picnic lunch.

When an inventory of available weapons disclosed that nobody owned a cannon, it was moved and seconded that one be built.

It was further proposed that the cannon be large enough to propel a 45-pound ball.

After the gun was built from parts of several scrapped cars it was loaded and fueled with ridge power for a trial run.

When the charge exploded the cannonball stayed put but the cannon itself recoiled over fifty yards into Stan Merrill's back yard.

The man who touched it off soared all the way to the general store at Goodwin's Mills.

When he finally returned to Arundel, he said he would have preferred a trip to Biddeford, but the angle of trajectory was wrong.

* * *

Recently there was a crisis of sorts up on the ridge, where the
fierce American desire for independence burns brightly. The folks
who stew, percolate, filter and bottle "ridge power" were alarmed
when sales declined.

The encroachment of highly publicized "natural" and "light" commercial beverages caused their dilemma.

Discerning consumers were not drinking so much delicious ridge
power because they believed it would weigh them down and they
would be too slow on the draw to grab the gusto.

Advertising budgets were scarce on the ridge, but ingenuity is
abundant.

At first the boys thought a new bottle design should replace the
traditional jug — which must be balanced on the shoulder. Then it
was remembered that used bleach bottles are inexpensive and that it
is downright patriotic to continue recycling them.

Large companies extol their own marvelous processes, emphasiz-
ing cleanliness and quality ingredients; but their ideas are impractical
here.

Ridge methods are secret and so speedy that the product is into
the bottle and subsequently into the customer before you can say
"natural light."

Sometimes the best solution is the simplest, and simplicity tri-
umphed when it was decided to water down precious ridge power.

Thus a beverage which is naturally natural became lighter by adding inexpensive Arundel well water that contains no calories. Sales
are booming again as ridge runners punish the pistons and outrun
disappointed and enraged treasury agents. Some time ago in my
Arundel Diary I failed to mention that we do not have a police department as such.

However, we do have an alert and efficient sheriff's· department patrol. Last week they received an FBI communication featuring six photos of the same fugitive.

Three days later they wired Washington to say, "We have captured the first five criminals and are looking for the sixth."

* * *

Summer is here and Arundel is alive with activity. Each of the roads is accented with new tire marks that attest to nocturnal maneuvers long after the squealing has died away.

Flowering dogwood lines much of the roadsides toward Kennebunkport, making driving a fragrant delight.

Only a trace of smoke issues from the stills on the ridge as careful operators maintain proper combustion and a steady stream of ridge power pours from copper tubing.

It was a stroke of genius to package liquor in used bleach bottles this year. A half gallon from the package store in Kennebunk contains 59 ounces, but a bleach bottle holds a full 64.

A major crisis arose when ridge runners declined to transport their usual loads, bemoaning the gasoline shortage.

So the latest word is that there will be roadside stands for dispensing this unusual beverage to happy folk. If one can imbibe a water glass of the straight product and still walk away, he will be entitled to a free tee shirt stenciled "I guzzled." The shirt may be reversed, displaying its plain side when used for burial. El Numbo, Torpedo Juice, Mind-in-a-fog and Whew are new bottle labels recently delivered hot off the press.

Although the side effects of ridge potables have yet to be examined, one operator who is nearly edentulous uses it to soothe his one remaining tooth. Last week, when his fuel supply was low, he used some to fire the still and the resulting intense heat melted the machinery. Ridge power will be added to gasoline when engines have been modified to accommodate the added octane.

Last year, when news of the plentiful supply of ridge power reached Washington, an agent was dispatched to find the still and the owner in the act of operating it. Everyone admitted the existence of the still and the identity of the owner but wouldn't tell where it was. After several frustrating days the man became desperate, for he had to make a report, but he had an inspiration and collared the still owner's little boy.

He said "Sonny, I understand your father has the biggest still in southern Maine," and the kid said "That's right."

"Tell me where it is?" he asked, and the lad said "No."

"I'll give you two dollars," he said and the kid said "OK" and told him.

As the agent turned to go to his car the kid said "Mister, I'd like to have my money." The man said "I'll pay you when I get back." The boy said "I've gotta have my two dollars right now."

The agent asked why, and the little kid said "If I know my old man, Mister, you ain't comin' back."

* * *

# ALLEN D. BROWN

*"Cap'n Perc Sane" is the literary creation of Allen D. "Mike" Brown, writer, editor, fisherman and Down East philosopher.*

*Born in Belfast, the son of a commercial fisherman, Brown has served as editor of a number of weekly newspapers in the coastal region. The letters of Cap'n Perc Sane began appearing regularly in that bible of the fishing industry, the* National Fisherman *— then the* Maine Coast Fisherman *— in 1962.*

*His writing is somewhat reminiscent of the early 19th century Maine humorists. It is essentially an oral approach, dropping Gs and vowels and containing some deliberate misspellings to effect more of a spoken than written style. Yet, like Bill Clark and John Gould, Brown draws upon true-to-life composites of his friends and neighbors in forming the characters who populate Saturday Cove, the fictional setting of these stories.*

\* \* \*

## LETTERS FROM CAP'N PERC SANE

Saturday Cove
Maine

Dear Editor,

Shorty Gage hauled all his lobster gear last weekend. Said t' hell with it. Winter's here n' the lobsters ain't. The wind's up n' the price is down.

Short thinks lobstermen should be paid year 'round like schoolteachers, whether they fish or not. He says if fender makers n' lightbulb changers can have a guaranteed income, so should lobster catchers. Short says the only thing guaranteed lobstermen is they will end up with longer arms than most humans, a 10-year-old pickup truck n' a rusty citizen's band radio.

Shorty says it's bad enough that the Good Lord made him a lobsterman, but then turned right around and didn't give him brains enough t' realize it.

"And I'll be damned," Shorty says, "if'n it ain't harder n' harder every year t' make the price of a six-pack of beer f' when company drops in." He said company.

"First, there ain't no lobsters," he says, "n' second, by the time I buy the bait, build a trap n' rig it, gas the boat, haul all day n' then argue all night why lobsters cost so damn much with a short-panted dude from Sioux City, I'm plum wore out."

Sam Wheeler asked Shorty why he didn't start a kangeroo ranch if'n he didn't like lobstering. Shorty told Sam t' go t' hell.

Shorty was doin' all this carryin'-on talkin' while he was haulin' his boat inta' the alders with his pick-up truck. He'd just get her comin' a little when the rope would break or someone would yell that his rear axle was settin' astern. Shorty's truck doors don't work so he'd hafta' crawl out the back winda every time this happened. It was hard t' tell where the philosophy left off n' the swearin' began.

Beulah Banning didn't help matters none a' tall. She was down t' the shore collectin' feelin' stones. Well, she said she was. She was actually there t' aggravate Short. Does it every year when he hauls his boat.

Beulah is chairman of the town's three Democrats which Short refers to as a nest of sea urchins. Politics are bad enough but advice from Beulah on how t' haul a lobsterboat just about curls Shorty's felt innersoles.

Beulah remarked t' Sam, who was sittin' in the sun, that if'n Mr. Gage would put rollers under his cradle rather than seaweed,

the boat might haul a dite easier. Shorty, through Sam, said if widder Banning gained a couple more pounds, she'd be eligible t' get documented.

Beulah is sensitive 'bout her weight, which Short knows only too well, so she went home with only half a grain bag of feelin' stones.

Pud Hall was clammin' while all this was goin' on. Pud has a motorcycle with a sidecar which he delivers clams with. He had four or five rockers n' was startin' his clam delivery when Short yells to him. Said he needed a tow so Pud hooks his motorcycle t' the front of Short's pick-up.

Pud revved up his cycle, Shorty climbed through his back winda n' yelled something that sounded like "Head 'em up! Move 'em out!" n' then there was this terrible crash.

When I left the Cove, Pud's sidecar was severed n' four yards inta' the alders. Shorty's truck rear end was athwartships n' Sam was still sittin in the sun whittlin' lobster plugs.

Best regards,<br>
Cap'n Perc Sane

* * *

Saturday Cove
Maine

Dear Editor,

The Cove is frozen in. Solid, shore t' shore. The old tide heaves n' pushes all day making chunks around the edges n' black cracks through the middle but that giant slice of ice pie clings like a burr on a shaggy dog.

Sam Wheeler was telling me 'bout his uncle Simon n' Jesse Foster. He was telling me how they got froze in at the Cove quite a spell back.

Seems Jesse n' Simon never got along a' tall. Never spoke, not even t' fight. How they could sail a coaster for years was a mystery. But for ten years they hauled kiln wood t' Rockland aboard this silent schooner.

Sam told me 'bout how the first one up in the morning would start the galley stove, fry his breakfast eggs n' ham n' perk just one cup of coffee. After he'd finish, he draw a bucket of water n' douse the fire. The second man in the galley would have t' start from scratch.

Jesse n' Simon would swap off being captain — Jesse on even numbered days n' Simon on odd. The schooner, Harmony, sailed equally well for either man.

Fittin' out in the spring, Jesse n' Simon would take port or star'bard f' working. Things would go fairly well 'til they reached the keel — then they both would paint sort of sideways which left a few holidays.

Why they never spoke has plenty of versions. One is that Simon sold Jesse a blind mare. The mare fell inta' Jesse's well one night n' it took four days t' block n' tackle it out.

'Cause the well was ruined, Jesse had t' haul water for the Mrs. from a spring a mile from the Cove. His mare being drowned beyond repair, he bought a mule for a water hauler. The mule kicked

Jess on the second trip n' Jess lived the rest of his life with a left leg that had a port tack.

Anyway, the day the Harmony froze in was one of them biters in January. The boys had been t' Rockland n' put inta' the Cove long about mid-afternoon. She was skimming then. Jesse was cap'n, it being the 22nd. Instead of dropping the hook out aways, Jess brought the Harmony smack t' the center of the Cove.

Simon, crewing, dropped anchor, dropped sails n' dropped down to the galley for a cup of coffee. After he'd doused the fire, he came on deck n' see that Jesse had taken the punt n' gone ashore. This left an already cold Simon with a short freezing swim.

That time of year picnickers were rare. Simon paced awhile but see that a swim was the only way. He shed his sheepskin n' rubber boots n' dove. Most Cove swimming records were broken that day. Before Simon got home his clothes were iron. The last few steps he had t' hop as his pants were frozen straight down like rain gutters.

His wife dragged him back of the kitchen stove, some say with ice tongs, where he stayed for eight hours. When he got so he could bend an elbow, he gurgled down a gallon of straight West Indies rum. This brought back his color somewhat.

Meanwhile, back at the Cove, Jess had been ahind a rick of alders having humorous convulsions. After his belly healed, he spread the word 'round the Cove of Simon's winter dip. When Simon, with sort of a bluish tinge, got outa' bed a week later he heard the whole story.

Well, the winter git colder n' the Harmony stuck tighter. The silent schooner groaned like a frozen oak in a gale. Neither man went near. Come spring, the Harmony was sold to a Stonington man.

The wives signed the papers.

Best regards,
Cap'n Perc Sane

\* \* \*

Saturday Cove
Maine

Dear Editor,

Most lobstermen are liars. Sitting around coal stoves on crisp nights, they lie more n' ever. People dropping in the store for some rat cheese and hearing the story 'bout Clipper Raye n' Aroostook lobsters would naturally think it 'bout the biggest whopper they ever heard. Well, sir, it t'was the truth as sure as fog in August.

His certificate read Romero Rupert Raye. And that ain't no name t' tote if you're gonna fool around lobstering. Clipper came about 'cause of his never taking down his riding sail. Left it up from April 'til November.

He was a Cove boy too — makes some of us sorta' proud.

One spring, Clipper said he'd had enough of pot-haulin' — said he was going 'bout as far away from salt water as the price of his boat could take him. And that's how he ended up in Aroostook County.

Nobody heard much from Clipper for pretty near a year. Then Burt Haynes n' Martha took a little vacation up that way. It was from Burt that we got the story.

Clipper had landed in Caribou with 'bout a leaky skiff price in his pocket. He rented a little shed outside of town and 'bout all a passer-by could hear for a couple of weeks was this hammerin' like all hell had broken the dike. Then some of them farmers begin to get mighty curious.

One night, a delegation of appointed paid a call on Clipper. He was cordial n' all, inviting them to sit after all the pleasantries was exchanged. Then the spokesman for the lot quite pointedly asked him what the hell he was making. Clipper allowed they were lobster traps. That raised a little fertilizer dust off their eyebrows. The spokesman then told Clipper that there weren't any lobsters up there in Aroostook County — 100 miles from the coast. Clipper allowed that there was; that everybody just thought there wasn't and didn't fish for 'em. He drove that barb home a little by asking if anyone there had set any pots. They left with the barb still in 'em.

The next most uncommon sight these good farmers was treated to, was a rented truck chugging down the Maine Street of Caribou loaded with 'bout 50 of Clipper Raye's lobster traps. And it chugged right outa' town and inta' the woods.

It was one of them warm spring mornings that bring the town prophets out from the front of their stoves and space them along main streets, that they next see the Aroostook lobsterman. The same rented truck, chugging still, hauls up in front of the chain store. Clipper docks her gently n' eases outa' the cab — rubber boots — oilskins — the whole works. He goes 'round back, drops the tailgate (which was most ready to fall off anyway) n' sets on the sidewalk, two bushel of the best looking lobsters that ever crawled a bottom.

The prophets eased in on Clipper, much like a cat would an eagle. Most of them potatomen never saw a lobster, but a drummer allowed to all that they were sure enough real. After all the prophets had their eyeful, Clipper lugged 'em inta' the chain store where he dickered a fancy price — peach basket n' all.

This went on way inta' the summer. Aroostook lobsters were outselling beefsteak — n' Clipper was getting rich. Hardly anybody questioned where he caught 'em. Those that would, got a mumbled "lake" reply from Clipper.

The Sea n' Shore Dept. sent a warden up t' check out the rumors, but Clipper told him that tidal water and his badge ended 'bout 100 miles SE. Next they sent up a Fish n' Game warden n' Clipper asked t' see the paragraph on lobsters. They were still holding conferences in Augusta when fall came and found the Aroostook lobsterman purring down the main street of Caribou with all his gear aboard a new truck.

In October, Clipper sold all his gear, new truck, ranch house, and 200-foot barn to a syndicate of town prophets. He wrote out pretty detailed instructions to 'em how to set, what lake, mud bottom or gravel — and then took off. Some say he went to **South America.** But nobody heard from Clipper Raye from that day.

There was an incident about a week after he left when a big truck, leaking water from the back, pulled inta' the police station n' the driver inquired as to the whereabouts of R. R. Raye, but nobody paid it never a mind.

The prophet syndicate shortly folded up and went back t' raising potatoes. And as I said before, folks around Sat'day Cove are kinda' proud of Romero Rupert Raye, the Aroostook Lobsterman.

Best regards,

Cap'n Perc Sane

\* \* \*

Saturday Cove

Maine

Dear Editor,

The annual Cove Christmas party will be held as usual this year at the schoolhouse. And, as in past years, it will feature the famous Gage eggnog. This is one case of **Barbados rum, the white** of one pullet egg n' three stirs with a two-tined fork.

Shorty Gage is the punchmaster 'cause he claims he's the only one that knows the recipe.

Shorty used t' be the whole party, Santa n' all. But Beulah Banning won out f' Santa a few years back by drawin' the shortest salt fish strip. Beulah makes a better Santa anyway with her 300 lbs. Beulah does things big as Santa. She even painted her oilskins red.

Beulah's oilskins are special-made and it was quite a sacrifice.

Pud Hall gets the tree this year. This wasn't a unanimous vote 'cause Pud never goes far t' get anything. Pud was the tree-getter three years ago n' chopped down Sam Wheeler's lawn fir. Sam had bird suet hangin' in it n' Pud never even took it off — just left it on f' decoration.

Sam got so damn mad at Pud he wouldn't open his present. That was three years ago n' those tunafish sandwiches must be pretty dried out by now.

Shorty's Friendship cousin Slats Farnum is also a problem. Slats gets t' anticipatin' that Gage eggnog right after he wakes up in the mornin'. He's feverish 'long 'bout 8:30 n' starts drinkin' beer. The party isn't until after supper Christmas Eve so Slats has 'bout a 36-bottle head start on the festivities.

Most years Slats never gets t' the nog even if'n he makes the party. He staggered in right in the middle of Silent Night last year, fell over Beulah's yellow tomcat n' skidded right up under the tree.

Beulah let out a helluva roar n' started runnin' around lookin' for her cat n' Slats seeing those red oilskins rushin' about thought the schoolhouse was on fire n' jumped right out through the window — sash n' all.

Amos Drinkwater is Beulah's great-grandfather. Nobody knows how old Amos is. Some say 109. Anyway, Old Amos, as he's known, goes t' the Christmas party.

Old Amos can't hear too well n' he thinks the party is town meetin'. They always let Amos vote 'cause they don't want t' hurt his feelin's. They get out the ballot box n' everything. He votes straight Republican every Christmas.

The old maid Berry sisters also go. They always have a mug or two of Gage nog which is a comedown from the chokecherry wine they make in their cellar.

'Fore Pud Hall got promoted t' tree-getter, it was his job of gettin' the fire goin' party mornin'. Pud took his job mighty serious when he was younger n' there never was a hotter schoolhouse in the country than that at the Cove on Christmas Eve. One year it was so damn hot, they called a recess so's everybody could go home n' take off their long underwear.

But the Gage nog usually irons out all the Cove difficulties n' punchmaster Shorty emerges the hero. It's powerful touchin' long late in the night t' see Short with his arm half way around Beulah singin' White Christmas, n' White Christmas, n' White Christmas.

Best regards,

Cap'n Perc Sane

* * *

# 9

# *From Away*

# EDMUND WARE SMITH

*Edmund Ware Smith (1901-1967), author, editor and widely-known authority on the life and lore of the north woods, became a Mainer by stages, first as a summer visitor and finally as a permanent resident beginning in the 1930s. Edmund Smith's literary wares appeared in the Saturday Evening Post, Field and Stream and the Ford Times, a magazine which he served as managing editor for several years. The following piece gives the insider-outsider's perspective to the Maine way of life.*

\* \* \*

## HOW TO GO NATIVE IN MAINE

The subject of the natives of Maine versus the summer people and tourists is so complicated that it can be approached only by a gymnast or preferably a trapeze artist of eccentric talent.

I almost qualify. I have been teetering on the tight wire of the matter ever since my father and mother dragged me from a comfortable home in Boston to the Spar Hawk Hotel in Ogunquit, where my second cousin Warren played piano in the summer orchestra. At the time of this baptism, I was seven years old. I have never been the same since, and I am glad of it.

Most of the rest of my life, and surely the best of it, has been spent in Maine trying to go native. The effort has failed. I have written eight volumes about Maine's wilderness and its people, owned two homes on its endearing land, known five of its Governors, and spoken from a lectern at its University. I have been a legal resident for twenty years, and when I am out of the State, my home-sickness is a thing of renowned agony.

But even with a record such as mine, you are up against a dead stymie. For unless you were born in the State and can prove it, there is no such thing as total acceptance. If you entered life only ten feet short of the State line while your mother was being rushed by ambulance toward a Maine maternity hospital, you're still "from away." Don't fight it. Just make the best of it.

But while the natives form a fraternity you may never quite join, they offer you — tacitly — a series of steps toward the achievement of their trust and affection.

The first step is marked "Tourist." Here you could remain under scrutiny for years. They like to look a man over carefully. If you keep coming back each season, it proves you must like them, so there must be some good in you. And therefore, you advance to "Summer Visitor," or "Summer Person." Try to make it the former. It's nearer the native heart.

As a Summer Visitor, you're a known regular. Presently, you buy a house on the seacoast, or on a lake shore, or on a country lane. You plant a mailbox on a cedar post. Comes a year when you install a heating system. You buy storm windows, a snow shovel, a banjo clock, and a cat. You sell your house in Jersey and move to Maine. You now classify as a "Year-Round Summer Person." In order to hold this position, it is well to tough out a few winters with no Miami.

When, with the passing years, you have worn out several sets of snow tires and long underwear, paid many taxes, raised a succession of vegetable gardens, and become a legal resident, you qualify for the highest attainable accolade. You are now "From Away." Strive for nothing beyond this. You've had it.

Here's why: In a typical Maine coast town — call it Far Castle — the natives are outnumbered five to one. This of itself could be disturbing to them. Strangers, with wealth from outside, have gradually acquired their venerable homes, or built new ones on the land of their forefathers. True, the town's economy has improved. Far Castle's master carpenters are at work. So are its boat builders, innkeepers, plumbers, and lobstermen. The picture is rosy, the dependence mutual. So why the reticence and reserve?

The fact is that Far Castle's natives have lived here for six and seven generations. This is true, rock-hard identity. It is nonnegotiable. No matter who has taken title to their property, he is still, in a sense, a licensed visitor. If this seems odd, ask yourself how you'd feel if a total stranger up and bought your great-great-grandfather's house and moved it, beam by hand-hewn beam, to a new site down the road? There goes your roof and ridgepole. There goes the room where you were born. What is left? The fact that you were born there!

If the tourist bears this in mind, he will have a better time in Maine. He will start with the right attitude. But he should also consider a few simple rules of behavior that should further amicable relations with the natives.

Don't try to imitate the native dialect. It may not sound as peculiar to you as yours does to them.

Beware of calling them "characters." You may be one yourself.

If you are loaded with money, don't wave it around. Spend it.

Don't pick bouquets of roses and peonies from the natives' flower gardens. It's stealing.

Be very careful with fire. Maine almost burned up in 1947.

In many states, the fine for throwing trash on the highway is a hundred dollars. In Maine, you can do it for less. But don't let the bargain tempt you. And don't, under any circumstances, picnic on a native's lawn without first asking his permission. Here's what happened to some foreigners from Connecticut who did.

After the picnickers left, the owner of the lawn went out and gathered up the sardine cans, eggshells, beer bottles, and grapefruit pelts and packed them in a carton. He had the car's license number and, with the aid of a State Police friend, located the owner's address.

Taking the carton, he drove the three hundred-odd miles to the Connecticut address, dumped the package on the erstwhile picnicker's front lawn, and rang his doorbell. When the offender appeared, our man said:

"I'm returning what you loaned me last Sunday. I think you'll find everything just as you left it for me."

Of course the above incident is extreme. Actually, there are innumerable strong, warm friendships between Far Castle's natives and its tourists, or Summer Visitors. They deepen with the years.

One thing I have noticed: At the Summer Visitor level the aspirant is often inclined to rush right on toward a higher acceptance status. But haste can set you back or at least extend probation. However, I know a man who got away with it. But he used native ingenuity.

The boundary between non-native George Blake's property and native Lucius Harper's is a brook, or ditch, about two feet wide. George, who had recently acquired his house and land, had a wonderful idea for a good-neighbor gesture. He would build a small bridge across the brook. It would invite and beguile his native neighbor. They would walk to and fro across the bridge and be friends.

George built the bridge secretly in his barn and installed it after dark. The idea was to surprise, as well as please, Lucius Harper. But when George looked out in the morning and saw his bridge, he was thunderstruck. Centered on the five-foot span, smack on the boundary line, was a sign that said: NO TRESPASSING.

It was a cruel rebuke, and George was crestfallen. But he revived when he realized that if his native neighbor really resented him, he would have sawed the bridge in half exactly on the boundary line. Seized with inspiration, George went to work in his barn with paint and brush. Next morning, it was native Lucius Harper's turn to be astonished. Midway across the bridge was a new sign: TOLL 10¢.

The word spread through Far Castle like a sheet of flame. Natives and visitors drove by to see what each new bridge sign had to say. CAPACITY—ONE, NO FISHING, DETOUR, SINGLE LANE, LOAD LIMIT—2 LBS., RING ONCE FOR BEER, and WHEEL-CHAIR TRAFFIC ONLY were but a few of the sightseers' rewards. With George and Lucius tossing the ball back and forth, the show lasted all summer, and by mid-sweet corn season, George Blake was strictly "From Away."

For one and all, the fair land of Far Castle is to love, cherish, and obey. Its pine forests, misty spruce headlands, islands in the sea; its gulls and gray ledges; woodsmoke, storms and sunlight, haunt and hold visitor and native alike. Since both are searching for the same thing, it seems wonderfully appropriate that the definitive statement on each other is a collaboration between a native and non-native who have been close friends for three decades.

The man from away is a retired university professor. The native is a plumber, still plumbing at eighty, lean as a rasher of string, and dean of the Far Castle sages. I am honored — at least, I think so — to be both the hero and the victim of the interchange between these sabre-witted gentlemen. It leaves me feeling like a mixed metaphor.

Said the professor to the plumber:

"Do you know this new guy, Smith, that just moved into the old Hopkins place?"

"Ed Smith?" said the plumber. "Why sure, I know him."
"What's he like?"
"He's just like one of us natives."
"That's no compliment."
"I didn't intend it should be."

\* \* \*

# KENNETH ROBERTS

*Kenneth Roberts (1885-1957), famous for his vivid, carefully researched novels of the colonial and Revolutionary periods* (Arundel, Rabble in Arms, Northwest Passage), *made his home at Kennebunkport. Fiercely loyal to his native state, he once attacked the historian Arnold Toynbee in a long* Saturday Evening Post *article for what he took to be Toynbee's slighting reference to Maine in* A Study of History.

*Roberts couldn't abide the idea of Maine as Vacationland and he wrote a number of essays lamenting the despoliation of the state's natural attractions. He once caused a stir by urging members of a local garden club to go forth "with ropes and grappling hooks" to tear down billboards along Maine roads.*

*He had the Mainer's traditional disdain for those out-of-state invaders, the city-bred "sports," who looked upon the north woods as a great national park where they could be served with quaint restorative slices of wilderness life for the price of a fishing rod and the hiring of a Maine guide. It was in this perverse spirit that Roberts wrote the following story.*

\* \* \*

## THE LURE OF THE GREAT NORTH WOODS

One of the universally accepted truths in this skeptical world is the lure of the great north woods.

The chief foundation of the lure appears to lie in the belief that only in the great north woods may man's overwhelming desire to catch edible fresh-water fish be gratified.

For a matter of three hundred years, poets have harped on the desirability of going back to the north countree, where the towering tops of the stately pines make banners of the clouds; on the joys of faring forth along the gypsy trail, and laving the face in crystal streams at dawn among the hills; on the pleasures of resting in flowery meads while larks and throstles make glad the day.

Most of the poets who have sung of the winelike air and the wholesome fare of the glorious north countree have made lilting references to the rise of speckled beauties to the brilliant fly: to the thrilling leaps of the salmon king who boundeth up the ice-cold stream in pursuit of his evening meal of fishermen's hooks; to the outthrust jaw of the nimble bass who goeth south with an eighty-dollar reel or words of that general import.

In other words, poets have always assumed and apparently will always assume that when one gypsies into the great north woods, one should attach sandpaper to the soles of the shoes to avoid slipping on the fish.

Poets, furthermore, seem able to reach the heart of the great north woods in one deft, sinuous leap. Whether a poet practices the art of poetry in Detroit or West 195th Street, he invariably eliminates the involved transfer from his home to the Great Outdoors, precipitating himself abruptly into soul-stirring quatrains about deftly casting a scarlet fly upon the foam-flecked pool, or how the trout leaped up at dawn to greet the rising sun.

"Come," says one of these poets — a leading advocate of gypsying away into the unspoiled Northern wildernesses, "Come when the leaf comes, angle with me; come when the bee hums over the lea; come with the wild flowers — come with the wild showers — come when the singing bird calleth for thee!"

One who reads this outburst in behalf of angling and the untrammeled wilderness feels that the journey from the tumultuous and fishless marts of men to the perfumed leas where the wild bee hums is as simple as obtaining an election to the National Geographical Society.

The gay enthusiasm of the poets is admirably supported by the artists who paint the rugged north country for magazine covers and calendars. The background of these paintings is virgin forest; the immediate foreground is filled with a likeness of a gentleman picturesquely disguised in wading boots, corduroy trousers, flannel shirt and battered felt hat, busily engaged in tearing a reluctant trout from his natural surroundings. One foot is planted on a moss-covered rock; the other rests beneath the surface of the torrent — presumably on a fish; his right hand deftly manipulates the rod; his left hand thrusts a landing net beneath the body of the trout which stares horror-struck at its captor. The careless smile on the fisherman's face shows clearly that the whole business is attended by a minimum of fuss and exertion.

In short, those persons who have been in a position to give publicity to the great north woods have for many years been subject to what the Freudians might call a north-woods lure-complex. Just as the younger dramatists and novelists interpret everything in terms of sex, so do north-woods enthusiasts interpret everything connected with the north woods in terms of lures.

Thus has arisen the universal acceptance of the lure of the great north woods. Persons who have no idea where the great north woods begin for luring purposes are well acquainted with the fact that the lure exists. It is a great basic fact of American life, like the Constitution of the United States, the heroic spirit of 'seventy-six, the consumption of baked beans in Boston and the words of the Star-Spangled Banner — one of those basic facts concerning which little is actually known, and most of that little erroneous.

For a number of years the art of fresh-water angling in that section of Maine in which I happen to live has gradually become less and less a matter of fish-capturing and more and more a labor of worm-chaperoning. In other words, when one extracts a choice parcel of worms from the depths of the tomato bed and fares forth into the flowery meads where the bee hums over the lea with the idea of catching himself enough speckled beauties for a mess, the net result of his faring is usually to give the worms a free excursion.

If angleworms in southern Maine — and the same thing is doubtless true in many sections of America south of the great north woods — were endowed with intellect and familiar with modern advertising methods, there would be signs in worm language in centers of worm population urging worms to become fish-minded — to Get a Lift with a Fisherman.

I cannot deny that trout are still to be found in the crystal streams outside the great north woods section. They are, however immature. They can no more make a mouthful of a medium-sized angleworm than a small boy can engulf a Virginia ham in one bite. By comparison with the speckled beauties encountered outside the great north woods, a sardine is a roistering hellion of a fish.

The reason for the immaturity of trout near inhabited areas is said by some to be due to the fact that small tin automobiles are easily obtained by the young and careless. The automobiles make it possible for them to repair in large numbers to every crystal stream and foam-flecked pool in the countryside. Arrived there, their natural lack of intellect causes them to ignore the fishing laws and retain even the smallest speckled beauty capable of digesting a worm.

For some years I annually took a little group of worms on a personally conducted tour of the local leas. On each occasion, as I wearily replaced the worms in the tomato bed at the end of the day, I resolved that on subsequent years I would forsake the haunts of men and small tin automobiles and turn to the foaming stream and the trackless forests of the north countree. Only there, I felt sure, could one go fishing and return with fish instead of with all the original worms.

Eventually the lure of the great north woods became so powerful that I broke away from the ties that bound me to civilization and went a-gypsying on the open road into the north countree with three fellow gypsies.

I had, I may add, conducted exhaustive researches into various sections of the great north woods, and had been assured by anglers of ability and experience that the country in the vicinity of a certain lake which lies in the shadow of the Height of Land on the Canadian border — Canoodlekook Lake for the purposes of this narrative — contained the very essence of north-woods lure.

It was miles from the railroad; through its primeval forests roamed the deer, the bear, the porcupine; at night, when the pale light of the moon silvered the towering tops of the giant pines, the forest glades echoed to the contralto screams of the hairy-eared lynx.

Further investigation uncovered the fact that a delightful cottage, set down on the lake shore in the midst of this wilderness, could be rented for any desired period. Not only did the persons who rented this cottage — known as Hokum Cottage for the purposes of this narrative — secure the services of its caretaker, Jake Short, enthusiastically characterized by the owner of the cottage as the best guide in the whole north country, but they also secured the use of a cook stove, ice box, bathroom complete with shower bath, and beds that would, in the owner's words, accommodate three people comfortably and four if necessary.

Since it was obvious that any person desiring to gypsy into the north country would deserve to lose his gypsying license if he wished for more than this, Hokum Cottage was engaged and urgent messages dispatched to western Pennsylvania, where two of the gypsies awaited the word to start their dash for the great north woods. Equally urgent messages were also dispatched to Jake Short, the paragon of north woods guides, instructing him to have all in readiness.

When forces were joined in southern Maine it was apparent that among the most noticeable omissions from poems extolling the lure of the open road and the great north woods is information concerning the amount of baggage and supplies to be taken by fisherman gypsies.

Since Canoodlekook Lake lies miles from the railroad in the depths of the virgin forest, the trip had to be made by automobile; and space was consequently limited. Each gypsy, after urging the other three to restrict his personal belongings to the smallest possible compass, craved the privilege of carrying some trifle unhesitatingly condemned by the others as unnecessary.

One gypsy was refused permission to take an army revolver for defense against bears on the ground that if he met a bear, he could pretend not to see it.

Another was asked not to include rubber boots, since wet feet were to be expected on a fishing expedition. If one got into really deep water, the others argued, the boots would fill, and the owner might drown. Unmoved by these arguments, the owner of the rubber boots persisted in carrying them, thus taking up space which the other gypsies wished for themselves.

A third gypsy insisted on taking a small wire-haired fox terrier, admittedly of no assistance in the capturing of fish, because there was nobody with whom he could be left if not taken. Protests were unavailing, because the owner of the terrier was also the owner of the automobile.

A fourth gypsy wished to take an Airedale terrier on similar grounds; but since the Airedale's master didn't own the automobile, the Airedale remained at home.

The party was divided into two schools of thought concerning the amount of provisions to be taken.

One school of thought maintained that since Jake Short, caretaker of Hokum Cottage, was the best guide in the whole north country, he would without doubt await his wards with a commodious basket of brook trout, a batch of sody biscuit, a pan of flapjack batter, a hot griddle, and all the other knick-knacks that play such a large part in the luring power of the great north woods.

The other school of thought held that Jake Short would be devoting his brain-power to discovering new fishing grounds for his employers and would consequently have little or no time in which to bother with ordinary food.

The first school of thought advocated taking nothing of an edible nature; the second advised taking everything, from salt to canned salmon.

A compromise was finally effected and into the interstices between the gypsies, the rubber boots, the tackle boxes, the extra overcoats and sweaters, the wire-haired terrier and the fishing rods were packed two loaves of bread, a slab of bacon, a slab of salt pork, a can of coffee and a can of tea.

A stop was made in the beautiful city of Portland for the purpose of adding to the already large supply of wet- and dry-flies possessed by the party. While a careful study of flies was being made at the counter of a sporting goods emporium, the eye of one of the gypsies was attracted by a box of small bottles bearing the inscription, *"Fiz-*

faz: *original fisherman's protection against mosquitoes, black flies, midges and all other stinging insects.* **Rub well into face, neck, ears, hair, hands and garments; renew when necessary.** *Price 35 cents."*

Another gypsy spied a box of tubes labelled, *"Zoonga Paste: original sportsman's aid.* **Absolutely prevents black flies, midges and mosquitoes from biting. Squeeze paste into palms of hands; rub well into face, neck, ears, hair and beard.** *Price 35 cents."*

Poets who have sung the glories of the great north woods, and of angling when the bee hums over the lea, have had nothing to say about pausing on the edge of flowery meads amid the piping of throstles to rub Fiz-faz or Zoonga Paste into the face, ears, and hair. According to the poets, an angler abstracts trout from the great north woods without having his attention distracted by extraneous matters; but according to the evidence on the counter of a reliable sporting goods store, all genuine fishermen are obliged to keep themselves as well oiled as a mogul engine.

\* \* \*

The gypsy trail led through the mountains and into rugged country. Flowery meads and leas grew fewer. The towering pines of the great north woods appeared in greater and greater numbers. There was, however, no perceptible diminution in the number of small tin automobiles.

By midafternoon the party left the railroad far behind and entered the true north woods that march back from the shores of Canoodle-kook Lake. Across the lake were mountains shrouded in heavy mist. No sound broke the ominous silence of the great north country save the hoarse squawking of small tin automobiles that passed briskly along the highway. When the gypsies drew up before the door of Hokum Cottage, nestled in a rough-looking mead or lea on the lake shore, they were greeted by the finest guide in the whole north country, Jake Short himself. Jake was young and fair-haired — an upstanding, clean-cut young American, and obviously one of the finest products of the great north woods.

Releasing the wire-haired terrier and throwing the creels from the windows of the automobile, the gypsies descended and surrounded Jake.

"Anything to eat in the house?" one asked.

"Potatoes," Jake said.

"Anything else?"

"No," Jake said.

"We thought maybe you'd have some trout for us," an optimistic gypsy murmured.

"I would if I'd known you wanted some," replied Jake cheerfully.

"Well," the optimistic gypsy said, "it's early. Let's go catch some. Where can we go, Jake?"

"Well," Jake said, "to tell you the truth, I got so much work to do around here, opening these cottages and cleaning up, that I can't guide you for three-four days. I'm sorry I said I would, but that's the way it is. I didn't expect to haf to open up these cottages and get 'em cleaned, but now I got to open 'em and get 'em cleaned up, so I got to open 'em and get 'em cleaned."

"The idea is, then," the pessimistic gypsy said, "that these cottages have not only got to be opened, but cleaned as well."

"Yes," said Jake, the prince of guides. "Yes, I got to see to opening 'em and cleaning 'em."

"Well," said the gypsy who had brought rubber boots, "I suppose you've got another guide for us."

"Well, no, I haven't," Jake admitted, "but I can get you one tomorrow morning."

"Is he as good a guide as you are?" the optimistic gypsy wanted to know.

"Well, he's a good guide," Jake said unemotionally.

"Get us two guides," the pessimistic gypsy said. "Then maybe both of 'em together will be as good as one real good one."

"All right," Jake said. "Now I got to tend to opening these cottages and cleaning 'em up."

"How about helping us carry our luggage before doing your opening and cleaning?" suggested one of the more despondent gypsies.

"Sure," said the finest guide in all the great north woods. Picking up two fish-baskets, one in each hand, he set off for Hokum Cottage with the easy lope of the trained woodsman, leaving the gypsies to follow with the rest of the luggage. Dropping the creels on the porch, the wonder-guide continued on through the house and was about to vanish into the great Northern wilderness when an agonized cry stopped him in his tracks. "We haven't anything to eat for supper," a gypsy protested, "or for breakfast either. Can you get us something?"

"Sure," said the ever reliable Jake. "What you want?"

The gypsies racked their brains. They could think of nothing but ham and eggs.

"Ham and eggs?" the prince of guides asked. "Sure! What time you want 'em?"

"By half-past six tonight at the latest," the optimistic gypsy said.

"All right," Jake replied, with a look of intelligence in his keen blue eyes.

One of the gypsies showed signs of excitement. "What are these blankety-blanked little blank-blanked specks on my hands that itch so?"

"Them's midges," Jake explained. "You'll swell up nice if you let 'em bite you."

"Say," said another gypsy, who had been exploring the upper regions of Hokum Cottage, "there's a bath upstairs, just as the owner claimed; but there's no water. The shower won't work, and neither will anything else!"

All four gypsies turned expectantly to the efficient caretaker and guide, Jake Short. He nodded soothingly and with an air of going for help, bolted hastily through the back door and vanished among the somber pines that hovered ominously over the rear of Hokum Cottage. Those melancholy trees appeared to sigh, as if in gloomy premonition of a sad event — and rightly; for Jake, the super-guide, didn't return that night, having contracted — as the gypsies learned from other sources on the following day — to guide a young lady to a dance.

Guide or no guide, and food or no food, however, the party had taken the gypsy trail for the express purpose of sampling the lure of the great north woods. Making a hasty change of costume and anointing themselves with Zoonga Paste and Fiz-faz, they collected their tackle and embarked in a rowboat. The owner of the rubber boots wore his rubber boots in the boat, although repeatedly reminded that he was in no danger of wetting his feet unless he fell overboard.

As the boat pushed off from shore, a brisk rain descended, and the gypsies were accompanied by a swarm of midges, black flies and mosquitoes. It seems odd that in all the years during which poets have sung of the lure of the great north woods, not one of them has made even passing mention of midges and black flies. It seems so peculiar, in fact, that it gives rise to the suspicion that the poets of the great outdoors and the gypsy trail and the rugged north countree have never been north of Portsmouth, N. H., or fished for anything larger than sunfish.

The rain fell more briskly. The hardier of the black flies and midges crawled up sleeves and down neckbands in an effort to escape the inclement weather, but still the gypsies rowed back and forth across the lake, dragging artificial lures of various sizes before the indifferent gaze of the trout and salmon reputed to lurk in its cool depths. Nothing, however, developed — barring blisters on the hands of the rowers and an increase in the rainfall.

As dusk descended, the gypsies landed to discover three other fishermen also knocking off for the day. The optimistic gypsy hailed them with the frank, free camaraderie so characteristic of life in the great north woods.

"Hey," he said; "been out all day?"

One of the party turned and eyed him morosely; then replied, with all the heartiness of a big, virile, outdoors man: "Sure!"

"How many did you catch?" asked the optimistic gypsy, scraping black flies and Zoonga Paste from an eyebrow.

"How many what?" the outdoors man asked hoarsely.

"How many lakers or salmon?"

The strange fisherman looked fixedly at him; then silently climbed into an automobile and lurched away.

One of their guides, left behind with the traps, stared tolerantly at the gypsies. "They didn't ketch nawthin'," he said. "They ain't ketched nawthin' today nor yesterday nor the day before that nor the day before that."

The gypsies retired thoughtfully to the interior of Hokum Cottage. The whereabouts of the best guide in all the great north woods remained a mystery; in the so-called bathroom there was an echoing void where water should have been.

Supper consisted of boiled potatoes, bread and bacon. This may be considered a good meal in certain parts of Ireland, provided there's enough of it; but it met with small enthusiasm in gypsy circles because of the scarcity of bacon and moistness of the potatoes, each one of which, for unknown reasons, cherished in its heart a soggy spot reminiscent of prehistoric watermelon.

It should be added, in closing the record of the first day's activities in the great north woods, that mattresses in Hokum Cottage were evidently made on specifications customarily used in the preliminary construction of asparagus beds.

Their bottom layers seemed to be old tin cans, discarded bicycles and broken rock. Over this, apparently, had been spread sod, corn husks and horse-chestnut burrs.

All through the night the rain thundered on the roof of Hokum Cottage while the four gypsies sought with plaintive groans to adjust themselves to pallets that squeaked and rattled. Awed, perhaps, by these cataclysmic sounds, the noisy denizens of the great north woods for once were still.

In the morning the sodden gurgling of the rain was neutralized by the dropping of stove lids in the kitchen of Hokum Cottage, the smashing of kindling wood against table legs, the cheery crackling of flames, the rumble of masculine voices.

Investigation of these pleasant sounds showed that Jake Short, the finest guide in all the great north woods, had emerged from his trance for a sufficient time to secure the services of the two required guides, and that it was they who wrestled with the cook stove and prepared the matutinal ham and eggs, griddle cakes and coffee.

Possibly it would be better to say that it was one of them who prepared these things; for one of the new guides, Tom Mudgett by name, was of no use in the house except as a persistent narrator of romances calculated to raise the drooping spirits of discouraged fishermen.

While the other guide, Eddie Skeegins, cleverly manipulated a pan of fried potatoes, a hot griddle covered with batter, a clutch of fried eggs, and coaxed a panful of tea to that stage of development known in the great north woods as "stout," Tom draped one knee over the other, crossed his arms limply, looked worried and told his simple, manly story.

\*   \*   \*

"Three of us," he said, "was up to the Beaver Dam a couple of weeks ago and caught seventy-two of the nicest trout ever you see, didn't we, Eddie? 'Nother good place is over to the Inlet. Four of us was up there three-four weeks ago and got so many we could only fish an hour and a half, wasn't we, Eddie? Dunno what those fellers want to talk about not gettin' no more fish in the lake. Gorrymighty, I been out on that lake twenty-seven time this year and ain't never come home skunked, have I, Eddie?"

Not until the eyes of the four gypsies protruded slightly from over-indulgence in griddle cakes, did they feel they were in a position to give undivided attention to the matter of Tom Mudgett's record-breaking trout catches.

"You certainly know where the fish are, Tom!" declared the optimistic gypsy. "Where'll you take us when the rain lets up?"

Mr. Mudgett looked even more worried. "Well, I dunno," he said finally. "The water'll be pretty high after this rain. I dunno where's the best place to go."

"How about the Beaver Dam where you got the seventy-two nice trout?" a gypsy asked.

"We kin go up there," Mudgett admitted. "Some people go up there and get a fine mess, and some go up there and don't get nawthin'. We might get nawthin'."

"Maybe the Inlet would be better, if you caught your baskets full in an hour and a half," suggested the optimistic gypsy.

"Yeah," Mudgett said, "only lots of times fellers go up the Inlet and never ketch a fish. Can't tell about the Inlet. We might ketch some and we might not. Ain't no way to tell. So many fellers come around here in automobiles that you can't never tell when a stream is all fished out."

"If you always have good luck on the lake, Tom," another gypsy suggested, "maybe the lake would be the best place."

"Yeah, it might," Mudgett agreed, "only you might sit out there three-four days and never git a smell of a bite."

"Then there isn't any place around here where we'd be sure of getting a few fish?" he was asked. Mudgett scratched his head dolefully and said he didn't know as there was.

The optimistic gypsy, to relieve his feelings, left Mr. Mudgett's presence and tried the shower bath to see whether it had started to work. It hadn't.

\*    \*    \*

By noontime the rain had ceased and the sun was struggling to appear. After a light collation of fried potatoes, fried eggs, thick-cut bacon, tea sufficiently stout to sear an oilcloth table cover, and a mound of flapjacks and maple syrup, the four gypsies rubbed themselves well with Fiz-faz and Zoonga Paste and fared forth into the rugged Northern wilderness.

Two gypsies, under the tutelage of Eddie Skeegins, entered a rowboat in company with the usual mosquitoes, black flies and midges, and rowed slowly up and down the lake for the remainder of the afternoon. Seemingly the fish were in a coma. They were indifferent to lures: apathetic toward every delicacy with which their jaded appetites were spurred.

The other gypsies, under the guidance of Tom Mudgett, bounced off into the wilderness in the automobile, left it by the roadside and plodded two miles up one side of a hill and down its far side to the Beaver Dam. Here an enterprising coterie of industrious beavers had dammed a brook until it had overflowed its banks and formed a desolate-looking bog from which emerged a forest of dying tamaracks. Access to the waters of the bog was had by means of a raft capable, if carefully handled, of holding one person. Persons not

using the raft were at liberty to cast their flies among dead trees and roots in the hope of miraculously avoiding the tangled snags and somehow catching fish.

There was a plethora of trout in the waters behind Beaver Dam, for they could be felt struggling valiantly to get the bait into their mouths. After four hours of diligent fishing the two gypsies and their guide had hooked 37 speckled beauties, 26 of which had been thrown back to mature. Eleven had been kept, though there was a strong suspicion in the gypsies' minds that when Tom Mudgett passed judgment on their length, he brought them within the law by stretching them a quarter-inch.

At sundown the gypsies and their guide, abandoning the exciting sport of measuring adolescent trout, plodded over the hill and down to the automobile. The creel containing the eleven fish was placed on the running board to be stowed away by that keen-eyed woods-man, Tom Mudgett.

Conversing cheerily, the little party started back for Hokum Cottage, secure in the knowledge that the evening menu of fried potatoes, fried eggs, fried ham and fried tea would be augmented by eleven fried trout.

They drew up with a flourish before the cottage door and descended merrily from the automobile, happy and serene after their hours among the snags and mud of the great north woods.

Then, like a flash of lightning at a wedding, came the storm.

"Where," the pessimistic gypsy asked ominously, "is the creel with the trout?"

"It's in the automobile," said Tom Mudgett, ever ready with an answer and always wrong.

"Let's see it," the pessimistic gypsy demanded.

Tom Mudgett sprang to the automobile and looked within. The creel was not there. He lifted the driver's seat and looked beneath. It was not there. He felt in his pockets. It was not there. He looked on top of the automobile and under it. The creel was not there. In short, it wasn't anywhere. It had been forgotten.

"You had it!" Tom Mudgett said to the pessimistic gypsy, unaware of the slogan "The customer is always right."

"I put it on the running board!" the pessimistic gypsy declared.

"You had it," Tom Mudgett repeated.

On the verge of exploding with emotion, the pessimistic gypsy rushed into the cottage and tried the shower bath. It was still dry. He leaped into the automobile and bounced back to the spot where the creel had been placed on the running board. It wasn't there. Obviously it had been picked up by somebody in a small tin automobile.

Somewhere, no doubt, the warm rays of the westering sun were illuminating the innocent features of the happy man who had stumbled on the eleven trout. Somewhere the fried food of the great north woods was being sweetened and neutralized by eleven succulent speckled beauties.

But in the hearts of those who had caught the eleven speckled beauties there was a seething whirlpool of human emotions; a mastodonic bitterness.

\* \* \*

Things seemed brighter on the following morning. A brilliant sun shone through the kitchen window, lightly kissing Eddie Skeegins as he toyed skillfully with the fried eggs, fried ham, fried coffee and fried flapjacks. Bright and early the four gypsies, attended by Eddie and Tom Mudgett, king of creel-forgetters, set off down the road for Derry Stream — a clear, cold mountain brook that bounded from the primeval forest, brawling among mighty boulders in all the many tongues of the great north country.

In Derry Stream the gypsies emulated the debonair gentlemen who, on calendars, stand so easily and so boldly in raging torrents. They waded the icy waters, casting their flies in spots where speckled beauties might lurk. Unfortunately, nothing worked for them as it does for the gentlemen on the magazine covers and the calendars.

There is grave doubt, too, that these debonair fishermen of the calendars would seem so debonair if they made free with the boulders and log chutes — especially the log chutes — in that section of the great north woods adjacent to Lake Canoodlekook. A log chute is a smooth slide arranged to facilitate the passage of logs over an unusually rocky section of a stream employed for logging operations. A log chute is so covered with a slick and slippery coating that one who steps on it is in imminent danger of losing not only his footing, but his dignity, his breath, the seat of his trousers,  and the lower edges of his pelvic bone.

The rubber-booted gypsy attempted to strike the attitude common to fishermen on railroad posters. After wrenching his back and bouncing on five boulders in falling, he sank in eight feet of water. Several hundred gallons of water passed through him before he was rescued.

Another gypsy, stepping carelessly on the upper end of a log chute, traveled down it on that portion of his anatomy designed for such trips. When taken from the pool at the bottom, he was drained by the suspension method.

After four hours of careful fishing, Tom Mudgett had one one-pound speckled beauty. Eddie Skeegins had nine small trout, the pessimistic gypsy had four minnows which came slightly within the law, and the other gypsies had nothing at all.

On returning to Hokum Cottage the four gypsies watched Eddie Skeegins prepare to fry the ham, eggs, tea, griddle cakes and trout. They tested the shower bath. It was still out of commission. They stared speculatively at the lumps on the surface of their mattresses. Then, after devouring their lunch, they silently entered their automobile and started at top speed away from the north countree and all the witchery.

\* \* \*

Here and there, no doubt, the lure of the great north woods still exists; but in only one place may it infallibly be found. I refer, of course, to a book of poems.

\* \* \*

# PETE DALY

*Pete Daly, a native of Hart, Michigan, moved to Maine in the mid-1970s and has served variously as district correspondent, staff writer and editorial writer for the Guy Gannett newspapers of Portland.*

\* \* \*

## HOW TO SPOT A TRUE MAINER

Dear Ma,

You sure picked the right time to make your first trip out here to Maine. Reliable sources have reported sightings of *Maniac rusticas,* otherwise known as the true Mainer, at various locations across the Maine landscape this summer, and in broad daylight!

True Mainers, especially the more colorful species inhabiting coastal and rural areas, have not been commonly seen in public during the summer months since the Maine Turnpike Authority was established back in '41 (during the Days of Infamy, I think it was.) Legend has it this shy and clever creature was driven to cover by the cyclical tribal migrations of peoples from the north and southwest of Maine, peoples that quickly laid temporary but tenacious claim to the state's beaches, public ways and service industries.

Well, Ma, things are different this year due to the Arabs, as you folks back there in middle America know. The flow of tourists to the Pine Tree State hasn't dried up, but it definitely is down dramatically. Why, I even heard a guy from Saco bragging that he'd crossed and then recrossed Route 1 on a recent Sunday afternoon with impunity.

Word of the sightings of true Mainers has spread so fast that the National Geographic is planning to send its crack team of photographers and writers here.

Here's how to recognize a true Mainer while driving, going to the beach or talking to strangers.

It's not easy, since many people in Maine go out of their way to convince you that they are Mainers, though it is common knowledge that a mortgage or a Maine in-law does not a true Mainer make. Why, you might think you're looking at a true Mainer when it's just another immigrant like myself, imposters from New Hampshire or even one of the several species of tourist that will undoubtedly get here somehow.

I've also included some advice on how to approach a *Maniac rusticas* without scaring it off.

*DRIVING:* True Mainers exhibit a baffling trait when behind the wheel. They are considerate. While preparing to drive through an intersection, a car approaching from the opposite direction will casually make a left turn directly in front of you. You have just sighted a true Mainer.

Do not be offended, since you will quickly learn that should *you* indicate a desire to make a left turn at an intersection, a true Mainer will stop in the middle of the intersection (perhaps backing up several dozen cars) and kindly give up the right of way.

The best rule of the road in Maine is patience, Ma. If, for instance, you have a Mainer turn left in front of you, and you then turn right directly behind him, he will immediately slow down as though he were en route to the town office to pay his taxes.

This illustrates the realistic nature of the true Mainer, for when one is at the head of a line of cars, one need not drive fast to keep up.

Autos left abandoned in the street are probably owned by true Mainers attempting to purchase something nearby, or perhaps just visiting another true Mainer.

Do not, repeat *DO NOT,* under any circumstance attempt to negotiate the Maine Free Left Turn in front of an oncoming vehicle bearing Massachusetts license tags.

As a matter of fact, Ma, it behooves any motorist from virtually any state except Massachusetts to avoid that state's drivers at all cost.

Another species of motorist that you should not confuse with the true Mainer is *The Canadian.* At some point during your Maine summer vacation, you will be exiting the Maine Turnpike when suddenly you are met by a large Ford or Chevrolet filled with all sizes of dark-haired, sunburned people, moving in reverse down the exit ramp against the flow of traffic. Do not be alarmed. It is only a Canadian who has had a change of mind.

*AT THE BEACH: Mainiac rusticas* has been seen at the beach in record numbers this year. He is known by his proclivity to search out the most remote section and to do so rarely in numbers exceeding

two or three. He can be seen slowly sipping cold beer — never Perrier water — and he could be reading anything from the Sunday Telegram to the Wall Street Journal.

Anyone with a copy of Down East magazine is probably not a true Mainer but more likely a retired New York City banker "summering" in Maine.

The true Mainer so seldom enters the Atlantic Ocean, and so

briefly when he does, that for many years it was commonly believed no true Mainers could swim.

If you see anyone in very skimpy attire swimming briskly from ice floe-to-ice floe during a cool day at the beach, you are observing *The Canadian* again, most likely of the Montreal subspecies. Do not disturb him, Ma, because he's got to squeeze a whole year of swimming into two weeks of vacation.

*SPEECH AND DRESS:* It is their manner of speaking that enables one to most quickly identify the true Mainer. True Mainers don't really say "ayuh" except for a few planted by the Chamber of Commerce every year at Windjammer Days in Boothbay Harbor.

Don't be fooled by any New Jersey sociologists or Massachusetts pottery makers, many of whom have immigrated to Maine since it became trendy on Sept. 3, 1975 (you remember, Ma, that was the date I moved here?) and have been practicing their "ayuhs' prodigiously ever since.

The fact is, a true Mainer begins his "ayuh" (when he says it at all) with an almost inaudible gasp. I don't know how it would be spelled but I know for certain it can't be imitated, even by Marshall Dodge. Just listen to "Awnt" Ginny sometime.

Don't refer to Lizzie's Aunt Ginny in Lewiston as "Ant" Ginny. Out here it's "awnt." Mainers can spot us Middle West natives every time because we tend to enunciate from our nostrils down.

In Maine, coffee with cream and sugar is called coffee "regular."

And whereas we folks back home would say, in the course of a mild argument, that Texas is big "and so is Alaska," the true Mainer will say, "and so *isn't* Alaska." Don't ask me why.

Look at the feet you see in Maine. Are they shod in funny-looking boots reminiscent of a platypus? Those are "Bean boots," actually for hunting or fishing, and the person wearing them is most likely (a) a Maine Times reporter, (b) a Maine Times subscriber, (c) a junior high school student from Cape Elizabeth, or (d) an immigrant or tourist.

Many true Mainers do in fact have a pair of these fine boots, but you won't see them wearing them unless you happen to be out hunting or fishing.

A visit to L. L. Bean is fun, Ma, but you might not see a true Mainer at all.

If you manage to corner a true Mainer, here is what you should and shouldn't mention if you desire a pleasant conversation: Don't mention the nuclear power plant peril unless you happen to be on Exchange Street in Portland. Don't mention the advantages of nuclear power unless you happen to be in Wiscasset. Do mention the earthquake.

Do or do not mention Gov. Brennan, depending on whether you are standing on Munjoy Hill or Caratunk. The same goes for ex-Gov. Longley, only reverse the locales.

Don't mention slot machines unless you and the Mainer are working them at the time. It's okay to mention Atlantic City, but don't mention Old Orchard Beach to a true Mainer unless he or she lives in or south of Old Orchard. Don't bring up the topic of where Maine "really" begins. You'll just become confused.

By all means bring up Andre the Seal — unless you've already talked about Joe Brennan with a Mainer from Munjoy Hill.

It's okay to talk about taxes, unless you work for the government. It's okay to talk about the government only if the Mainer isn't so employed.

And since you are not from Maine, Ma, don't even think of mentioning moose hunting, Massachusetts real estate developers, nuclear waste disposal sites, the bottle bill and New Hampshire, or Maggie Smith's library.

Maine is a great place and when you discover true Mainers, it's even more fun.

Love,                                                                                     Pete

# EDWARD M. HOLMES

*From a literary standpoint, Edward M. Holmes ranks as high as any writer in this collection. An emeritus professor of English at the University of Maine, Holmes's finely-crafted tales have appeared in a number of Maine and New England periodicals. They have also been collected in three anthologies: "Driftwood" (1972), "A Part of the Main" (1973) and "Mostly Maine" (1977).*

*A transplanted New Jerseyite, Holmes established his roots in Maine in 1939, living variously at Winter Harbor, Tremont, Great Gotts Island, Boothbay Harbor, Princeton, Ellsworth, New Vineyard, Old Town and finally Winterport. This restless movement has informed his writing. "I never write about places I don't know first hand," says Holmes.*

*His occupational experiences have been as varied as his residential settings. In addition to teaching, he's been a seaman, newspaper reporter, Wall Street clerk, department store salesman, lobster trucker, carpenter, school principal and organizer of health cooperatives and credit unions.*

*In "The Panhandle Portrait" we discover a new twist to the classic tussle between the Maine native and the Maine resident who's "from away."*

\* \* \*

## THE PANHANDLE PORTRAIT

All of us that congregate down to Joe Ramsey's now and then knew about the Morrison fellow's plan to buy Uncle Merle Hanscom's Panhandle nearly as soon as Uncle Merle did. I don't know but sooner. Not that the Morrison man is any great talker, but he has a wife and two three young ones and dinner-table talk the same as anyone else. So if his son, who seems to spend no less than two-thirds of his time with Phipp Schuyler's daughter, who raises no serious objections to that — if his son, as I say, was to mention it to her, and back at her house she told Phipp, who would talk about it to Aaron Abram (who works in Phipp's boat shop), and on his way home from work Aaron give it to Phil Dexter, who is almost always the first one after supper down to Joe Ramsey's Information Center — if a string of things like that happened, which seldom fails, you can see how we might know about it before Carl Morrison ever stopped in at Uncle Merle's to suggest it.

Not, you understand, that it was any great news. Uncle Merle's property kind of nestles inside the Morrison place like a kitten against a soft sofa-cushion, except for a strip about seventy-five by thirty with a tall, lean, grayboarded antique of an out-house standing up there at the end of it like it was on guard duty. Nobody has used that out-house, not even to stash any fishing or farming gear in, since before Pearl Harbor. Even for Uncle Merle, who is more ornery and contrary minded than most, it was not too handy.

So a few nights later, when Uncle Merle dropped in at Joe Ramsey's to buy him a loaf of that fog-like bread, a half-pound of cheese, a dozen eggs, and some chewing tobacco, Phil Dexter took his eyes off the game on the checkerboard long enough to say to Uncle Merle he understood Merle was about to sell his Panhandle to that Morrison fellow.

"And why not?" Uncle Merle said. "It don't do me no good, and I can look at it just the same whether I own it or not."

"There ain't no doubt of that," Phil said.

"His money is just as good as anyone else's," Uncle Merle said, like somebody was going to contradict him. Uncle Merle is living on his Social Security checks plus what he still can dig out of the clam flats when he feels like it; we can't see that he is suffering any, but obviously a little extra cash would taste good, like icing on the cake.

"It sure better be," Phil said. "Thing you want to watch for, Uncle Merle, is next thing you know he will be buying the whole property out from under you, house and all."

"I guess there ain't much danger of that, not while I got half a brain left."

"Keep a sharp lookout, Uncle Merle," Phil said.

And that might have been the end of the whole business, except that the next evening when Aaron Abram was walking down the road past the Morrison place, he stopped to pass the time of day with Carl Morrison who was out there clearing bottles, cans, and candy wrappers out of that bushy hedge he has which fences off his yard from the rest of us trekking up and down the highway to no particular purpose. When anyone talks with Aaron, one thing leads to another quite fast, and before he even knew it perhaps, the Morrison fellow let slip that the reason he was buying the Panhandle was to get rid of that goddamned out-house which soared up across his view of the sunset like a cigar butt stuck in an icecream sundae.

If Morrison had known what Joe Ramsey's was like perhaps he would never have said it, but obviously he didn't. He has not lived here over a year or two now (come here from the city, like some others, trying to find a place fit to live in, I guess), and it takes time for a man to get all his bearings. Fact is, Aaron told us that one day when Morrison and him had been talking (Aaron will talk to anybody that will listen) and Aaron said he had to be on his way, Carl Morrison asked where he was bound, and Aaron said "Prayer meeting."

"Prayer meeting! On Tuesday night?" Carl asks him.

"Every night," Aaron says.

"Who does the preaching?"

"All hands," says Aaron, and even then, it seems, Morrison didn't catch on to what he was talking about.

So of course word about Carl Morrison's wanting to buy that land so he could tear down the out-house and get it out of his view of the sunset filtered through all tongues at Joe Ramsey's in about ten minutes, and an hour or two later had reached nearly every corner of Oak Harbor, north, east, south, and west. Nor was it long, of course, before it got back to Uncle Merle Hanscom, and once it did, mister, I want you to know he was some goddamned put-out. He wasn't going to have no newcomer barge into town and and buy up land just so he could tear down Merle Hanscom's out-house. Be goddamned if he was! So he goes up to Morrison's and tells him he's changed his mind about selling that parcel and the deal is off.

Morrison, polite as can be, says he's sorry to hear that, but maybe he had not figured the value just right and would Uncle Merle feel better if he was to get about half again as much?

Uncle Merle says no, he would not.

So Morrison says how about twice the price, which was going it real steep since the land wasn't worth more than about a fourth of what he had offered in the first place.

And Uncle Merle says no, it is not for sale, and goes off like he was mad, which I daresay he was, at that.

Which left Carl Morrison puzzled, of course, and after a few weeks (late in April, I'd say) he started dropping in at Joe Ramsey's Information Center himself, evenings, buying a little of this or that, leaning against a post and watching the checker game, and getting a word in now and then about nothing in particular, until we got used to his being there. Naturally somebody asked him, the second or third night he was there, about the land deal, and he said it was off (which we all knew anyway), and that he didn't even have the beginning of a notion why. Nobody was going to come right out in the open and tell all they knew, but one or two did allow that Carl should understand Uncle Merle was a strange character, contrary as a hog on ice, and if anyone wanted to get him to do something, he would have to approach Uncle Merle when the phase of the moon was just right, or such a matter.

None of that was really much help, of course, but some time the next week Aaron Abram walked home from Ramsey's the same time Carl Morrison did and told Carl that Uncle Merle had got wind of the idea Carl wanted to tear down that ramshackle old out-house, and being odd anyway, had taken offense and would be damned if he'd sell. "So that's it," Carl Morrison said.

"Yessir, that's it."

"The money ain't going to make no difference."

"I should judge not," Aaron told him.

"Well, now at least, I've got something to think about," Carl said.

For a time nothing happened. Then one day in May, Carl Morrison's wife brought one of them folding chairs out to her side yard, put an easel and a framed canvas in front of it, and set there with brushes and tubes of paint, and a small piece of plywood to smear things on, and painted herself a picture of the view to the westward — or so we took it. The day after that she was out there again, but that wasn't all: Carl was there too with the same equipment (except no chair: he stood up to do *his* painting) about thirty feet away from where she was and looking at things from a little different angle. Day after that, their son was out there with them, and more of the same equipment. It was like they were forming a kind of painters' semi-circle all concentrated on Merle Hanscom's Panhandle.

Strange thing was, though Merle Hanscom see his neighbors there suddenly all turned into artists, he didn't seem to give much of a cuss: it was their place, and if they wanted to act like lunatics on it, that was up to them.

But not so with the rest of us. I want you to understand, mister, the bunch down to Ramsey's was some damned curious trying to figure out, first, what that Morrison fellow thought he was up to, and next, what them pictures, if they really was pictures, looked like. Trouble was, Carl Morrison had quit coming in to Joe Ramsey's altogether and didn't even walk the town roads neither; if he had to go fifty feet, he did it in that car of his with the throttle two-thirds open if not more so, so even Aaron got no chance to talk to him. And if his son was saying anything more to Phipp Schuyler's girl, we never learned of it. Aaron wouldn't go up to the house and ask them outright, or just look over their shoulders neither, though there was plenty down to the store tried to get him to do it. Aaron felt friendly with Carl, but not so friendly that he could do a thing like that and feel comfortable about it.

Then the next week they had company, a man and a woman from away somewhere — Pennsylvania, to judge by the license plate — and every day it wasn't rainy *they* were out there doing the painting, and one or two of the Morrisons besides. It began to puzzle us what on earth they could ever do with so many pictures of one place; it wasn't after all, like they was in the postcard business. And then, in a way, we found out.

Up the road a piece from Joe Ramsey's is a thing called The Country Store, which it isn't, of course. There is nothing country about it. It opens only from late May to October, and for the most part takes in tourists — or that is, usually only tourists offer to go in there. It is filled with a mixture of all kinds of culch that they call "crafts," for some reason or other, plus a few beat-up lobster buoys. Charlie Ramsdell's daughter and son-in-law started about the time they got through going to college and couldn't think of nothing better to do. It is a harmless enough outfit, I guess; brings in a certain amount of income for that couple to pay their taxes with, and maybe some over, or so they tell me.

Well, Phil Dexter was walking past it one day, which he has to do anyhow to go aboard his boat or just to join the group down to Ramsey's and he see that Philadelphia car outside The Country Store, and Carl Morrison and them guests of his carrying armloads of framed pictures into the place. Now that news roused us up quite a bit, and after we had talked it over for a time, and stirred it up, and looked at it this way and that, three or four of us went along to that crafts outfit to see what was going on. The car wasn't there any more, and Charlie Ramsdell's girl looked kind of tickled to see us come in, and then asked what she could do for us.

I told her I didn't rightly know, and she said perhaps what we would be most interested in was the new Oak Harbor art exhibit. I stared at her for a few seconds. "I guess that's right," I said.

She pointed over across the store. "Well, it's right in there, in that room," she said.

And it was, a separate room, a kind of shed off the main building, and not a thing in it to speak of except all them pictures, framed and hung up on the wall, and every last one of them, of course, featuring Merle Hanscom's out-house like it was the Eiffel Tower or something. Some of them was done in deep, heavy, thick paints you could almost bite into, and others was in light colors, airy and fancy, as if the sun was shining right through them the whole time. And one or two was just black and white. They come in all sizes, and all prices, mostly expensive, according to the little sticker of paper down under the frame of each one. Also the artists seemed to have a lot of different notions about just what Merle Hanscom's antique out-house looked like.

We glanced them all over, with a number of comments not too complimentary, and went out without buying nothing, which didn't seem to bother Charlie Ramsdell's girl in the least. Back at the store the news of the exhibit begun to spread quite fast, but Phil Dexter couldn't wait: he had to trot right up to Merle Hanscom's and fetch him back to The Country Store to see how famous his out-house had got. He wouldn't tell Merle what it was all about, just made him come with him and kept him curious enough so he would.

Wellsir, Merle looked them pictures over, and those of us that was watching him was hard put to it to tell how he felt. He done a little quiet growling, like a dog that isn't angry yet but just ain't friendly, yet it seemed to me, the more he looked the redder his face got. He didn't ignite though, and when he set off for home he was only muttering a bit.

What set him off, finally, was what he found when he got abreast of Morrison's. What he saw there was no less than eight people all setting behind easels and all painting pictures of Merle Hanscom's out-house. Some of them was holding a paintbrush up straight, eyeing the building with it across the top of their thumb like they was measuring it with a ruler. And there was one fellow going from picture to picture, apparently pointing out to the artist what he, or she, was doing that was, or wasn't just right.

Time he got to the house, Uncle Merle was almost running. He stopped long enough in his shed to fill a one-quart can with kerosene, strode out there to the end of the Panhandle, opened the door, doused the inside of the building in good shape, and with one stroke lighted a match and threw it inside. Then he stepped back to watch.

Now I want you to know that place made quite a goodlooking torch for a few minutes. There was some wails and shouts from over in Carl Morrison's lot, but Uncle Merle never even turned his head to look, and most of the crowd kept right on painting. They were an art school, we found out later, one that Carl Morrison knew the teacher of, and Carl had persuaded them to come over from Knox County and do some landscape scenes from his property. One or two of them run to the house to get to a telephone and call the fire department, but Morrison suggested (so Aaron told it after he talked with him later) that perhaps they should wait long enough to see if the fire was going to spread. It didn't. The place blazed up and fell over on its side. Then Uncle Merle walked slowly back to his house, returned with two buckets of water, and wet down the grass around what was left of the boards still burning. He never so much as looked over to where that art school was hard at work.

That was all near the beginning of the summer, which by now is almost over. The grass has growed up and covered the burned embers where Uncle Merle had his fire, and he acts like he was quite satisfied still to be owning that Panhandle. Down to Joe Ramsey's we are sure Carl Morrison is satisfied. And Aaron Abram, who has been up there to find out, says that couple that runs The Country Store ain't complaining, even if there is an eighth-of-an-inch of dust over all them paintings. They even sold one of them, he said though they didn't recall who it was bought it, and Aaron told them if the fellow paid so much as a dollar, he was beat out of fifty cents, an idea that down to Joe Ramsey's Prayer Meeting nobody disputes.

\* \* \*

# 10

# Characters

# ROBERT P. TRISTRAM COFFIN

*Robert P. Tristram Coffin (1892-1955) was an enthusiastic and prolific celebrator of Maine values. Born in Brunswick, educated at Bowdoin (and Princeton and Oxford), he produced more than three dozen books of verse, biographies, novels and essays on Maine.*

*Coffin's view of his state and his nation was relentlessly positive and optimistic. America, he wrote, "is promises — promises kept."*

*In 1942 Coffin published "A Book of Uncles," a collection of short character sketches about members of his family who seemed blessed by a uniform strain of captivating eccentricity.*

*"Most of my uncles were off center somewhere or other," he wrote. "One was always off his balance when he got on the subject of the Civil War. He had been in it, and he got madder than a hornet whenever he thought over what the Rebs had done to his company's supply of pork one night. His whole view of four years of American history was warped by the loss of some spare-ribs."*

*In the following story, Coffin shows how one otherwise undistinguished uncle made his mark on history by being in the wrong place at the right time.*

\* \* \*

## MY ONLY FAMOUS UNCLE

I had only one famous uncle.

He became famous in the way any man would choose if he had the chance. By accident, without any exertion on his part.

You remember how the saying runs: "Some are born great, some achieves greatness, and some have greatness thrust upon 'em." Well, Uncle Shubael did.

Uncle Shubael was a modest and quiet man. Perfectly contented. He never wanted to be singled out or pointed at, even among uncles. He just wanted to be allowed to be one of the crowd. He just wanted to be left alone. He had a fine moustache, and it curled up nice at the ends. But it wasn't any bigger than most men wore in his day, and it didn't curl up at the ends any more than the moustaches on other men who had curly hair and a naturally jaunty and upcurling disposition. Uncle Shubael was strong. He could lift a two-hundred-pound cake of ice with one hand, on a hot Summer's day, at a picnic, if women were around and looking on. But there were always two or three other men at all the family picnics who could lift a three-hundred-pound cake and take the eyes of the ladies right off Uncle Shubael. Uncle Shubael liked ladies. But he didn't like them more than other men who had fine moustaches and strong backs. He did not like them in a way that made him come first with them. He liked them only a little bit harder than average.

Uncle Shubael was a pretty large man, but not so large as to be devastating. He did not have to have a special rocker built for him as my Uncle Amos did. The usual pint-sized moustache cup did for him for his breakfast coffee, though he drank it full five or six times. I suppose he was a handsome man. Certainly he looked like a very handsome man while you were looking at him. But when you looked away somewhere else, you forgot at once how handsome he was. You remembered him as a sort of average handsome. Average square Yankee head, square Yankee face, and fairly average very blue eyes. I think his hair was light brown. Average light brown, that is. And though it curled, it didn't curl enough to make it stand out much.

This uncle of mine had a big family. I remember a lot of boys. But they, too, were kind of average. They did not tower above my regiment of cousins. They did not shine or rankle much. In any rumpus we had, you could count on finding their chunky, square bodies and butts wedged right into the middle of us all. They weren't either at the bottom or the top of the heap. Always middling.

Like their father. Most of them could throw me, underholts or up-
perholts. And did. And sat on me. But they did not sit on me hard
enough to knock the wind out of me and make me remember the
shape and heft of their sternness.

Well, there Uncle Shubael was. Living an average life, eating
average meals, begetting average Yankee boys, and making average
love to women who were probably average women. And he might
have remained so and gone on to an average end if Fate hadn't
singled him out to become famous. But Fate did.

Now Uncle Shubael was a mason. And when I say that, I mean
the kind of man who lays up stone. I don't mean the kind of man
who goes around with an apron in front of him and says solemn and
secret words King Solomon used to say and takes good care of all his
brothers' widows. Uncle Shubael *was* that kind of mason, too, as a
matter of fact, and he did take care of a lot of widows also, all in
the line of duty, of course. But that kind of masonry had no part in
his getting to be famous. Uncle Shubael was a man who laid up
stone and brick in a profession older than King Solomon's time.

He was a brick-mason. Maybe not much above the run-of-the-mill
bricklayers, but he could lay up brick all right. I used to watch him
by the hour when he was laying up a chimney. And he let me help.
He laid it up fast, and he kept me stepping, fetching him his brick.
The chimney just soared up, through two floors a day. And he made
my tail smart with the flat of his trowel when I dropped an armful
of brick on his right foot's corns, accidentally.

The way Uncle Shubael got famous was this: He was plying his
useful profession away from home, for once. In Salem, Massachusetts. I don't know what tempted so quiet and contented and un-
pushing an uncle that far away from my Maine village, but something
did, and there he was. Maybe there were an unaverage lot of average
ladies in Salem, Massachusetts. But there Uncle Shubael was. And
he was doing well. He had been doing well all that Fall.

But it came on the Thanksgiving season, when men think of their families, and so Uncle Shubael decided he would spend the feast in the bosom of his. So he packed up his duds in his portmanteau, took his kit of tools, and booked passage on the steam-cars to Boston, and went down to the pier to take the boat. The boat was the way the average Maine people came home from making their fortunes in Boston then. My uncle went upon the boat and stowed his gear aboard.

Now it lacked some two hours or so, Uncle Shubael discovered, before the boat sailed.

And Uncle Shubael got dry. Uncle Shubael always got dry when he was waiting or when he was concentrating very hard on things. He got dry especially at our picnics. And no mere lemonade could quench him. He had to have stouter stuff. And he brought it along at our family picnics, unbeknownst to his quiet and less than average wife, in flat bottles that fitted the fine curve of his shapely hip. But he had no such bottles here at the Boston boat.

So Uncle Shubael went back uptown. He went in search of refreshment and to while away the time.

As he walked along, he came to a narrow street, and looking down it, he noted an arm extended from the wall, and in that arm's fist was a bell. It was the ancient hostelry known as the *Bell-in-Hand*, on Pye Alley. My uncle was cheered by the sight, he went to the *Bell-in-Hand* and entered thereinunto. He started in doctoring for dryness. He was a good doctor for that.

Now my uncle was also the soul of conviviality. And there entered into the inn several citizens of Boston, seeking to doctor for dryness, too. My Uncle Shubael hailed them, they came to his table, they joined him in his drink, they became fast friends. My uncle set up the drinks. They set them up back. My uncle could not, of course, fail to join them in all the toasts they drank to this and that, to average ladies, unaverage ones, to Uncle Shubael, and to one another. Time wore on.

The ale that afternoon in the *Bell-in-Hand* in Pye Alley was the mellowest Uncle Shubael ever dipped his brown-gold moustache into. It lifted him up. It lifted him up from an average good mason into a fine open-hearted fellow ready and able to say the first and last word on the biggest subjects of the world. It lifted him up into a man ready to set them up to any who came along. And new citizens of Boston came along. They fell in with Uncle Shubael. And Uncle Shubael grew, and they grew with him. Uncle Shubael drank and discoursed brilliantly. The crowd of listeners grew, and the separate listeners grew. They all drank and grew. And time wore on.

Time wore on more and more. Suddenly Uncle Shubael sat up and pulled his turnip of a Waterbury out of his waistcoat pocket. It was the Waterbury his own father had given him on his twenty-first birthday and his wedding night combined. And now Uncle Shubael looked on it, and his countenance was troubled. For he saw how thin time had worn. He stood up.

"Gentlemen," said he, "I've a boat to catch. I am afraid I must say farewell."

"We will catch the boat with you." And the gentlemen of Boston rose with my uncle.

"No, I beg of you. Let me go alone. For I must go fast. I have but three minutes to make the boat. I must hurry."

"We," said the citizens of Boston, "will hurry with you."

My uncle looked at his tankard. It was still half full. It seemed a shame to leave such liquor. Against his better judgment and the Waterbury's hands, he took the rest of his ale. It was the half tankard too many. And Fate schottisched off to play her next trick in human history.

Uncle Shubael poured out of the *Bell-in-Hand*. And the citizens of Boston poured out with him. Uncle Shubael ran for it. And the citizens ran with him. They all poured down the hill towards the wharf.

Now my uncle was a very good runner. He had won the hundred-yards'-dash for married men I don't know how many times at the

Baptist picincs. With the married women looking on. But now with
no women looking on he broke all his old records on the Boston
cobbles. He took off his hat, as he ran, took off his coat, and his
waistcoat. He hung them on his arm. Behind him, the Boston citizens
took off theirs and hung them on their arms, too. They could not
keep up with my uncle, but they kept him in sight, and they cheered
him and themselves on.

So they all, the citizens of Boston and my uncle, came to the
Atlantic.

When my uncle reached his pier, he saw there were eight feet of
dark water between him and his boat's deck. And it was widening.
For the boat was backing out of the slip. But that did not bother my

Uncle Shubael. For Uncle Shubael had also won the running-broad-jump many times at picnics. He could do eighteen feet, if enough ladies were looking on, cold. And warmed with the *Bell-in-Hand* ale, no knowing what feet he could add to the eighteen! The water of Boston Bay was widening at his toes, but my Uncle Shubael curled his moustache back in scorn to see it. He threw his hat and coat and waistcoat ahead of him upon the moving deck of the boat. He drew calmly back for his take-off.

But as he drew back for his take-off, Uncle Shubael backed straight into the arms of a Boston policeman, and quite a large one, and very Irish. The policeman's arms closed on Uncle Shubael.

"You must not commit such a folly," the man of the Boston law said.

"Unhand me!" said my Uncle Shubael. "I can make it easy. Let me go."

"No," the policeman said firmly, "I cannot permit you to risk your life."

"No," said the citizens of Boston, for they had by now come up, too, "we cannot permit you to risk your life." And they laid hands on my uncle also.

Uncle Shubael might have got away from the law, but the citizens of Boston were too much for him. He stood imprisoned in arms. He stood and watched his boat and his coat and hat and waistcoat move away into the mist of Boston's Bay. He stood with his pants hiked up at the knees for his flight through the air that was never now to be. His tools and his clothes and even his Waterbury had made the boat. But Uncle Shubael himself had missed it.

And by that fact Uncle Shubael became forever famous. By that simple act of missing a boat he became a marked man. He was known forever after as the man who missed the boat.

Wherever the family gathered, this uncle of mine was the center of interest and admiration and concern. Aunts brought him the largest doughnuts. Small boys stared at him with wide eyes and hung at the seat of his trousers wanting to touch him. All women smiled on him and ran to fetch him the largest fractions of the best pies. Men stopped talking when he entered the room. People turned and looked at him on the street. He was pointed out to strangers in the town. Awe whispered the words: "That's him. That's the man who missed the boat! Yes, Sir!"

With no more exertion than that, my uncle became a famous man, a great man, for life.

Uncle Shubael was an angry man, at the time. He was angry at missing the boat. He even took the policeman who had protected him so well and sat down on him hard on the dock. The citizens of Boston had to take my Uncle Shubael off. They smoothed him out, and the policeman out. And finally they all went back to the *Bell-in-Hand* together and had another cup all around. And the Boston citizens helped my uncle find a lodging place for the night, *sans* hat, *sans* coat, *sans* Waterbury. Uncle Shubael went innocently to sleep, as a child might. But he was a marked man, a man Fate had exalted. And his average square Yankee head was towering among the immortals. He was the man who missed the boat.

It was a pretty important boat to miss. For it was the *Steamer Portland*, and this was her last trip. It was Thanksgiving time of the year 1900. And the *Portland* steamed out of Boston Bay, in all her splendor of Brussels carpets and band playing *Casey Would Waltz with a Strawberry Blonde*, women shining in mutton-leg sleeves, and new polished cuspidors. She went out all gilt and brass and glass and Victorian elegance. She sailed out crowded with holiday people and my uncle's mason-kit and clothes and Waterbury watch and hat, and she ran into the no'theast blizzard of a century, with the snow coming level like steel filings. And she went down with all on board. No person lived to tell what happened. The *Portland* went out into the blinding snow and melted away into history.

I can still remember those level javelins of hail and hard snow-flakes as they roared in over our farmhouse that night on the edge of the hissing cauldron of the Atlantic Ocean. Our farmhouse shook over us and sobbed through all its timbers. The night was wild with a million banshees riding their snorting horses in from sea. The coast people trembled and looked at one another over the smoky lamp-globes with eyes gone wide and faces gone white. They thought of the homecoming ones. And with the wild dawn, word came that the *Portland,* white wedding-cake of a steamer and the Maine coast's glory, was missing. The word of doom spread. The day wore on. And many a Thanksgiving table was left unset, or the family sat there and ate in silence with a dark stranger sitting in their midst as they wept at their eating.

Uncle Shubael's family sat in mourning at their darkened feast. And the door came open, and Uncle Shubael came back to them from the grave. He burst upon his sorrowing family, radiant, with a whole day's sleep and a whole night's making him shine. He had come by the steam-cars. For his family he had come back from the land no traveller returns from. He had overslept from the ale and the conviviality of Boston all day and had come on the evening train. He had heard the news. He wore a grin for good luck's sake. And he was a man famous forever. He was a great man now. He belonged with history.

That was the only uncle I had who became great. He was the man who missed the boat.

* * *

# HAROLD BOYLE

*Maine being a rural state, there is little in the store of humorous literature with an urban base. The writings of Harold J. Boyle, a late-blooming Maine humorist, are an exception.*

*Born just before the turn of the century, Boyle served for four decades are a quiet, competent, hardworking reporter and finan-*

cial editor for the Portland newspapers. He retired abruptly in 1962, nerve-frayed and pumped out, and went to live with a niece in Massachusetts. Ten years later, a remarkably re-invigorated Boyle returned to the city room and began a new career as one of Maine's most charming and engaging columnists. His stock in trade is the remembrance of things past in Maine's largest city, recounted in a whimsically entertaining style.

Boyle's nostalgic first-person narratives are in the classic Yankee-humorist line of Seba Smith and Artemus Ward. In place of the innocent rustic is the wide-eyed young reporter bemused by the breezier newsroom spirits about him in the Portland of the 1920s and 1930s. Charlie, the sidewalk lawyer and street-wise friend of the young reporter, figures in many of Boyle's captivating reminiscences.

* * *

## CHARLIE WAS A SIDEWALK LAWYER

I remember when Charlie, the young reporters' friend and short-order cook here, was a sidewalk lawyer for a spell. He worked in MacDonald's Restaurant at Exchange and Middle Streets on the last shift, midnight to 8 o'clock. Not feeling particularly tired after that usually quiet stint, he got into the habit of spending a few hours in Municipal Court. Either Samuel Bates or Judge Joseph Connolly was county attorney at the time — it was in the early 1920's — and both put on a show at most sessions.

Charlie became intensely interested in the cases, absorbed quite a bit of petty criminal law and even served as a spare juror in Superior Court now and then.

He would come into the editorial office of the old Portland Press evenings and ask if the court reporter covered the case of so-and-so and what Sammy Bates said in presenting the evidence. After a while he felt proficient enough to criticize the attorneys.

"I'd like to have the other side," he would say, in reviewing a case he heard that morning. "I think that Joe Connellan should have taken that one upstairs." That meant an appeal, of course. (Connellan was one of the prominent attorneys of his day). Or he would make this observation: "Most lawyers don't know when to stop milking. They get a full pail and keep on talking and lose the case." One day he said: "I tried to signal Joe Connolly that he had a pailful but he kept on talking." Connolly, who afterwards was named a Superior Court Judge, did not need Charlie's signal, I'm sure.

Charlie's favorite story about the Portland Bar went this way: A prominent business man here was bitten by a dog on State Street. He went to a well-known attorney on Exchange Street to ask about his chances for collecting damages. "The dog owner will pay $100 without going to court, I'm sure," the businessman was told. "Good," he said, "it's your dog, I've got witnesses and give me the $100." The attorney paid.

This story made a hit in the business district. So did its sequel. The next morning the business man received his bill in the mail: "For legal services in settling dog bite case — $100. Please remit promptly."

One day Charlie got a chance to practice his law in the editorial department, when a woman came to see Editor Harry Bigelow about her husband. He was in trouble. Bigelow quickly shifted her to me to take the story. He had been "surprised by three deputies" (our newspaper account read) while mixing himself a little batch of home-brew. Did they have a right to keep her husband in jail on the charge?

Charlie sat near me, tapping out a story about the coming visit of the Grand Sachem in the Red Men to Portland. He was all ears at the woman's request for legal advice, which was his field. "Lady," he said, breaking in on our conversation, "I'm not exactly a lawyer but I do know quite a bit about the law. They can't put him in jail for that."

"Oh, they can't?" she said. "Well, Mister, you got the case. That's where he is right now, in the Cumberland County Jail on Monroe Street. You got the case." A somewhat miffed Charlie stammered: "You didn't give me all the facts." She repeated: "You got the case. That's where he is, in jail. Now what do you think of that? You got the case, Smarty. He's in jail."

Editor Fred Owen, who just tolerated Charlie's hanging around the city room so much, exploded into one of the loudest laughs I had heard in years.

But Charlie was unperturbed at losing his first case. He resumed typing: "The reception to the Grand Sachem will start at 7:30 o'clock after which corn and venison will be served." Every Red Man knew, of course, that corn and venison meant beans and franks.

\* \* \*

## GATE-CRASHING IN THE OLD DAYS

About this time of year a half-century ago, Portland played host to the Western Maine Music Festival. It was a week-long series of concerts featuring a famous music personality of the day — Madame Nordica, Mary Garden, Rosa Raisa, Schumann-Heink, Pery Granger, Rosa Ponselle.

William R. Chapman and his wife developed the idea and it blossomed into one of the big musical attractions in Northern New England. It outgrew its first performances in the Armory on Milk Street, moving to the present Exposition Building.

The festival included a chorus of several hundred voices who were admitted at a reduced rate to hear the Metropolitan Opera stars and to sing. I think the 75-piece orchestra was recruited on the same basis — you got a close look at the singing star at a discount and you played, too.

Professor Chapman was overall conductor of the big assemblage. He also composed a few pieces, including the "Centennial March" in observance of Maine's 100th birthday in 1920.

Mrs. Chapman, a capable public relations assistant, usually visited the three Portland newspapers a week before the festival began, distributing a few complimentary tickets for the music critics and the editors. These disappeared about five minutes after she left.

Charlie, the young reporters' friend here and a short-order cook, gate-crashed one concert in 1920 or 1921. It was no mean feat because the Chapmans held free passes to a minimum and maintained an elaborate system to keep free riders out.

I never knew why Charlie wanted to go to the big concert featuring Rosa Raisa, "Metropolitan Opera star," that night. I always suspected his favorite musical selection was "Yankee Doodle." An advance program in the Press that morning announced she would sing three arias in French, Italian and Russian, real heavy stuff.

Charlie came into the editorial office that afternoon and asked our music critic, Tena Jordan, for a pass. She told him she was lucky to have one herself because the bigwigs in the business and advertising departments threw their weight around and grabbed the others. It was an old newspaper custom.

That galvanized Charlie into action. It was a challenge, as they say today. He took a piece of stationery and typed on it: "Introducing Steadman Smythe, a music critic on the Boston Evening Transcript. Any curtesy (he mispelled that word) you extend to him will be appreciated by the Boston Transcript management."

"That ought to do it," he said to me. "Who is Steadman Smythe?" I asked. "Me," Charles said. "Sounds like a Boston Transcript name, doesn't it?" The Transcript at that time was the most prestigious newspaper in New England. It was the official social organ of the Beacon Hill jet set. "I know how to handle the professor (Chapman)," Charlie added.

I had my misgivings and told him he might get into trouble. But, for some reason, he was determined to hear Rosa Raisa sing. You couldn't buy a ticket anyway, he explained. The Exposition Building was a complete sellout.

The story I pieced together afterward went something like this: Charlie got by the ticket taker, who sent a message to Conductor Chapman that a Boston Transcript critic was in the house. But Chapman and his wife had taken the "ree-al" Transcript music critic to dinner that evening and were, in fact, with him when the message came.

Chapman, who was quick to spot a freeloader, said: "Get the imposter!" (The Transcript music critic had the very plebian name of Brown and was, according to our music critic, a guy who took quite a bit of getting used to.

Soon every usher was looking for Charlie, who suddenly sensed there was something wrong. Almost in a panic, he spotted George Knight of Yarmouth, a friend, who played one of the three bass

violins in the orchestra. Charlie wormed his way through the brass and tympani sections and crouched down near Knight, telling him he was in trouble. Knight, a fellow Red Man, I believe, agreed to help a brother in distress and told him to stay there.

To those in the audience, Charlie looked like a spare bass fiddler ready to take over if one of the trio collapsed when they played the thunderous "1812 Overture." Although he could not read a note of music, he kept his eye on Brother Knight's score all evening.

Both Chapman and his wife took turns scanning the big audience through opera glasses, looking for the imposter. Every usher had been alerted to find Charlie and throw him out in the middle of an aria, if necessary. But none, including Conductor Chapman, suspected that Charlie was right under the orchestra leader's baton.

Charlie was in fine spirits as he related his experience to the staff the next day. "That Rosa Raisa got away with some bum notes in a couple of her trills," he said. "I know," he added, "because I was so close to her I could have spit on her gold slippers."

About a month after the successful gate-crash, Charlie and I were alone in the editorial office when Professor Chapman bobbed in. He walked over to Charlie, who seemed to turn slightly pale. I knew he went in for dramatics and I expected him to say: "At last, imposter, we meet. Put up your dukes!"

But he only wanted to know when Editor Bigelow would be in. Then he shook hands with a surprised Charlie and me and disappeared. It was a closey for Charlie.

* * *

## THE DAY HARDING WAS ALMOST ASSASSINATED

I remember the day President Harding came to Portland in the summer of 1922, and the news wire services almost sent out a story that someone tried to assassinate him here.

My friend, Charlie, short-order cook, bouncer and sidewalk lawyer, was in on that one.

For weeks the old Daily Press and the Evening Express carried stories about Harding's coming visit with Portland's U.S. Senator Fred Hale. He was to stay overnight at the Hale homestead on Pine Street and drive to Poland Spring the next day for a round of golf. Harding was a tolerably good golfer; Hale broke 100 now and then. The two were close friends and inseparable golfing companions. Hale had told the President so much about the famous Poland Spring golf course that he wanted to try it.

One day the Press carried a story that a well-known Congress Street candy maker (now out of business) would present Harding (or his wife) with a ten-pound box of chocolates made especially for the occasion. I'm not sure but we may have had a picture of him with the box of candy on the front page.

Harding's trip here was to include a ride down Congress Street in an open car with Hale, a short pause in Monument Square, then full speed to Poland Spring. Somewhere, possibly on the sidewalk in front of the Hale home, the formal presentation of the candy was to take place. But there was a snafu at the start of the procession, and the candy maker was unable to get through the crowd to the President. He was left stranded on Pine Street.

A friend who had a car drove him to the Press where he hoped to get help. By the time he got to Monument Square Harding's car was slowly moving through crowds to the City Hall. The candy maker rushed into the editorial office, almost into the arms of Charlie, who wore a sailor straw hat with a red, white and blue ribbon and gold letters that read: "Red Men for Harding." It was his big day.

"Grab the taxicab in front of Guppy's and head him off at Woodford's Corner," Charlie said. "He's going to stop there for a few minutes."

It was like Charlie to know something that none of us knew. In a

last minute change, Harding did plan to make a brief stop at Woodfords and shake hands with a few solid citizens there.

The lone taxi in Monument Square was available, unfortunately,
and it shot down Preble Street with the candy maker for Woodfords.
It was stopped once to let the President's car whiz by. But the
Harding car didn't stop, only slowed down in front of Odd Fellows
Hall at Woodfords Corner. In desperation, the disappointed candy
maker forced his way through the crowds and tossed the candy to a
Secret Service man on the running board of the President's car. He
kicked it, and in seconds several other Secret Service men appeared
from nowhere and seized him. The evidence was all over the ground,
ten pounds of chocolate covered the area.

The incident happened so quickly that neither Harding nor Hale
noticed it at the time, the Portland senator said later. There was a
temporary panic in the crowd, but it ended quickly. The candy
maker was given a "tongue banging" by the Secret Service, as Charlie
called it.

Someone with a nose for news telephoned the Associated Press in
Monument Square that a bomb had been thrown at the President,
"but it didn't go off." An Express reporter stationed in the Square
telephoned the facts: A box of candy had been tossed toward the
President's car, but it was deflected. Nothing else.

Charlie told me he never would have revealed the Woodfords stop
if he thought the candy maker would have panicked when he realized
all his plans had failed.

"It's a wonder the guy wasn't shot," Charlie said. It was, too.

\* \* \*

# ERSKINE CALDWELL

*Erskine Caldwell is, of course, renowned as a novelist of the Deep South* (Tobacco Road, God's Little Acre). *However, early in his writing career he spent about five years in Maine and wrote a number of short stories which displayed early his talent for capturing the character and flavor of regional settings. "The Corduroy Pants," written when Caldwell was still in his twenties, is a first-rate example that downeast humor can be mastered by an outsider of ability.*

\* \* \*

## THE CORDUROY PANTS

Two weeks after he had sold his farm on the back road for twelve hundred dollars and the Mitchells had moved in and taken possession, Bert Fellows discovered that he had left his other pair of corduroy pants up attic. When he had finished hauling his furniture and clothes to his other place on the Skowhegan road, he was sure he had left nothing behind, but the morning that he went to put on his best pair of pants he could not find them anywhere. Bert thought the matter over two or three days and decided to go around the back road and ask Abe Mitchell to let him go up attic and get the corduroys. He had known Abe all his life and he felt certain Abe would let him go into the house and look around for them.

Abe was putting a new board on the door step when Bert came up the road and turned into the yard. Abe glanced around but kept on working.

Bert waited until Abe had finished planing the board before he said anything.

"How be you, Abe?" he inquired cautiously.

"Hell, I'm always well," Abe said, without looking up from the step.

Bert was getting ready to ask permission to go into the house. He waited until Abe hammered the twenty-penny into the board.

"I left a pair of corduroys in there, Abe," he stated preliminarily. "You wouldn't mind if I went up attic and got them, would you?"

Abe let the hammer drop out of his hands and fall on the step. He wiped his mouth with his hankerchief and turned around facing Bert.

"You go in my house and I'll have the law on you. I don't give a cuss if you've left fifty pair of corduroys up attic. I bought and paid for this place and the buildings on it and I don't want nobody tracking around here. When I want you to come on my land, I'll invite you."

Bert scratched his head and looked up at the attic window. He began to wish he had not been so forgetful when he was moving his belongings down to his other house on the Skowhegan road.

"They won't do you no good, Abe," he said. "They are about ten sizes too big for you to wear. And they belong to me, anyway."

"I've already told you what I'm going to do with them corduroys," Abe replied, going back to work. "I've made plans for them corduroys. I'm going to keep them, that's what I'm going to do."

Bert turned around and walked toward the road, glancing over his shoulder at the attic window where his pants were hanging on a rafter. He stopped and looked at Abe several minutes, but Abe was busy hammering twenty-penny nails into the new step he was making and he paid no attention to Bert's sour looks. Bert went back down the road, wondering how he was going to get along without his other pair of pants.

By the time Bert reached his house he was good and mad. In the first place, he did not like the way Abe Mitchell had ordered him away from his old farm, but most of all he missed his other pair of corduroys. And by bedtime he could not sit still. He walked around the kitchen mumbling to himself and trying to think of some way by which he could get his trousers away from Abe.

"Crusty-faced Democrats never were no good," he mumbled.

Half an hour later he was walking up the back road toward his old farm. He had waited until he knew Abe was asleep, and now he was going to get into the house and go up attic and bring out the corduroys.

Bert felt in the dark for the loose window in the barn and discovered it could be opened just as he had expected. He had had good intentions of nailing it down, for the past two or three years, and now he was glad he had left it as it was. He went through the barn and the woodshed and into the house.

Abe had gone to bed about nine o'clock, and he was asleep and snoring when Bert listened at the door. Abe's wife had been stone-deaf for the past twenty years or more.

Bert found the corduroy pants, with no trouble at all. He struck only one match up attic, and the pants were hanging on the first nail he went to. He had taken off his shoes when he climbed through the barn window and he knew his way through the house with his eyes shut. Getting into the house and out again was just as easy as he had thought it would be.

In another minute he was out in the barn again, putting on his shoes and holding his pants under his arm. He had put over a good joke on Abe Mitchell, all right. He went home and got into bed.

The next morning Abe Mitchell drove his car up to the front of Bert's house and got out. Bert saw him from his window and went to meet Abe at the door. He was wearing the other pair of corduroys, the pair that Abe had said he was going to keep for himself.

"I'll have you arrested for stealing my pants," Abe announced as soon as Bert opened the door, "but if you want to give them back to me now I might consider calling off the charges. It's up to you what you want to do about it."

"That's all right by me," Bert said. "When we get to court I'll show you that I'm just as big a man as you think you are. I'm not afraid of what you'll do. Go ahead and have me arrested, but if they lock you up in place of me, don't come begging me to go your bail for you."

"Well, if that's the way you think about it," Abe said, getting red in the face, "I'll go ahead with the charges. I'll swear out a warrant right now and they'll put you in the county jail before bedtime tonight."

"They'll know where to find me," Bert said, closing the door. "I generally stay pretty close to home."

Abe went out to his automobile and got inside. He started the engine, and promptly shut it off again.

"Come out here a minute, Bert," he called.

Bert studied him for several minutes through the crack in the door and then went out into the yard.

"Why don't you go swear out the warrant? What you waiting for now?"

"Well, I thought I'd tell you something, Bert. It will save you and me both a lot of time and money if you'd go to court right now and save the cost of having a man come out here to serve the warrant on you. If you'll go to court right now and let me have you arrested there, the cost won't be as much."

"You must take me for a cussed fool, Abe Mitchell," Bert said. "Do I look like a fool to pay ten dollars for a hired car to take me to county jail?"

Abe thought to himself several minutes, glancing sideways at Bert. "I'll tell you what I'll do, Bert," he proposed. "You get in my car and I'll take you there and you won't have to pay ten dollars for a hired car."

Bert took out his pipe and tobacco. Abe waited while he thought the proposition over thoroughly. Bert could not find a match, so Abe handed him one.

"You'll do that, won't you Bert?" he asked.

"Don't hurry me — I need plenty of time to think this over in my mind."

Abe waited, bending nervously toward Bert. The match-head crumbled off and Abe promptly gave Bert another one.

"I guess I can accommodate you that little bit this time," he said, at length. "Wait until I lock up my house."

When Bert came back to the automobile Abe started the engine and turned around in the road toward Skowhegan. Bert sat beside him sucking his pipe. Neither of them had anything to say to each other all the time they were riding. Abe drove as fast as his old car would go, because he was in a hurry to get Bert arrested and the trial started.

When they reached the courthouse, they went inside and Abe swore out the warrant and had it served on Bert. The sheriff took them into the courtroom and told Bert to wait in a seat on the first row of benches. The sheriff said they could push the case ahead and get a hearing some time that same afternoon. Abe found a seat and sat down to wait.

It was an hour before Bert's case was called to trial. Somebody read out his name and told him to stand up. Abe sat still, waiting until he was called to give his testimony.

Bert stood up while the charge was read to him. When it was

over, the judge asked him if he wanted to plead guilty or not guilty.

"Not guilty," Bert said.

Abe jumped off his seat and waved his arms.

"He's lying!" he shouted at the top of his voice. "He's lying —
he did steal my pants!"

"Who is that man?" the judge asked somebody.

"That's the man who swore out the warrant," the clerk said.
"He's the one who claims the pants were stolen from him."

"Well, if he yells out like that again," the judge said, "I'll swear
out a warrant against him for giving me a headache. And I guess
somebody had better tell him there's such a thing as contempt of
court. He looks like a Democrat, so I suppose he never heard of
anything like that before." The judge rapped for order and bent
over towards Bert.

"Did you steal a pair of corduroy pants from this man?" he asked.

"They were my pants," Bert explained. "I left them in my house
when I sold it to Abe Mitchell and when I asked him for them he
wouldn't turn them over to me. I didn't steal them. They belonged
to me all the time."

"He's lying!" Abe shouted again, jumping up and down. "He
stole my pants — he's lying!"

"Ten dollars for contempt of court, whatever your name is," the
judge said, aiming his gavel at Abe, "and case dismissed for lack
of evidence."

Abe's face sank into his head. He looked first at the judge and
then around the courtroom at the strange people.

"You're not going to make me pay ten dollars, are you?" he
demanded.

"No," the judge said, standing up again. "I made a mistake. I
forgot that you are a Democrat. I meant to say twenty-five dollars."

Bert went outside and waited at the automobile until Abe paid
his fine. In a quarter of an hour Abe came out of the courthouse.

"Well, I guess I'll have to give you a ride back home," he said, getting under the steering wheel and starting the engine. "But what I ought to do is leave you here and let you ride home in a hired car."

Bert said nothing at all. He sat down beside Abe and they drove out of town toward home.

It was almost dark when Abe stopped the car in front of Bert's house. Bert got out and slammed shut the door.

"I'm mighty much obliged for the ride," he said. "I been wanting to take a trip over Skowhegan way for a year or more. I'm glad you asked me to go along with you Abe, but I don't see how the trip was worth twenty-five dollars to you."

Abe shoved his automobile into gear and jerked down the road toward his place. He left Bert standing beside the mailbox rubbing his hands over the legs of his corduroy pants.

"Abe Mitchell ought to have better sense than to be a Democrat," Bert said, going into his house.

* * *

# 11

## Versifiers, Rhymers & Outright Poets

# HOLMAN DAY, ETC.

*Outside of an arts colony or maybe a creative writing class, you can probably find more poets per square mile in Maine than any other spot in the universe.*

*For one thing, because Mainers tend to speak metaphorically and to employ the language with spare precision we have a lot of natural poets walking around who have never even dreamed of trying to put a verse down on paper. Many others have tried, with varying degrees of success. Every coastal village and upriver hamlet has its budding Byrons. Most labor in serene anonymity for the pure pleasure of the exercise; others offer their more cherished items for publication in the local newspapers and other sensitive publications.*

*From time to time anthologies of Maine poetry have been gathered by some literary society or other. Because such material leans heavily toward the sentimental and outright sappy, these heavy volumes tend to gather more dust than attention. But the bookshelves of Maine bulge with them, solid testimony to the inspirational nature of the Maine setting and character.*

*Some of our poets — many more than average, really — achieve recognition as important figures in the craft, from Henry Wadsworth Longfellow, a Portland native, to Robert Lowell, who summered at Castine on Penobscot Bay.*

*Some distance below the poetical output of such luminaries lies the comical verse, usually ribald and peppered with scatalogical rhymes, which has played a vigorous role in the oral tradition of rural Maine. Whenever the oldtimers congregated in illicit rendezvous of two or more and had their risibilities lubricated by the* latest batch of home brew, most were capable of reciting these naughty verses for hours on end without recourse to repetition, except on popular demand. Sadly, perhaps, we have no examples to offer here, although the art is not altogether lost today.

What follows is a sampling of downeast humor — not all of it wholly typical — in the writings of some of Maine's better-known poets. They are:

HOLMAN F. DAY (1865-1935), was a popular backwoods novelist and humorous versifier in the early decades of this century.

Born in Vassalboro in 1865 he began his writing career, as proprietor and editor of the Dexter Gazette before joining the staff of the Lewiston Journal as roving correspondent. His job allowed him to travel into remote corners of the state, including the north woods, which later became the setting for more than 500 stories and 30 novels about Maine life.

Part of his duties at the Journal included writing humorous poems for the daily "State Chat" column. A number of these homely verses were collected in book form in 1900. The book, "Up in Maine," became an instant bestseller and launched Day on a career as a popular writer with a national audience. Although most of his stories were set in logging camps, he also wrote political novels and sea stories and dabbled in stage writing.

In the 1920s Day formed a silent film company in Augusta and produced a number of two-reelers starring the popular actress Mary Astor. He eventually drifted to California where he produced movie scenarios and conducted a radio program in which he related Yankee stories in a downeast dialect. His earning power never came up to his high standard of living, however, and he died in genteel poverty in Hollywood in 1935. He was buried in an unmarked grave in the family plot in a Vassalboro cemetery. In 1948 former classmates of Day's from Colby College raised a marker at the site of his burial *in memory of one of Maine's most popular — but now largely for-gotten — humorous poets and storytellers.*

*As for the other poets who appear in this section, none except Artemus Ward could by any stretch of the imagination be character-ized as humorous poets, although all of them incorporate vital aspects of Yankee humor.*

*EDWIN ARLINGTON ROBINSON (1869-1935), born at Head Tide and raised in Gardiner — the model for his "Tilbury Town" poems — was a major American poet. He wrote long narrative poetry in blank verse painting psychological portraits of New England characters.*

*"Miniver Cheevy," the poem which first brought Robinson national fame, is included here not because it is particularly comical — it is not — but because it contains those elements of irony and pessimism which underly much of what constitutes the essence of Maine wit. This particular example of dreamy stoicism represents downeast humor raised to a high art.*

*EDNA ST. VINCENT MILLAY (1892-1950) was born in Rock-land, grew up in Union and in later years summered on Ragged Island in Casco Bay. One of the best-known poets of the 1920s and 1930s, she wrote of love and life with a lyrical freshness which at-tracted an almost cultish following among young Americans of the period. "The Penitent," in its way, reflects the same downeast qualities as "Miniver Cheevy," only at a much gayer level.*

*ROBERT P. T. COFFIN (1892-1955), whom we encountered in a previous chapter in prose form, received the Pulitzer Prize for poetry in 1936 for "Strange Holiness."*

\* \* \*

# HOLMAN DAY

## AUNT SHAW'S PET JUG

Now there was Uncle Elnathan Shaw,
— Most regular man you ever saw!
Just half-past four in the afternoon
He'd start and whistle that old jig tune,
Take the big blue jug from the but'ry shelf
And trot down cellar, to draw himself
Old cider enough to last him through
The winter ev'nin'. Two quarts would do.
— Just as regular as half-past four
Come round, he'd tackle that cellar door,
As he had for thutty years or more.


And as regular, too, as he took that jug
Aunt Shaw would yap through her old cross
    mug,
"Now, Nathan, for goodness' sake take care!
You allus trip on the second stair;
It seems as though you were just possessed
To break that jug. It's the very best
There is in town and you know it, too,
And 'twas left to me by my great-aunt Sue.
For goodness' sake, why don't yer lug
A tin dish down, for ye'll break that jug?"
Allus the same, suh, for thirty years,
Allus the same old twits and jeers
Slammed for the nineteenth thousand time
And still we wonder, my friend, at crime.

But Nathan took it meek's a pup
And the worst he said was "Please shut up."
You know what the Good Book says befell
The pitcher that went to the old-time well;
Wal, whether 'twas that or his time had come,
Or his stiff old limbs got weak and numb
Or whether his nerves at last giv' in
To Aunt Shaw's everlasting chin —
One day he slipped on that second stair,
Whirled round and grabbed at the empty air
And clean to the foot of them stairs, ker-smack,
He bumped on the bulge of his humped old back
And he'd hardly finished the final bump
When old Aunt Shaw she giv' a jump
And screamed downstairs as mad's a bug
"Dod-rot your hide, did ye break my jug?"

Poor Uncle Nathan lay there flat
Knocked in the shape of an old cocked hat,
But he rubbed his legs, brushed off the dirt
And found after all that he warn't much hurt.
And he'd saved the jug, for his last wild thought
Had been of that; he might have caught
At the cellar shelves and saved his fall,
But he kept his hands on the jug through all.
And now as he loosed his jealous hug
His wife just screamed, "Did ye break my
   jug?"

Not a single word for his poor old bones
Nor a word when she heard his awful groans,
But the blamed old hard-shelled turkle just
Wanted to know if that jug was bust.

Old Uncle Nathan he let one roar
And he shook his fist at the cellar door;
"Did ye break my jug?" she was yellin' still.
"No, durn yer pelt, but I swow I will."
And you'd thought that the house was a-going
    to fall
When the old jug smashed on the cellar wall.

* * *

## A. B. APPLETON, "PIRUT"

Abbott B. Appleton went to the fair
*(Sing hey! for the wind among his whiskers),*
Saw curious "dewin's" while he was down
    there
'Mongst the gamblers, the sports and the frisk-
    ers.
He carried his bills in a wallet laid flat —
An old-fashioned calf-skin as black as your hat;

He was feeling so well he was easy to touch —
Then he hadn't as much; no, there wasn't as
   much.
He noticed a crowd 'round a pleasant-faced
   man
Whose business seemed based on a curious plan;
He asked for a quarter from each in the crowd,
Put the coin in his hat, and he forthwith al-
   lowed
That simply to advertise he would restore
His quarter to each, adding three quarters
   more.
Now Abbott B. Appleton he did invest —
Anxious to share in these spoils with the rest.
Man asked for ten dollars, and Abbott, said he:
"Why, sartin!  And then we'll git thutty back
   free."


But the man who was running the charity
   game
Informed him it didn't work always the same,
And Abbott B. Appleton got for his ten
A smile — and the man didn't play it again.
Then Abbott, in order to make himself square,
Got after the rest of the snides at the fair.
He hunted the pea, but he never could tell
When "the darned little critter" was under
   the shell.
He shot at a peg with a big, swinging ball,
Five dollars a shot — didn't hit it at all.
And he finally found himself "gone all to
   smash,"
With wisdom, a lot — and two dollars in cash.

Abbott B. Appleton cursed at the fair
*(Sing fie! for a man who 'tended meetin'),*
And he said to himself, "Gaul swat it, I swear
Them games is just rigged up for beatin'.
I thought they was honest down here in this
    town;
I swow if I hadn't I wouldn't come down;
But if cheatin's their caper I guess there's idees
That folks up in Augerville have, if ye please.
I'm a pretty straight man when they use me all
    square,
But I'm pirut myself at a Pirut-town fair.
I won't pick their pockets to git back that
    dough,
But I reckin' I'll giv' 'em an Augerville show."


Abbott B. Appleton "barked" at the fair
*(Sing sakes! how the people they did gather),*
And  his cross-the-lot voice it did bellow and
    blare
Till it seemed that his lungs were of leather.
He said that he had there inside of his pen
Most singular fowl ever heard of by men:
"The Giant Americanized Cock-a-tco,"
With his feathers, some red and some white,
    and some blue.
He promised if ever its like lived before
He'd give back their money right there at the
    door.
Then he vowed that the sight of the age was
    within.
" 'Twill never," he shouted, "be seen here agin.
'Tis an infant white annercononda, jest brought

From the African wilds, where it lately was
    caught.
The only one ever heern tell of before,
All wild and untamed, that far foreign shore."


Abbott B. Appleton raked in the tin.
*(Sing chink! for the money that he salted.)*
Then he opened the gates and he let 'em all in,
And then — well, then Abbott defaulted.
It was time that he did, for the people had
    found
Just a scared Brahma hen squatting there on
    the ground;
Her plumage was decked in a way to surprise,
With turkey-tail streamers all colored with
    dyes;


And above, on a placard, this sign in plain
    sight:
"There's nothin' else like her.  I trimmed her
    last night."
In a little cracked flask was an angle-worm
    curled —
"Young annercononda, sole one in the
    world."
And another sign stated, "He's small, I sup-
pose,
But if he hain't big enough, wait till he grows."
And Abbott B. Appleton, speeding afar,
Was counting his roll in a hurrying car.
Saying still, "As a general rule I'm all square,
But I'm pirut myself at a Pirut-town fair."

* * *

## BALLAD OF OZY B. ORR

Here's a plain and straight story of Ozy B.
  Orr —
A ballad unvarnished, but practical, for
It tells how the critter he wouldn't lie down
When a Hoodoo had reckoned to do him up
  brown.
It shows how a Yankee alights on his feet
When folks looking on have concluded he's
  beat.
Now Ozy had money and owned a good farm
And matters were working all right to a charm
When he "went on" some papers to help his
  son Bill
Who was all tangled up in a dowel-stock mill.
Now Bill was a quitter, and therefore one day
Those notes became due and his dad had to pay
So he slapped on a mortgage and then buckled
  down
To pay up the int'rest and keep off the town.
Oh, that mortgage, it clung like a sheep-tick in
  wool,
And the more she sagged back, harder Ozy
  would pull;
But a mortgage can tucker the likeliest man,
And Ozy he found himself flat on hard pan.
He dumped in his stock and his grain and his
  hay,
He scrimped and he skived and endeavored to
  pay;
He sold off his hay and his grain and his stock
Till the ricky-tick-tack of the auctioneer's knock
Kept up such a rapping on Ozy's old farm

That the auctioneer nigh had a kink in his
  arm —
And it happened at last, 'long o' Thanksgiving
  time,
Old Ozy was stripped to his very last dime.
And he said to his helpmeet: "Poor mummy,
  I van
I guess them 'ere critters have got all they can.
For they've sued off the stock till the barns
  are all bare,
'Cept the old turkey-gobbler, a-peckin' out
  there;
They'd a' lifted him, too, for those lawyers are
  rough,
But they reckoned that gobbler was rather too
  tough.
So they've left us our dinner for Thanksgivin'
  Day;
Just remember that, mummy, to-night when
  you pray.
Now chirk up your appetite, for, with God's
  grace,
We'll eat all at once all the stock on the place."


But Ozy he was a cheerful man,
  A goodly man, a godly man —
He didn't repine at Heaven's plan, but he took
  things as they came;
And cheerfully soon he whistled his tune
  That he always whistled — 'twas Old Zip
    Coon,
And he whistled it all the afternoon with never
  a word of blame.

While all unaware of his owner's care,
The gobbler pecked in the sunshine there,
With a tip-toe, tip-toe Nancy air, and ruffled
    like dancing dame;
Till it seemed to Ozy, whistling still
    To the ripity-rap of the turkey's bill,
That the prim old gobbler was keeping time
To the sweep and the swing of the wordless
    rhyme:
    Pickety-peck,
    With arching neck,
The turkey strutted with bow and beck.
And a Yankee notion was thereby born
To Ozy Orr ere another morn.


A practical fellow was Ozy B. Orr,
As keen an old Yankee as ever you saw
A bit of a platform he made out of tin,
With a chance for a kerosene lantern within;
He took his old fiddle and rosined the bow
And took the old turkey — and there was his
    show!
You don't understand?  Well, I'll own up to
    you
The crowds that he gathered were mystified,
    too.
For he advertised there on his banner unfurled
"A Jig-dancing Turkey — Sole one in the
    World."
And the more the folks saw it, the more and
    the more
They flocked with their dimes, and jammed
    at the door;

For it really did seem that precocious old bird
At sound of the fiddle was wondrously stirred.
In stateliest fashion the dance would commence,
Then faster and faster, with fervor intense,
Until, at the end, with a shriek of the strings
And a furious gobble and whirlwind of wings,
The turkey would side-step and two-step and
    spin,
Then larrup with ardor that echoing tin.
And widely renowned, and regarded with awe,
Was the "Great Dancing Turkey of Ozy B.
    Orr."
And the mortgage was paid by the old gobbler's
    legs —
Now Ozy is heading up money in kegs.

He would calmly tuck beneath his chin
   The bulge of his cracked old violin,
He sawed while the turkey whacked the tin,
   the people they paid and came;
For swift and soon to the lilting tune,
   When he fiddled the measure of Old Zip
     Coon,
The gobbler would whirl in a rigadoon — or
   something about the same!
While under the tin, tucked snugly in,
   Was the worthless Bill, that brand of Sin;
And 'twas Bill that made the turkey spin with
   the tip of the lantern flame;
For, as ever and ever the tin grew hot
The turkey made haste for to leave that spot,
Till it seemed that the gobbler was keeping time
To the sweep and the swing of the fiddle's
   rhyme.

   Pickety-peck,
   With snapping neck,
The gobbler gamboled with bow and beck!
Does a notion pay?  It doth — it doth!
Just reckon what O. B. Orr is "wuth."

* * *

# ARTEMUS WARD

## UNCLE SIMON AND UNCLE JIM

Uncle Simon he
Clumb up a tree
To see
What he could see,
When presentlee
Uncle Jim
Clumb up beside of him
And squatted down by he.

\* \* \*

# EDWIN ARLINGTON ROBINSON

## MINIVER CHEEVY

Miniver Cheevy, child of scorn,
   Grew lean while he assailed the seasons;
He wept that he was ever born,
   And he had reasons.
Miniver loved the days of old
   When swords were bright and steeds were prancing;
The vision of a warrior bold
   Would set him dancing.

Miniver sighed for what was not,
   And dreamed and rested from his labors;
He dreamed of Thebes and Camelot
   And Priam's neighbors.

Miniver mourned the ripe renown
   That made so many a name so fragrant;
He mourned Romance, now on the town,
   And Art, a vagrant.
Miniver loved the Medici,
   Albeit he had never seen one;
He would have sinned incessantly
   Could he have been one.

Miniver cursed the commonplace,
  And eyed a khaki suit with loathing;
He missed the mediæval grace
  Of iron clothing.

Miniver scorned the gold he sought,
  But sore annoyed he was without it;
Miniver thought and thought and thought
  And thought about it.

Miniver Cheevy, born too late,
  Scratched his head and kept on thinking;
Miniver coughed, and called it fate,
  And kept on drinking.

\* \* \*

# EDNA ST. VINCENT MILLAY

## THE PENITENT

I had a little Sorrow,
Born of a little Sin,
I found a room all damp with gloom
And shut us all within;
And "Little Sorrow, weep," said I
"And, Little Sin, pray God to die,
And I upon the floor will lie
    And think how bad I've been!"
Alas for pious planning —
    It mattered not a whit!
As far as gloom went in that room,
    The lamp might have been lit!
My Little Sorrow would not weep,
My Little Sin would go to sleep —
To save my soul I could not keep
    My graceless mind on it!

So up I got in anger,
    And took a book I had,
And put a ribbon on my hair
    To please a passing lad.
And, "One thing there's no getting by —
I've been a wicked girl," said I;
"But if I can't be sorry, why,
    I might as well be glad!"

\* \* \*

# ROBERT P. TRISTRAM COFFIN

## THIEF JONES

The people living round the place
Called him Thief Jones to his face,
Thief was like a Christian name,
It had lost the smut of shame.
Thief's house was black and let in weather,
The ridgepole hardly held together,
The doorway stood at a lee-lurch.
Men often opened it to search
Among the litter of net-corks there
For a lobster buoy or pair
Of missing pants whose seat was sewn
With patches they could prove their own.
It got so, when a man lost track
Of anything, he took a tack
Down Thief's way and had a look.
The folks at Mundy's Landing took
Thief as they took foggy weather;
They'd learned to get on well together.

Thief never said a word if he
Happened to be in. He'd be
Glad to see the man and might
Help him straighten things out right —
"This rudder's yours, this anchor's mine."
He might invite the man to dine
On the hasty-pudding cooking
On his stove, after the looking.
Men liked to talk with Thief, he knew
Stories yellow, pink, and blue.

But though they liked to hear him lie,
They never halved a blueberry pie
From his cookstove's warming-shelf,
Thief ate his victuals by himself.

\* \* \*

## EASTER ORR

Easter Orr was natural bad,
He took the only horse he had
And cut one ear off in a fit
Of passion at the looks of it.
The horse bit back and laid his scalp
Open in a fringe like kelp.
Easter said he would not trade
His horse for any man God made.

\* \* \*

## LAZYBONES

Of all the Tipsham lazybones
    The Yanceys took the cake,
Only in blueberry time
    Did Mother Yancey bake.

And then it was but six or so
    Pies that had the pip,
And the soggy bottom crust
    Would sink an iron ship.

The Yancey boys went bare of foot
    Till the snowflakes flew,
And you could put in your right eye
    The corn Dan Yancey grew.

They were folks for whom the skies
    Were always low and murky,
They were always on hard-pan
    And poor as old Job's turkey.

One Winter when the bay froze up
    From Whaleboat out to Ram,
The Yanceys did not have so much
    As a knuckle-bone of ham.

They sat around their dying stove
    And worried at the weather,
The neighbors went and got a cord
    Of seasoned birch together.

They brought it to the Yancey home
    Where seven tall sons sat
Round the last stick of their wood,
    Crowding out the cat.

"Here you are, Dan Yancey, this
    Will keep you for a spell."
They left the wood and went back home
    Feeling pretty well.

But there was not a sign of smoke
    From the Yancey flue
Going up that afternoon
    On the Winter blue.

And when the dusk was coming on,
Dan came to Abel Leigh,
"Can't you send one of your boys
To saw my birch for me?"

\* \* \*

## MR. BURNS STARTS TO TOWN

The stars were burning through the frost,
The young new moon was going down,
A doorway opened on the night,
And Mr. Burns set off for town.

He set off quickly with his head
Ducked low down, and he went smart,
Behind him came a water pail,
It struck the ground and burst apart.

A sudden watery flower bloomed
Where Mr. Burns might well have been,
But he was halfway to the barn
In his best pair of trousers then.

Words came out behind the pail,
Woman words and close together,
But Mr. Burns was hitching up
In the smell of harness leather.

He slipped the headstall on the mare,
The sen-sen on his breath was sweet,
He made the traces fast, got in,
And headed his Dolly's nose upstreet.

Mr. Burns had had his way,
He'd got his town pants, he was free
And off for Saturday night, good ale,
And kinder female company.

Yet he could not resist the chance
To fling the last word through the door,
He drew up and flung the word
Into his house's glowing core.

He heard the taunt hit hard and deep
And cracked the whip across the mare,
His runners squealed upon the snow,
They leapt and went away from there.

But Mrs. Burns, as women will,
Was to have the last word yet,
She'd gone early to the barn
When she'd seen how the tide would set.

She'd gone there with an eagle's eye,
A handsaw, and determined tread,
She'd burned her husband's bridges so
They hung but by a slender thread.

So now when he put out his wings
To start on his victorious flight,
There came a sharp and ominous
Crack that ran across the night.

The mare went on, but not the sleigh,
Both fills broke off crisp and clean
And Mr. Burns who held the reins
Was somewhere sadly in between.

He left the seat and joined the stars
In spite of all his lordly girth,
But his beauty was too vast,
And Mr. Burns came down to earth.

He travelled for a little time
Upon his ample chest and thighs,
He felt the snow come in and cool
His ardor and his enterprise.

The reins burned through his hands at last,
And he slowed down and came to rest,
Half the snow upon the world
Was in his trousers and his vest.

Mr. Burns lay there, the sad
Ruins of a man, and heard
The rising tumult of the last
Word and word and word and word.

* * *

# 12

# Parody

# 'DOC' ROCKWELL

*George L. "Doc" Rockwell (1890-1978) began his show business career as a vaudeville performer with a comedy magic act, later turning to humorous monologues. He got his nickname from an act in which he delivered a mock medical lecture holding a banana stalk and comparing it to the human spine. As a radio comic he appeared frequently on the Fred Allen Show. Following his retirement in the early 1940s, Rockwell turned to writing and became a regular contributor of humorous columns to Down East magazine. The following piece was written for a Portland newspaper at the height of his national popularity as a broadcasting comedian in the 1930s.*

\* \* \*

## DISCOVERY OF BOOTHBAY HARBOR

Nobody knows exactly who the first settler of Boothbay Harbor was. But from all present observations it was some man by the name of either Brewer, Giles, Greenleaf, Dodge, McKown, Kelley, Lewis, Perkins or Reed. These people did for the Boothbay region what Brigham Young did for Salt Lake City and as a consequence the town received a charter from Sears, Roebuck & Company and was officially chartered in 1573.

Its geographical location makes it ideal as a summer resort. Situated at the extreme end of a peninsula, it is not easily accessible by railroad and accordingly is not visited by every Tom, Dick and Harry. This fact appeals to the families who would like to enjoy their own cottage without being swooped down upon by self invited relatives and presuming acquaintances.

It is also the heart of the fishing and shellfish industry of the northeastern part of central southern Maine. If the lobsters caught within five miles of Boothbay Harbor in a single day were laid end to end on the Postoffice steps, it would keep many people away from the window and give the clerks a better chance to read the postcards.

There are many other towns and villages within a short distance and Boothbay Harbor has a drawing population of several thousand and a painting population of about the same number especially during the Summer when the artists are here. Some of these people are interior decorators and do wonderful work with Jamaica ginger and vanilla extract. All of which makes it hard to believe that Boothbay Harbor is located in the temperate zone. But it is.

The climate is ideal for raising blueberries, whiskers, and money to buy the minister a new carpet sweeper for the parsonage. The Winters are mild and the Summers are cool, many people sleeping under blankets every night as protection against the mosquitos, which seem to be able to penetrate any number of sheets. But mosquitos are only found in a very few places and there are really no pests with the exception of several young men who have been paying for their tuition in some barber college for the past 10 years, by selling subscriptions to the Saturday Evening Bath.

The principal industries of Boothbay Harbor are the manufacture of grandchildren, good dispositions and reasons why the Eastern Steamship Company won't run a boat here from Boston. The government consists of a Board of Selectmen, several women's societies and the Civic Club.

If you would like further information about anything in this region listen in on any of the 18 party telephone lines. You can't go wrong in Boothbay Harbor — without everyone knowing it.

\* \* \*

# DONALD C. HANSEN

*Donald C. Hansen is director of the editorial pages of the Guy Gannett newspapers of Portland. A native of Presque Isle, he was a reporter and editor of weekly newspapers in Brunswick, Boothbay Harbor and Rangeley before joining the Portland papers in 1959. As a political reporter Hansen frequently employed a humorous approach in his columns for the Portland Press Herald. Here are two examples.*

\* \* \*

## AN UTTERLY CHARMING EVENT

"I hope," said the office's leading advocate of stripping newspaper writing of any last vestiges of male chauvinism, "that if you cover Jadine O'Brien's congressional announcement that you won't stress the color of her dress."

Well, for heavens sake, I know better than that. So I was pleased when the boss told me to scoot on out and cover Jadine's press conference this week when she announced that she would seek the Democratic First District congressional nomination. I arrived early at the O'Brien hotel headquarters. Jadine was busy making last minute changes in her announcement speech so I chatted instead with Jack O'Brien, the candidate's handsome husband.

Jack was wearing a chic grey suit for the occasion, set off by a blue and white shirt and one of the new wide ties, a sea blue I believe, which are so in style at the moment.

Jack wore his hair as he usually does, a slight wave in front and cut fashionably long in the rear.

The candidate's husband was effusive as always. "May I get you a cup of coffee," he asked with a fetching smile. "Or would you prefer tea? I believe we have both."

As candidate O'Brien was still busy with her speech I gratefully accepted the offer of coffee. "Oh dear," he said. "I'm so sorry but the cream hasn't arrived yet. Dana's gone to get it."

Dana, Jack explained, is the husband of Jean Childs, who is the manager of the O'Brien campaign. "We're the best of friends, Dana and I," Jack explained. "We play golf together and have wonderful times."

Jack, over coffee, said he was pleased that his wife had decided to run and that he was looking forward to the campaign.

While Jack and I discussed the upcoming campaign (Jack is surprisingly knowledgeable about politics for a man; "I like to keep up

on current events," he said modestly), candidate O'Brien and campaign manager Childs were planning strategy and campaign issues.

"Oh, here's Dana now," Jack said, as Mr. Childs entered with the cream.

"Goodness, I hope I'm not late," Dana said, cleverly arranging the coffee and sandwiches on a beautifully arranged buffet. "This is real cream," he said. "Not milk, mind you, but real cream."

Dana's outfit was just as stunning as Jack's. He too wore a grey suit (I'll bet they go shopping together) and had his hair done much like Jack's.

Dana explained that while his wife Jean is managing the O'Brien campaign he is keeping busy with his hobby — a string of harness horses which he keeps at his wife's home in Westbrook. I have been there and I can tell you that Dana's stables are spotless. He beamed when I told him so. "Well, I do like to keep things looking well," he said, blushing becomingly.

Both Jack and Dana explained while some husbands might be content merely to work, they personally felt that men had a responsibility to contribute in the field of public service as well. Jack, for example, is a member of a group devoted to good works which meets every other year in Augusta. "We meet and discuss issues and pass laws," he said. "I find it exciting."

Dana is a former member of the group and was once elected the leader of the organization. Now that he's a former member, he said that he devotes as much time as he can spare away from his family in assisting the group in their discussions. "We call it lobbying," Dana said. "We former members try to help the present members make the proper choices."

"Goodness, they are helpful," Jack interjected. "Dana's been a jewel helping us out."

The room was beginning to fill up with reporters and supporters of candidate O'Brien and Dana excused himself to serve coffee to the late arrivals.

I asked, in the moments we had left before the press conference began, if Jack was looking forward to the campaign.

"Oh my yes," he said, his blue eyes twinkling. "The campaign's just begun and already I'm as excited as a schoolboy. I think it's marvelous."

We could have chatted on for hours but the press conference began and Jack went off to listen attentively to candidate O'Brien's announcement speech.

\* \* \*

## ODIN FRANKLY AND THE LITTLE PEOPLE

Odin Frankly, to his very great surprise, became one of the casualties in Tuesday's elections. Frankly, who since 1970 has served in the Maine House of Representatives from the class town district of Lakeland, Hardfield and Rockton, was defeated Tuesday by his arch political foe, former state Rep. Curtis Bagley.

Frankly lost, curiously enough, because he over-estimated the political clout of the midget vote.

"The little scudders didn't come through for me," Frankly said in some heat yesterday in an election post mortem. "They must of stayed home."

The seeds of Frankly's defeat were sown, he conceded, in the halls of the House of Representatives during the last season. "I made the mistake of listening to some of the debate," he said, "and what I heard got me all confused."

Frankly said that the idea of winning re-election by unifying the midget vote behind him arose after he began listening to other House members discussing the wants and needs of "the little people back home."

"I remember this debate over a tax bill," Frankly said, "and Jim Dudley he gets up and says he's going to vote against it because it'll hurt 'the little people back home.' And so I got to figuring that Jim wins real easy every time he runs and the reason must be because he's got all the little people supporting him."

Frankly continued to listen to the debate and, sure enough, House members in their speeches more often than not alluded to the "little people" in their district.

"I was surprised at first because I couldn't see how midgets could have so much political influence," Frankly said, "but every time somebody'd get up to talk he'd mention them and tell how they wanted him to vote.

"Sometimes a House member would say he was going to vote against some bill or other because it wasn't in the best interests of the little fellow. Or that he'd got some calls from the little people back in his district. But one thing was clear enough to me," Frankly said, "it was plain nobody was going to vote against the little people back home."

Once the session was over Frankly went back home and devised a re-election campaign built around the support of the little people in his district. "Now I'd never actually seen any of them in Lakeland, Hardfield or Rockton but I figured they had to be living here in some numbers because it was plain they was everyplace else and taking a lively interest in state politics too."

Frankly's campaign turned out to be the largest tiny campaign in state history. It opened, as Frankly's campaigns always have, with

a Labor Day speech over in front of Needham's Hardware and Grain Store. Frankly spoke earnestly about his hopes for the future of the little people in the district but as his eyes scanned the crowd he was disappointed to see his audience composed of listeners of average size or larger.

"That's when I made my first mistake," he admitted yesterday. "I got worried about not seeing any of them in the audience so I ended up by pledging that if I was re-elected I'd sponsor a bill to give everyone in the district who was under four feet tall $1,000."

Gladys Sharpe, who was covering the speech for the Hardfield Herald, went back to the office and wrote a story that delicately suggested that Frankly had got hold of some bad cider. That only made Frankly all the more determined to stick by the little people and in his next speech he reiterated the promise and added that he was "1,000 per cent" committed to the idea.

Frankly next took $50 from his campaign war chest and had signs painted proclaiming "Singer's Midgets For Frankly" and then nailed them up on trees all over the district.

He had tiny label buttons made to be distributed to the little people.

And still the little people in the district failed to turn out at Frankly's rallies and campaign stops.

He became obsessed with finding the little people whom he was convinced abounded unnoticed in the district.

When Frankly and his opponent Curtis Bagley capped the campaign with a face to face debate at the Lakeland Grange Hall on election eve Frankly said he was confident that "every Munchkin in the district knows I'm on their side," and promised that if he won he'd start a fund to erect a statue of Tom Thumb on the Rockton town common.

Bagley won in a landslide and Frankly is still trying to figure out why.

* * *

# PETER AGRAFIOTIS

*Born in New Hampshire in 1947, Peter Agrafiotis is the youngest and least traditional of the downeast humorous writers represented in this collection. His style is deliberately irreverent and mocking. He is the editor of VACATION CLUE ("America's Only Vacation Magazine That's Sarcastic"), published annually at Cape Neddick in southern Maine. Agrafiotis, who is also a talented modern impressionist painter, chronicles the adventures of the fictional Tatnic, a community unlike any other in Maine. He is currently at work on a novel, "The Times of Tatnic."*

\* \* \*

## BUILDING YOUR OWN CLAM TRAP

Don't get us wrong, we're not suggesting that someone on a two-week vacation from Albany try to master the art of clam-trapping. Learning to trap clams with any degree of deftness takes years of practice — in fact some of the old-timers say that clam trappers are born, not made. And we know that most people would rather spend their time browsing.

Even if one were to spend the whole summer on the coast the license fees and cost of a canoe and life jacket make clam trapping prohibitive for all but the most desperate. However, the growing demand for clam traps for coffee tables and hampers back in the suburbs makes building your own a valid alternative in these days of unemployment.

Cherrywood makes the most durable and attractive clam trap, and the cheapest place to find cherrywood is right at the orchard. Cherry-farmers, like most professionals, take Wednesday afternoons off, so this would be the best time to hunt for your stock.

Next you will need a mirror for the inside of the trap. Clams being very gregarious creatures, their own reflections are the best lures. The mirror from your motel room will do nicely.

Once you have the clam in the trap the problem is getting him to stay there. Metal, of course, makes the strongest door and the iron grates over sewers inlets are favored by locals, though a hibachi grill will serve as well. Both can be picked up anywhere. The trip mechanism may take a little ingenuity.

* * *

## NEW COMMUNITY COMES TO YORK COUNTY

Of course we all love the quaintness of traditional Maine life — the rustic old worn farms, the clam trappers heading upstream in their canoes, the humorous spectacle of the fisherman trying to keep up payments on his color TV from the proceeds of his catch. But progress is inevitable, even in Maine; it is promised that a better life is on the way.

Country City Estates of Kansas City, Kansas, and Kansas City, Missouri, has just unveiled its plans for Kansas City, Maine. The Maine condominium settlement is to be a beach and hillside community carved out of useless sections of Wells and the Kennebunks.

Says Country City President Frank Czar: "This will put York County right on Route 1 of American life." And typical of modern American life, Kansas City, Maine, will be complete with a colonial village wax museum, an "oldsters" golf course, Kentucky Fried Chicken, McDonald's, a Cambodian refugee camp, and a Shugg reservation. Country City has purchased from the bankrupt former owners of a former ski resort the earth surfaces of the mountain down to two feet deep and plans to move them to the sites of the future impacted-cluster condominiae to afford views of the ocean from up to 50 percent of the apartments. The marshes will be converted into beaches with sand from the former Ogunquit dunes, acquired by Country City from the Army Corps of Engineers.

Asked why he chose York County, Country City Estates President Czar said he and his wife had vacationed here last year and fallen in love with the place and wanted to spend some time here each year. "And I'm the kind of guy that has to keep busy," Czar says.

\* \* \*

## THE BARBER CROTTY AND THE GROCER MAXWELL

In the village of Ogunquit on a day in the time when 50¢ yielded change from a barber, the grocer Maxwell crossed from his store to the shop of the barber Crotty and took his shave, paying with a half-dollar of lead. Crotty dropped the coin to his counter where it landed with a "thunk." But he thanked the grocer and gave him a quarter in change. Late in the afternoon of that day the barber put the lock on his door and, as was his custom, crossed over to Maxwell's store for the groceries for his evening meal. His bill of $.75 he paid with a quarter and that same "half-dollar." Maxwell put the money in his till and bid him thanks and good night. The next morning Maxwell was back at the barber shop for his shave with the lead coin. That evening Crotty returned it for his groceries. This situation continued throughout the week, and then the next and the next. Soon the townspeople were placing bets on which one would be the first to lose his sober expression at the sight of the coin. Years passed and bets went uncollected as neither man flinched. A few of the older bettors died and the betting began to get more serious — the barber and the grocer were now both old men — which one would outlast the other? When Crotty died everyone mourned and waited the appropriate time to ask the grocer about the coin. But no matter how they beseeched him, Maxwell would make no reply. And no matter how they guessed, the bets were called off — that Crotty was buried smiling was deemed insufficient proof.

* * *

## A RECIPE FOR DOGFISH TAIL PIE

The popular belief that there is always big money in fishing the waters of the Maine coast is not quite true: it is a fact that the Maine fisherman has his lean times like the rest of us. This does not keep the dinner-table atmosphere from remaining unfailingly festive and

colorful. One of the favorite "leantime delicacies," dogfish-tail pie, originated quite by accident when a local lobsterman coming home after baiting his traps with cut-up dogfish, threw a tail to his cats. In the ensuing fight the tail flew into the cherrypit pie crust on top of the stove. Distracted by the ruckus, the wife, unnoticing, poured in the cherry-pits over it and slid the pie into the oven. After the evening chowder was polished off, out came the pie. "It's too tart," said the wife. "It's yecky," said the daughter. "Good cherry pit pie," said the fisherman, and it wasn't till he got a bone stuck in his throat that he found out what made all the difference.

Back home in the suburbs you don't have to have a cat-fight to have good dogfish-tail pie. Just kick the tails around the kitchen floor a few times and make sure they go into the pie under the cherry pits. If our salty Maine taste is tarter than yours, add a half cup more molasses.

* * *

## CALENDAR OF SUMMER RELIGIOUS EVENTS

The indigenous peoples of York County are, of course, the Shugg Indians. Their intermarriage with the Prohibitionists from Europe who began settling here in about 1956 has produced some charming religious customs. The summer months abound with religious rituals that will delight as many visitors as they may dismay.

June 21st — The Ceremony of the Summer Solstice. This is begun by the tossing of the golden frisbee by the most beautiful young native. The designated one may be either a boy or a girl, as sexual discrimination (and even differentiation) is to the Shuggs unknown. The ritual progresses with large numbers of the young gathering on the beach and exchanging consciousness constricting drugs. (The legalizing of the sale of alcohol to the Shuggs has cut the number participating in recent years.) The youths, all having taken a vow of nonattainment, sit down on the sand and remain motionless for up to three months.

July 1st — The Competition of the Masters. Business success being a high form of religious attainment to the natives, proprietors of all kinds of establishments meet to practice smiling and other techniques of ingratiation they may expect to find useful in their daily rituals and to pray for a good tourist crop.

July 6th — The Congregation of the Mid-Wives. This festival is limited to the most enlightened of the population — women over 60 years of age. The participants, all dressed in flower print costumes, gather to eat cottage cheese and talk about their operations.

July 14 — The Ceremony of the Full Moon. In this ritual men who have taken vows of celibacy congregate in the Ogunquit dunes to chant and practice acupuncture on each other.

June 3-Sept. 15th — The Communing of the Heroes. In this masculinity rite well-groomed males from 25-60 years of age gather at night to imbibe large quantities of intoxicants, eat Heroes, and relate stories of sexual prowess while vying for the attentions of the serving girls.

Aug. 10th-26th — The Parade of the Virgins. In this festival scantily-clad native and pilgrim girls gather on the beach to offer their bodies to the Sun God. (This is also a fertility ritual.)

Sept. 5th — Departure of the Pilgrims. This is the most joyous and colorful display of the religious season. With clamor and pageantry to rival the Israeli fleeing Egypt, the pilgrims pack up their tribes and the garish ornaments they have purchased from the Shuggs and begin the return journey to their home villages to spread the wisdom they have gained during their summer retreat. The departure is followed by nine months of silent meditation by the Shuggs.

\* \* \*

# KENT WARD

*A native of Aroostook County, Kent Ward began his newspaper career as editor of his hometown weekly, the now-defunct* Limestone Leader. *In 1962 he signed on with the* Bangor Daily News *as Rockland bureau chief and quickly rose through the desks to become assistant managing editor.*

*Ward writes a widely-read weekly column, "Maine Watch," in which he comments pungently upon the Maine social and political scene. His writing style seems almost a deliberate parody of the tough-talking, metaphoric journalese of an earlier era, a countrified version of Walter Winchell, say, or Westbrook Pegler.*

*For that reason he is included in this section.*

\* \* \*

## MAINE WATCH

The lunkheads who hang out down in Washington and smoke funny cigarettes that inspire them to hatch marvelous ideas like Affirmative Action, OSHA and the nine-digit Zip Code have come up with a real beaut this time.

The Town of Rockport has been informed by the feds that if it wants a $22,500 handout to study the town's sewage disposal problems it is going to have to hire a member of a minority group as a "public participation coordinator" for $1,800.

Since your chances of finding a minority person in Rockport, Maine, are roughly akin to you finding me in one of those Unisex hair salons where the guys with the bouffant hairdos come out looking prettier than a lot of the gals on their way in, town fathers have had to reach all the way over to North Windham to find someone willing to take the money and run.

"That stuff might work okay in Los Angeles or Boston, but it's a bit much here," Rockport Town Manager Paul Weston has complained to the Maine Congressional delegation in a message which he might as well have filed with Ronald McDonald for all the good it will do.

I mean, I really can't picture a Congressional delegation that gets all drooly over the prospect of giving $81 million of your money to our one true minority getting too terribly disturbed over the Town of Rockport laying another 1,800 bananas on someone they have to drag in from North Windham to meet federal guidelines for staking out a piece of The Rock.

If you are as unworldly about such things as I am you quite possibly have always wanted — but never dared — to ask just what a "public participation coordinator" does to earn his keep. (Yes, friends, six months ago I didn't know what a Public Participation Coordinator was. Now I are one.)

Well, our guy Emmett Meara down in the NEWS Rockland Bureau — who has about as much tact as you would expect any laid-back Irish journalist to possess — fired that question point-blank at Weston the other day and got a baleful stare and a whole bunch of silence for his trouble.

How the hell should *he* know? Weston undoubtedly felt like replying.

Instead, he set his jaw and 'splained to ol' Emmett: "I do not like the situation, and I hope that the Environmental Protection Agency changes the situation. But when I've complained to the Boston office they say, 'You guys import food and clothing, so why don't you import some minority workers?' "

Doesn't that sound like any Boston office you've ever dealt with? What have we got — about eight per cent unemployment — and those turkeys want us to bring in someone from away to be our Public Participation Coordinator?

Down the road a little further in the Town of Union, according to Meara, authorities have had to reach all the way to Illinois to scrape up *their* minority firm to handle a federally funded job that any number of locals could be doing while they are out looking for work.

And you're out there dawdling over your oatmeal and still wondering why this country is going under?

Moving right along, I guess I ought to remind you that you shouldn't go wandering into Moose Country north of the Canadian-Pacific tracks next week unless you do so in your armored personnel carrier.

There are two reasons for this:

1. You will be protected from the most assuredly vicious Maine Moose, a large animal with an unnerving habit of glomming up behind you and nudging you so you will ask it to pose for pictures with the wife and kids. This play-acting may fool the tourists from Fall River, but not the Maine Inland Fisheries and Wildlife Department, who recognize the moose for what it is: a thoroughly dangerous animal that must be eliminated for its own good.

2. You will be protected from the 700 Great White Hunters who have been given a week to clear the area of the species in order to save it from extinction.

The state's week-long "experimental" moose season is on next week, offering comic relief from the nuclear referendum tedium of Tuesday next.

The comedy will come, of course, about the same time as the "experiment," which will constitute the dragging of the first large and decidedly dead bull moose from without the lily pads in some swamp about 20 miles from the nearest tote road.

Along about that time you should be wishing that you owned the local skidder or helicopter-and-skyhook concession up back of Greenville some place.

One piece of advice to those who may not be included in the Maine 700 authorized to zap a moose: Do not be driving through Moose Country on your way to a bank heist, unless, of course, you plan to do it with something subtle like a note to the teller accompanied by a Molotov cocktail.

Anyone caught in Moose Country with guns in their pickup and without a moose conservation permit in their L. L. Bean knickers will be slapped in the slammer so quick it will make one's head spin. And that comes from the Head Beagle of the warden service himself.

One other thing.

In the event that there are some among the Maine 700 who are not quite sure what a moose standing in a frog pond in the Maine wilderness looks like, I offer the accompanying illustration. Clip and insert in your ammo pouch for handy reference. Aim for the middle of the white stripe that the warden service has contracted with a minority firm to paint on 700 of the animals.

\* \* \*

## KISSING AND MAKING UP

The recoupling of Greta and John Rideout, those madcap zanies in Oregon who played out their marital difficulties on prime time television and then decided to kiss and make up, probably didn't surprise one police officer in the entire world.

An officer doesn't have to be on the force very long before he learns that the quickest way to come by a fat lip and severe scratches about the face and arms is to attempt to settle a good old-fashion rip-roaring domestic squabble.

I know some officers who would rather spend six weeks directing the five o'clock traffic across the Bangor-Brewer bridge in grossly inclement weather than proceed to 164 Turkey St. to check out the latest altercation between Captain Nice Guy and his charming wife, Ms. Godzilla.

A domestic squabble is your basic no-win situation for the cop on the beat.

Invariably, when the peacemaker steps between the two combatants, six-foot-three, 295-pound Capt. Nice Guy hangs a karate chop on him and Ms. Godzilla chooses the occasion to conclude that her new crockpot might make a nice impression on the officer.

As help arrives to cart the trooper into the waiting meat wagon, our charming couple kisses, makes up and begins planning the next Friday Night Fight.

I had the opportunity, along with half of the Bangor press corps, to observe first hand the kiss-and-makeup phenomena at a delightful little shootout a couple of towns down the river about a dozen years ago.

In that one, our hero, armed with a goodly supply of booze and bullets, held a platoon of local and state police officers, sheriff's deputies and nosey newsmen at bay until dawn's early light.

Bullhorns, ultimatums, scattered shots, screams in the night, emissaries trying to talk the man out of his madness, to no avail. The whole nine yards.

Keeping everyone honest by means of an elephant gun that he fired periodically from the window, this local version of Clint Eastwood holding off the horde storming Fort Apache wiped out two police cruisers, shattering their windshields and ruining, to no one's sorrow, a brand new police radar set.

He dispatched an innocent house cat to Kitty Heaven in front of the officers behind a barricade across the street as a means of impressing them with his marksmanship.

As quickly as police lobbed tear gas cannisters into his lair he would fling them back, offering candid comments about the ancestry of the lobbers as he flung.

When one of our bravest (read it numbest) photographers set up a camera and telephoto lens on a tripod and zeroed in on the Fuhrer bunker, our main man, convinced that the enemy was about to launch a mortar attack, sent a couple of volleys into the press corps.

As the motley pack scattered around a nearby house it was met with a snarling German Shepherd approximating the size of a small horse. Rather than face Old Shep in his native habitat, the ever-alert newsmen bolted back into the line of fire.

Meanwhile, back up on Hill 109, Quick Draw McGraw was placing a provocatively attractive bullet hole through the pantsleg of State Trooper Bill Robinson, causing Robinson to poetically ruminate on the amount of paperwork it was going to take to explain THAT to the colonel in Augusta.

A state police sergeant ordered newsmen to smash a nearby street light so that Clint Eastwood would have to work harder for the good shot.

Now, you may have been the best street light liquidator on your block when you were a kid and no one was watching, but try putting one out with a rock while The Fuzz is supervising. The degree of diffi-

culty increases dramatically in proportion to the number of officers urging you onward.

Eventually, some television cameraman landed a lucky shot and beautiful darkness settled in.

Like all wild parties, this one began winding down when the sun came up and Davy Crockett tired of defending the Alamo.

He came out with his hands up, elephant gun broken down and guitar strapped across his back, and was hustled off to the local lockup to be reunited with his wife who had fled the premises in terror scarcely seven hours previously.

The next scene was right off the cover of True Romances.

"Get a load of this," a veteran trooper said to newsmen in the station house, inviting them to peer through one of those one-way windows that cops enjoy having in their shops, the better to observe you with, my dear.

In the next room it was kiss-and-make-up time for The Rifleman and his missus, locked in passionate embrace and wondering why in the world anyone had ever made such a fuss over them.

"Ain't love grand?" Trooper Robinson asked of no one in particular as he fondled the pants leg with the bullet hole in it.

"Yeah," growled Sgt. Ben Dunbar. "Let's go get some grub."

\* \* \*

## THE GASOLINE SHORTAGE

The governor told news reporters the other day at Augusta that he is confident that Maine residents will respond to his plea for voluntary conservation of gasoline for several reasons:

—We are frugal Maine Yankees;

—We have never had a helluva lot of anything, anyway, so one more shortage is no particular big deal; and

—We realize that if we don't give up our gasoline all of those tourists from New Jersey and Massachusetts won't have enough to drive their Winnebagos up this summer to help pollute Sebago Lake.

Oh, I can hear you muttering in your Gatorade now. There goes Ward again, exaggerating as usual.

To set your mind at ease on that point, let me quote from a news story filed by Dave Rawson, our operative in the State House, by whom the governor would never slip one. Wrote Dave:

"Brennan also said he doubted the state's tourist industry would be seriously affected (by a gas shortage). One of the reasons for asking Mainers to conserve, he said, was to assure there would be ample fuel for tourists."

Can't you just see old Molunkus Harry giving up his ration of gasoline and forsaking his daily drive into Mattawamkeag for a six-pack and a bottle of Thunderbird wine so the chairman of IBM can have an extra few gallons to buzz on into the Bar Harbor Yacht Club in his Mercedes?

His governorship could have talked all day without giving that as a reason for Maine motorists to cut back on gasoline, the Maine

Publicity Bureau and the Maine Hotel and Motel Association not-withstanding.

There was considerable discussion within this office the other night when that flock of eider ducks dropped out of the sky and into Brewer's Fast Food District, causing the birds to become quite dead when they struck the pavement.

A cynic on the copy desk speculated that when the birds found out that they were over Brewer they did the only honorable thing — they committed suicide.

I personally feel that the herd of birds had gotten wind of the governor's reason for conserving gasoline, figured they were in Alice's Wonderland, took a wrong turn through the looking glass in their haste to get the hell out before the tourists started arriving, caught an edge and wiped out in a most spectacular fashion.

* * *

# DON FEDERMAN

*For a time in the 1970's, until the law was repealed, Maine was the only place outside Nevada and Atlantic City where slot machines were legal. This gave rise to dreams among some Maine communities of becoming new gambling meccas of the East.*

*Entrepreneurs in the coastal resort area of Old Orchard Beach got carried away, advertising their attractions in a Boston newspaper. High rollers from away who made pilgrimages to Maine in response to these blandishments quickly discovered the stakes were severely limited by state law.*

*Don Federman, a copy editor for the Portland Press Herald, borrowed from the style of Damon Runyan in penning an imaginary account of two summer visitors' investigation of the action.*

# LETTER HOME TO VEGAS

Dear Al,

As you can see by the postmark, I'm on the East Coast for the first time since Crazy Eddie made the slammer for passing post time in Yonkers.

I should have stayed in Vegas. But you know me, Al, I gotta have action, and while The Strip is humming, there are times in August when the desert air seems to dull the dice, if you know what I mean.

Anyway, I'm sitting at the bar in Caesar's when Boston Charlie walks in, slaps me on the back and says, "Joey, look at this!"

So I look. What I see is a newspaper I have never seen before, and it is hard for the eyes to focus on where they should read. I mean, Al, with the New York News a person can get a fast handle on what is going on, but this one is called the "Globe" and right away I can see it is one of those news sheets you gotta belong to a club in order to have the time to get through.

"Where am I looking?" I ask Charlie, and he points to an ad at the bottom of the page which says, "CASINO GAMBLING."

"Look at that!" he cries. "Does that not delight the eye?"

"It does," I says, not wanting to hurt Charlie's feelings because I know how sentimental he can get at even the mere sound of a well-shuffled deck. "But what does this foreign press have to do with anything?"

"Joey, Joey," he says in a hurt way as if I had suggested all may not be kosher with the cards, "they do not call me Boston Charlie for nothing. This is my home turf, and I can see it has advanced much since the burning of witches and Forever Amber."

"I would not dispute you on your home ground," I says. "But what does this place called Old Orchard Beach, which I see by the ad is in the territory of Maine, have to do with the ways of worldly men?"

"You have heard, no doubt," says Charlie, "of such bankable names as Lowell, Saltonstall, Kennedy and Rockefeller?"

"I have," I says, "but I have not seen them in Vegas lately."

"That is because these people stay near their turf," Charlie explains. "They do not like waves of alien corn. The coast from Marblehead to Bar Harbor is their playground."

"You are sounding very knowledgeable this morning, Charlie," I says. "I sense great meaning in all of this. You are telling me these high rollers will now descend on the territory of Maine for their annual rest and recuperation from the rigors of clipping their coupons?"

"It is highly possible," answers Charlie, who is never one to overplay a hand.

Now, Al, it is with great awe that I am listening to these names. In fact, I am packed and in a DC-10 to Beantown before I turn to Charlie who is laying eight to five with all comers that the motor won't drop off.

"Tell me about the high rollers, again," I ask. "You know, the part about the Kennedys . . ." So Charlie goes through it once more being careful not to leave out the part about Jackie O and her buddies, and even tossing in King Saud and Billy C.

When we land, Charlie rents a limo and we're on our way north to the promised land. Honest, Al, it was like driving through Central Park for two solid hours. Never have I seen such a green jungle. Charlie kept warning the driver to be on the lookout for moose.

About the time I figure we've become another Lost Patrol, Charlie cries out, "We're here!" and we make a sharp right coming to a stop on a side street. Looking up, I spot a sign that reads, "La Salle de Poker." I can only make out one of the words, Al, but I get the message.

Inside, it truly does not look like Jackie O's summer hangout. There is this feeling in my stomach that all is not well, and people strolling around in 1920 bathing suits do not make me feel any better.

Sensing my distress, Charlie says, "Let us hit the tables." We walk over to one, sit down, and ask the dealer how much to get in. "Twenty-five," he mumbles, and I'm thinking this is not so bad after all, and my spirits once again are on the rise.

I toss in two tenners and a fiver. It is not without concern that I notice I am being handed back $24.75 — all in quarters. I turn to Charlie, but he is not there. I pick up my cards, and staring me in the face are four aces, king high. The greatest hand I have ever had in my life, Al, and the limit is a lousy twenty-five cents!

Ah, well, Al, such is life. You win some, you lose some. By the way, if you happen to run into Boston Charlie, inform him that all is forgiven. I mean, life may not be a bowl of cherries, Al, but then all a guy really needs are three in a row to be happy.

Your pal,

Joey

\* \* \*